D0216558

WILLIAM COWPER

Selected Letters

William Cowper (1792), by L. F. Abbott. National Portrait Gallery, London

WILLIAM COWPER

Selected Letters

Edited by
JAMES KING
and
CHARLES RYSKAMP

CLARENDON PRESS · OXFORD
1989

Oxford University Press, Walton Street, Oxford OX2 6DP

Oxford New York Toronto
Delhi Bombay Calcutta Madras Karachi
Petaling Jaya Singapore Hong Kong Tokyo
Nairobi Dar es Salaam Cape Town
Melbourne Auckland

and associated companies in
Berlin Ibadan

Oxford is a trade mark of Oxford University Press

Published in the United States
by Oxford University Press, New York

British Library Cataloguing in Publication Data

Cowper, William, 1731-1800
William Cowper : selected letters.
I. Poetry in English. Cowper, William,
1731-1800 Correspondence, diaries, etc.
I. Title   II. King, James   III. Ryskamp,
Charles, 1928-
821'.6
ISBN 0-19-818596-0

Library of Congress Cataloguing-in-Publication Data

Cowper, William, 1731-1800.
William Cowper, selected letters.
I. Cowper, William, 1731-1800—Correspondence.
2. Poets, English—18th century—Correspondence.
I. King, James, 1942-   II. Ryscamp, Charles.
III. Title.
PR3383.A44   1989   821'.6 (B)   88-28955
ISBN 0-19-818596-0

Set by Hope Services, Abingdon
Printed in Great Britain by
Courier International Ltd, Tiptree, Essex

For Our Mothers

Alice Gelinas King
(1909–1987)
and
Flora De Graaf Ryskamp
(1899–1986)

CONTENTS

INTRODUCTION

WILLIAM COWPER's letters are renowned for their seemingly effortless spontaneity, intimacy, and delicacy. Method, he once suggested, 'is never more out of its place than in a letter'. He also asked: 'If a Man may Talk without thinking, why may he not Write upon the same Terms?' Certainly, Cowper wrote letters quickly and decisively, and his manuscripts show little sign of hesitation or revision. Although they appear artless, such letters, in their 'familiar stile', as he himself realized, were the most difficult prose in which to succeed. Yet his fluent turns of phrase were obviously released at the moment pen was put to paper. Cowper commented facetiously on the virtues of his apparently haphazard method: 'When one has a Letter to write there is nothing more usefull than to make a Beginning. In the first place, because unless it be begun, there is no good reason to hope that it will ever be ended.' And then, in a more serious vein, Cowper said it was essential that one not write without thinking 'but always without premeditation'. As a result, Cowper 'speaks' to us in his letters, and this conversation is, by turns, filled with gossip, village news, advice, humorous anecdotes, and self-reflection. Above all, the letters display a lively mind monitoring itself and reporting its discoveries of the little joys of daily existence in a correspondingly lively manner.

Nevertheless, candour sometimes gives way to artfulness. There certainly are different selves in the letters in this volume. Young, self-confident Billy Cowper is a man of the world devoted to fashion in literature, clothing, and mode of life. Later, during his short-lived evangelical fervour, he writes with conviction of the power of God to transform his wicked self, but the language seems stereotyped. He can write letters of duty to Joe Hill and Margaret King, pious epistles to John and Mary Newton, and—often at the same time—vibrant, vivacious ones to William Unwin and Lady Hesketh. Particularly in these later years, Cowper distils a measure of intense joy out of the constant sense of impending gloom which threatens to swallow him. Ultimately there are the

letters when, exhausted by a constant battle against a hostile
God and a consuming belief in his own worthlessness, he
writes, perhaps too repetitiously and self-absorbedly, of the
stark pathos which invades every waking moment. In the end,
inner darkness prevails. Words, once the source of pleasure for
himself and others, no longer have any power.

Cowper's finest letters are those in which he reaches out to
the cosmopolitan, sophisticated London world he had abandoned in his early thirties. In this correspondence, he
describes his rustic scene in Buckinghamshire, the Olney
townspeople, his carpentry, drawing, gardening, and his wide
assortment of pets. The canvas upon which he paints this
domestic detail is often restricted to what he can see from the
windows of Orchard Side, his home at Olney. A little later, at
the end of the 1770s, from the stance of outsider, he comments
on the world of literature and, as ambition begins to dominate
his writing, he quests for fame.

Few writers have paid a greater tribute to friendship than
Cowper, who, although he often asked his friends for money
and gifts as well as admiration and support, in turn bestowed
unreserved devotion on them. He comforted the frequently
despondent William Unwin; he reassured John Newton that
his endeavours were worth while; he offered fatherly advice to
John Johnson, James Hurdis, and Samuel Rose; he com-
plimented the at times insecure Harriot Hesketh. When
speaking to intimates, he allows the strong resourceful side of
his character to emerge. But he was often deeply unsure of
himself.

In a delightful moment of self-abnegation, Cowper asked:
'Alas! what can I do with my Wit? I have not enough to do
great things with . . . I must do with it as I do with my Linnet,
I keep him for the most part in a Cage, but now & then set
open the Door that he may whisk about the Room a little, &
then shut him up again.' It is the paradox of Cowper's
existence that this uncaged wit, sparkling with evanescent
vitality, was snatched from a mind often mired in despondency.

The Chronology pinpoints the moments of success and
failure in Cowper's life, but a brief sketch may serve as a guide
to the turmoils which beset him. Cowper was born on 15
November 1731 at Berkhamsted, where his father John was

the rector of St Peter's Church. The Cowpers were a distinguished family, as was that of his mother Ann Donne. William was the fourth but first surviving child of the couple, and the young boy idolized his mother, whom he remembered as angelic. He was shattered when she died on 3 November 1737 of complications following the birth of John, her seventh but second surviving child. William never completely recovered from his mother's death, and in some chilling way melancholia invaded his being. In his school-days he was tormented by various bullies, but at Westminster he was eventually considered an excellent student, a good athlete, and a desirable companion. After an unhappy love affair with his cousin Theadora Cowper, he became a man of the town who dabbled in law. In 1763, however, a severe psychic crisis overwhelmed him when he felt unable to appear before the Bar of the House of Lords to defend his claim to a sinecure appointment. He attempted suicide. Eventually he was hospitalized at the 'Collegium Insanorum' of the kindly Nathaniel Cotton at St Albans, where he remained until 1765.

The remainder of Cowper's life at Huntingdon, Olney, Weston, and, eventually, Norfolk was spent away from his once-beloved London. At Huntingdon, he formed a close relationship with Mary Unwin, and he moved with her to Olney after her husband's death. As he himself recognized, he considered her as a generous and devoted mother. Late in the 1770s, the writing of poetry became Cowper's primary way of escaping from depression. In 1782, he published *Poems by William Cowper, of the Inner Temple, Esq.* and three years later followed *The Task*, the semi-autobiographical poem which made his name a household word for the next few decades. Success unleashed ambition, and from 1785 to 1790 he attempted to gain literary immortality by surpassing Pope as a translator of Homer. The mixed success of that undertaking dismayed him, but he nevertheless pressed on with an edition of and commentary on Milton. Despite his deep-seated admiration for that poet, whom he saw as a spiritual father, and the ensuing friendship with William Hayley, brought about by this venture, Cowper eventually abandoned the project. His mental condition worsened considerably after 1793, and in 1795 he and Mrs Unwin were taken to Norfolk by his cousin John Johnson. Cowper's last five years were especially sad. He heard voices and was unable, even momentarily, to subdue what he believed to be the wrath of an angry God. He died on 25 April 1800. During the long years of mental illness, he had made many efforts to quell his inner demons. In spite of his conviction of damnation, he emerges as courageous and even heroic.

The letters in this volume, representing less than a tenth of Cowper's known correspondence, come from every part of his life. They have been chosen to do several things: to show Cowper's extraordinary skill as a writer of letters; to display his personality in all its guises; to demonstrate his deep-seated commitment to friendship; to reveal his fine critical sensibility; to commemorate his interest in landscape, gardens, pets, and ordinary village lives and events. All of the letters are printed in complete form, following the text in our edition in five volumes of the *Letters and Prose Writings* (1979–86). We have not altered the text, but we have modified openings and closings in accordance with the principles of the *Selected Letters* series.

Full information on the condition and location of the holographs is to be found in that edition, as are details concerning the dating assigned to letters in which Cowper did not provide such information. We have tried to make the annotation as brief and as informative as possible. In giving documentation on the persons, places, historical and contemporary events, and books mentioned by Cowper, our intention has been to clarify his references and to present unobtrusively sufficient information for an understanding of the context in which Cowper wrote.

We are grateful to Dr Margaret M. Smith of the Index of Literary Manuscripts for drawing our attention to the presence at Dr Johnson's House in London of the holograph of Cowper's letter to William Unwin of 17 January 1782. We have used that manuscript as our copy-text; it replaces the printed source used in volume ii of the *Letters and Prose Writings*. The editors would also like to thank various critics, reviewers, and correspondents for their helpful suggestions and corrections, and the Social Sciences and Humanities Research Council of Canada for generous financial assistance.

LIST OF LETTERS

CHRONOLOGY

15 November 1731 (OS)	William Cowper born in the rectory, Berkhamsted, Hertfordshire; son of the Revd John Cowper, and of Ann, daughter of Roger Donne of Ludham Hall, Norfolk. [Cowper celebrated his birthday according to the New Style calendar on 26 November.]
13 November 1737 (OS)	Death of Ann Cowper.
c.1737	At school in Aldbury, Herts., under the Revd William Davis.
c.1737–9	At the Revd Dr William Pittman's boarding-school at Markyate Street, Herts.
c.1740–2	A boarder in the house of Mrs Disney.
April 1742	Enters Westminster School.
29 April 1747 (OS)	Admitted to the Middle Temple.
May 1749	Begins nine months at Berkhamsted.
1750–3	Is articled to Chapman, a London solicitor. He spends much time in the company of Theadora and Harriot, the daughters of his uncle Ashley Cowper.
c.1753–4	Abandons hope of marrying Theadora Cowper.
November 1753	Experiences his first period of depression.
June 1754	Is called to the Bar.
9 July 1756	Death of his father.
1756–63	Association with The Nonsense Club (Bonnell Thornton, Robert Lloyd, George Colman the Elder).
15 April 1757	Admitted to the Inner Temple.
1763	Dispute erupts over the Clerkship of the Journals of the House of Lords; is summoned to appear at the Bar of the House of Lords. Beginning of his

	second period of depression. Makes his third suicide attempt on the eve of his examination at the House of Lords. On the urging of his brother, he enters Dr Cotton's 'Collegium Insanorum' at St Albans.
July 1764	Recovery and beginning of conversion to evangelicalism.
June 1765	Leaves St Albans and settles in lodgings at Huntingdon.
c.September 1765	First acquaintance with the Unwin family.
11 November 1765	Becomes a boarder with the Unwins.
2 July 1767	Death of the Revd Morley Unwin.
14 September 1767	Arrival with Mrs Unwin at Olney, where the Revd John Newton had offered to find a house for them.
15 February 1768	Move to Orchard Side, Olney.
20 March 1770	Death of Cowper's brother John at Cambridge.
1771	Begins *Olney Hymns* in collaboration with Newton.
1772	Engaged to Mrs Unwin.
January–February 1773	Engagement is broken. Third period of severe depression.
April 1773	Moves to Olney vicarage under the care of Newton.
October 1773	Makes another attempt to commit suicide.
23 May 1774	Returns to Orchard Side.
February 1779	*Olney Hymns* published.
December 1780	'The Progress of Error' and 'Truth' begun.
January–March 1781	'Table Talk' and 'Expostulation' written.
Spring 1781	'Charity' written.
July 1781	Meets Lady Austen.
August 1781	'Retirement' begun.

1 March 1782	*Poems by William Cowper, of the Inner Temple, Esq.* published.
October 1782	*John Gilpin* written.
c.October 1783	*The Task* begun.
May 1784	First acquaintance with the Throckmortons.
24 May–12 July 1784	Final breach with Lady Austen.
October 1784	*The Task* completed.
November 1784	'Tirocinium' completed. The translation of the *Iliad* begun.
July 1785	*The Task* published.
October 1785	Resumes his correspondence with Lady Hesketh; receives financial assistance from her and 'Anonymous' (Theadora).
November 1786	Following Lady Hesketh's visit from June to November, Cowper, at the invitation of the Throckmortons, moves to The Lodge, Weston Underwood.
January–June 1787	Fourth period of depression.
September 1788	Translation of the *Odyssey* begun.
January 1790	First acquaintance with his cousin John Johnson.
July 1791	Translation of Homer published; begins making revisions soon after publication.
September 1791	Translation of Milton's Latin and Italian poems begun.
December 1791	Mrs Unwin's first paralytic stroke.
May 1792	Mrs Unwin's second paralytic stroke. First visit from William Hayley.
1 August– 17 September 1792	Cowper, Mrs Unwin, and John Johnson visit Hayley at Eartham, Sussex.
Autumn 1792	Renewed depression.
Autumn 1793	Further deterioration in Mrs Unwin's health. 'To Mary' written.
November 1793	Lady Hesketh arrives to take charge of Cowper and his household.

January 1794	Beginning of his fifth severe depression, from which he never fully recovers.
April 1794	Granted a yearly pension of £300.
17 May 1794	Mrs Unwin's third paralytic stroke.
28 July 1795	Cowper and Mrs Unwin removed by John Johnson to Norfolk.
17 December 1796	Death of Mrs Unwin.
November 1797	Final revision of translation of Homer begun.
8 March 1799	Revision of Homer completed.
19 March 1799	'The Cast-away' begun.
31 January 1800	Treated for dropsy.
22 February 1800	Confined to his rooms.
25 April 1800	Death.
2 May 1800	Buried in the parish church of East Dereham, Norfolk.

BIOGRAPHICAL REGISTER OF CORRESPONDENTS AND PERSONS FREQUENTLY CITED

AUSTEN, Lady, née ANN RICHARDSON (1738–1802). The widow of Sir Robert Austen. Cowper met Lady Austen in July 1781, when she took up residence with the Revd and Mrs Thomas Jones, her brother-in-law and sister, at Clifton, near Olney. About the end of January 1782, Cowper and Lady Austen quarrelled, possibly because she had made a veiled proposal of marriage to him. Their reconciliation took place in June–July 1782, but a final break occurred in the late spring or early summer of 1784. Lady Austen has been immortalized as the muse of *The Task*, and it is evident that Cowper admired her charm and wit. She had a satirical turn of mind, however, which she may have directed towards Mrs Unwin, who in all likelihood prompted both breaches with her rival.

BACON, JOHN (1740–99). Sculptor. A largely self-taught artist, Bacon had strong connections with Methodism and was a friend of Newton; it was through the latter that Bacon approached Cowper to praise his verse. A shrewd and sometimes grasping man of business, Bacon once suggested that he could execute all the national monuments at a price below that fixed by Parliament.

BAGOT, WALTER (1731–1806). Vicar of Blithfield and Leigh in Staffordshire. Bagot and Cowper were intimate friends at Westminster but drifted apart soon afterwards, and visited each other only twice in the years 1750–81. Bagot was very much like Cowper in his taste, gentle manners, and considerate humour. He had been a handsome boy but a slovenly dresser; he published poetry in his youth, and throughout his life he spent hours of each day reading the classics. When Cowper began his translation of Homer, Bagot visited and encouraged him, gathered subscribers on his behalf, and offered much-appreciated advice on the niceties of Greek grammar.

BODHAM, ANNE, née DONNE (1748–1846). Cowper's cousin, whom he called 'Rose'. She was the niece of Cowper's mother. Her husband Thomas was curate of Brandon Parva, Norfolk. Cowper was deeply touched when his old childhood playmate sent him the miniature of his mother by D. Heins.

BULL, WILLIAM (1738–1814). Pastor of Newport Independent Church. He had been educated at the Daventry Dissenting

Academy and took in students at Newport Pagnell. Cowper readily agreed, at his suggestion, to translate some of the verse of the French Quietist Jeanne Marie Bouvier de la Motte Guyon (1648–1717) into English. Despite his disapproval of Bull's religious opinions and love of tobacco, Cowper was continually moved by his friend's earnest admiration for him.

CARWARDINE, THOMAS (1734/5–1824). Hayley's close friend, who took a keen interest in Cowper. He held the livings of Earl's Colne and Little Yeedham, Essex, and was a prebendary of St Paul's.

CHAPMAN, Mr. Solicitor or attorney. Early in 1750 Cowper's father, anxious for him to acquire a practical knowledge of the law, sent William to Chapman's home, which was in Greville Street, in the heart of the legal district. The lawyer was a fair and honest person, but, with the exception of Edward Thurlow, Cowper heartily disliked his fellow clerks.

COLEMAN, RICHARD. Cowper's servant. Dick, the son of a drunken cobbler, was 7 or 8 years old in 1765, when he accompanied Cowper from St Albans. Cowper felt that he had rescued him from what would have been a life of degeneracy; nevertheless, Dick turned out to be a good-for-nothing.

COTTON, NATHANIEL (1705–88). Cowper's physician at St Albans. He had received his medical training at Leyden, and he had a considerable reputation for his humanitarian attention to the insane. His hospital for their care in St Albans had first been on a small scale, but before Cowper came to him he had moved to a spacious place called 'The College' or the 'Collegium Insanorum'. It was on Dagnall Street, not far from the abbey.

COURTENAY-THROCKMORTON, CATHARINE, née STAPLETON (d. 1839), and GEORGE (1754–1826). Catharine married in 1792 George Throckmorton, who by then had assumed the name of Courtenay on inheriting through his mother the estates of the Courtenays of Molland, Devon. The cheerful friendliness of this couple endeared them to Cowper and Mrs Unwin.

COWPER, ASHLEY (1701–88). Cowper's uncle and the father of Harriot and Theodora. By virtue of his sinecure office as Clerk of the Parliaments, he obtained £4,000 a year. William passed many happy hours at Ashley's house on Southampton Row when he was at Mr Chapman's. The proposed marriage between William and Theodora was forbidden by Ashley *c.*1756, although he relented in 1763. The immediate cause of William's mental breakdown in 1763 was the difficulties which ensued when his uncle nominated him as Clerk of the Journals. When Ashley denied Thea's hand, there was a very real tension between uncle and nephew, and, after his religious conversion, William looked askance at his uncle's worldly life and ambitions. Yet he admired his uncle's verse and he felt warmly towards him when he resumed his friendship with Ashley's daughter Harriot in 1785.

COWPER, JOHN (1737–70). Cowper's brother. Unlike William, John had always been studious, first at Felsted and then at Corpus Christi, Cambridge, where he served as Praelector (1765) and Bursar (1767). He was a poet himself—the brothers had exchanged now lost rhyming letters—and he was particularly talented in languages. He was an ordained priest in the Church of England and was appointed rector of Foxton in 1765. Although he sympathized with his brother's sorrowful plight in 1763, John was bewildered by that experience and had his brother hospitalized at Dr Cotton's. Subsequently, he was hostile to his older brother's evangelicalism, and a coldness developed between them. William travelled to Cambridge in 1769 when John first became ill. A breakthrough in their relationship occurred the following year when John was dying. During his final illness, John converted to evangelicalism and, at the same time, understood fully the crisis that had earlier dominated his older brother's life. For the first time, the two brothers shared a close bond of sympathy, and Cowper wrote of his brother's conversion and death in the second portion of *Adelphi*, the first part of which contains William's autobiography up to 1765.

COWPER, MARIA, née MADAN (1726–97). The wife of Major William Cowper, her first cousin; Martin Madan's sister and Cowper's cousin. An unusually accomplished person, she had wished to become an actress; later, she was deeply evangelical in her religious beliefs, and this was a bond with the poet.

COWPER, General SPENCER (1723 or 1724–97). First cousin of Cowper and Lady Hesketh. In the 1780s, the general became interested in the literary fortunes of his younger cousin, and he, together with Lady Hesketh, obtained opinions of men of letters as to the merits of the translation of Homer and helped gather subscribers to the edition.

COWPER, THEODORA (1734?–1824). Cowper's first cousin. In the early 1750s, William and Thea fell in love, but her father Ashley forbade the marriage c.1756—possibly because both his daughter and nephew showed a propensity to melancholia or, more likely, for financial reasons. Thea was profoundly disturbed by this, and she was further broken in 1763 when Ashley relented and Cowper then refused the match. Thea never fully recovered from this early disappointment and spent much of the remainder of her life in mental asylums or in seclusion. When Harriot resumed her friendship with William in 1785, Thea became the 'Anonymous' who supplied her cousin with many gifts, including a writing desk.

DUNCOMBE, JOHN (1729–86). Translator and reviewer. John Cowper and Duncombe must have known each other at Felsted School and Cambridge, and Cowper probably became acquainted with Duncombe through his younger brother. At school, Duncombe had a reputation for brilliance, and in 1756 and 1759 collaborated with his father William in translations of Horace, an endeavour in which Cowper assisted. Duncombe wrote many original poetical compositions and was an essayist and reviewer of considerable talent. From 1766 to 1786, he undertook the 'Review of Books' in the *Gentleman's Magazine*, and in this capacity it was he who most probably wrote the notices on Cowper's two volumes of verse for that periodical— the most important reviews to Cowper.

FUSELI, HENRY (1741–1825). Artist. Educated at the Zurich Collegium, he was learned in Greek, Latin, Hebrew, French, Italian, and English. When he established himself in London, he was employed as a professional reader by several firms, and, as such, was engaged by Joseph Johnson to offer 'strictures' to Cowper on his translation of Homer. Fuseli's assistance is graciously acknowledged by Cowper in the Preface to his translation, but he was frequently irritated by the artist's severe admonitions.

GREATHEED, SAMUEL (d. 1823). A pupil of Bull's who was also a friend of Newton. On their first meeting in June 1785, he struck Cowper as a well-bred young man, and he often escorted Cowper from Olney to Newport Pagnell for dinner at the Bulls. Greatheed showed interest in Cowper's work, although it is doubtful whether he exercised much influence over him. But he did accumulate biographical information for Hayley's use after Cowper's death, and he also preached Cowper's funeral sermon, in which his frank admission of his friend's derangements earned him the enmity of Lady Hesketh.

GREGSON, WILLIAM (1732–1800). Roman Catholic chaplain to the Throckmortons. He and Cowper became good friends, and the 'Padre' volunteered to transcribe portions of the translation of Homer.

HAYLEY, THOMAS ALPHONSO (1780–1800). Only child of William Hayley. He displayed signs of remarkable ability in the visual arts in his early teens and was encouraged by Wright of Derby, Romney, and Flaxman. From 1795 he was articled for three years as a resident pupil to Flaxman. In 1798 Thomas showed signs of ill health, arising from curvature of the spine, and returned to his father's house at Eartham, where he died two years later.

HAYLEY, WILLIAM (1745–1825). Poet and patron of the arts. He was educated at Eton, Trinity College, Cambridge, and the Middle Temple. In 1774, he purchased Felpham, near Eartham, Sussex, where many of his literary and artistic friends were summoned for long visits. He was a prolific writer of poems, plays, and tracts, and was known to hold radical political opinions. In 1792 Hayley wrote to Cowper when he saw an erroneous notice in a newspaper claiming that he and Cowper were writing rival lives of Milton. Cowper responded warmly to Hayley's effusions, and the two men quickly became close friends. After Cowper's death, Hayley employed Blake to provide illustrations for some of his publications, including biographies of Cowper (1803–4) and Romney (1809).

HESKETH, Lady, née HARRIOT COWPER (1733–1807). Cowper's first cousin and the wife of Sir Thomas Hesketh (d. 1778) of Rufford Hall in Lancashire. She was a well-known hostess, who was regularly in the company of ladies like Elizabeth Montagu, Frances Burney, Hester Thrale Piozzi, and Caroline Howe. Of a mercurial and haughty temperament, she bestowed unreserved affection on Cowper. She had been out of touch with her cousin for many years when she wrote to him in 1785 after the publication of *The Task*, and she henceforth devoted a great deal of time to his welfare.

HIGGINS, JOHN (b. 1768). A native of Weston and an admirer of Cowper's poetry. When Cowper learned that a young man of the neighbourhood could recite many of his poems by heart, he invited him to tea. The earliest known portrait of Cowper is a profile drawing which Higgins made in 1791. In 1792, he inherited the estate of Turvey Abbey, several miles from Weston, and regular contact between the two men ceased. However, Higgins's admiration for Cowper was unflagging, and he cherished his collection of relics of the poet (he constantly wore Cowper's shoe-buckles).

HILL, JOSEPH (1733–1811), often called Sephus or Joe. He was Cowper's closest friend during his Temple days. He had been bred early to the law, acted as a clerk in Chancery Lane, later qualified as solicitor and attorney, and became one of the Sixty, or Sworn Clerks in Chancery. He became a wealthy man, owing to the enormous esteem in which so many of his rich clients held him. During much of his life, Cowper was financially dependent on Hill, who handled all his monetary affairs and who from his own pocket made it possible for Cowper to live as a gentleman, though a poor one. Hill married Sarah Mathews in August 1771.

HURDIS, JAMES (1763–1801). Poet. In 1785, he had been appointed curate of Burwash, Sussex, and he remained there until he obtained the living of Bishopstone in 1791, which he held until his death. His earliest collection of poems, *The Village Curate* (1788), was a deliberate imitation of Cowper, and Cowper's publisher Joseph Johnson asked him in 1788 for an opinion of Hurdis's second volume, *Adriano*. Cowper revised that work for publication, as well as the tragedy *Sir Thomas More*. Hurdis first wrote to him in 1791, and subsequently sent numerous corrections to the translation of Homer. Hurdis resembled the late William Unwin, and Cowper responded strongly to this talented yet vulnerable young man, whom he assisted to obtain the Professorship of Poetry at Oxford in 1793.

JOHNSON, JOHN (1769–1833). Cowper's second cousin. After attending Caius College, Cambridge, he was ordained in 1793, in which year he was appointed a curate at East Dereham, Norfolk. He resigned that post in 1795 and became curate of Yaxham and Welborne. When he paid his first visit to Cowper in January 1790, the poet had not been in touch with any of his maternal relations for twenty-seven years. 'Johnny of Norfolk' took a kindly and devoted interest in his elderly relation; for his part, Cowper responded immediately to the vivacity and thoughtfulness of 'the wild boy Johnson', and this led to renewed contacts with his Donne relations, with whom he had spent many happy moments at Catfield as a child. John, prodded by Lady Hesketh, removed Cowper and Mrs Unwin from Weston in 1795 and took them to live with him in Norfolk. Johnson was inordinately attached to pedigree, and snobbery was his predominant flaw. He could also be incredibly naïve, as when, in an attempt to comfort Cowper, he cut a hole in the wall behind Cowper's bed through which he could whisper comforting thoughts. On balance, however, he was resolutely faithful to the older man, whom he venerated as a father. Cowper was also fond of John's sister Catharine (1767–1821).

JOHNSON, JOSEPH (1738–1809). Cowper's publisher and bookseller. From his establishment in St. Paul's Churchyard, he published important works on surgery and medicine as well as some of the most innovative works of poetry and prose of his time. Among his authors were Erasmus Darwin, Mary Wollstonecraft, Tom Paine, and Maria Edgeworth.

KING, MARGARET, née DEVEILLE (1735–93). Wife of the Revd John King, rector of Pertenhall, Bedfordshire, who had been a fellow student of Cowper at Westminster. More importantly, Mrs King had been a friend of Cowper's brother John, whom she had probably known when he was a student at Felsted and her father was the vicar there.

LAWRENCE, THOMAS (1769–1830). Artist. Lawrence was a young man of 24 when he went to Weston in 1793 to paint Cowper's portrait. But he was already on his way to fame: he had been invited in 1792 to paint George III. He was knighted in 1815 and became President of the Royal Academy in 1820.

MADAN, JUDITH, née COWPER (1702–81). Mother of Martin Madan and Maria Cowper; Cowper's aunt. Mrs Madan was the only daughter of Judge Spencer Cowper, Cowper's grandfather. A correspondent of Pope's, she curtailed her literary interests when she married Captain Martin Madan. After she came to know Lady Huntingdon and John Wesley, religion became the great solace of her life. Her letters to Cowper testify to their similar feelings about evangelicalism.

MADAN, MARTIN (1725–90). Cowper's cousin. Educated at Westminster, Christ Church, Oxford, and the Inner Temple, he was admitted to the Bar in 1748. In 1750, he was deeply moved when he heard John Wesley speak, took up itinerant preaching, and eventually was ordained deacon in the Church of England in 1757. He became much involved with the Wesleys, Lady Huntingdon, George Whitefield, and other distinguished Methodists. A man of extraordinary and sometimes reckless self-confidence, he published a number of religious works, but he grew infamous when in 1781 he published *Thelyphthora*, where he attempted to curb prostitution by suggesting that a man who has slept with a woman has married her. Some of those antagonistic to the book claimed, incorrectly, that he was an advocate of polygamy. Towards the end of his life, he translated Juvenal and Persius into English.

NEWTON, JOHN (1725–1807) and MARY, née CATLETT (1729–90). Newton, a fervent, dedicated, and sometimes over-zealous man, led a strange and adventure-filled life before becoming an evangelical in 1748. His autobiography, *An Authentic Narrative* (1764), tells the story of his life as the master of a slave-ship and of his conversion. Newton had first gone to sea in 1736 and had made six journeys before 1742. After his marriage to Mary Catlett on 12 February 1750, he made three further voyages, but in 1754, owing to ill health, he gave up the sea. After his retirement he became surveyor of tides at Liverpool for five years, using his leisure time for the study of Greek, Hebrew, and theology. He was, after some difficulty, ordained a priest in the Church of England in 1764. He accepted the curacy of Olney that year, where he remained until 1780, when he became rector of St

Mary Woolnoth in London. In addition to his contribution to the *Olney Hymns* (1779)—which were begun at his instigation—he was the author of a substantial number of tracts, including *Cardiphonia* (1781). Throughout the 1760s and 1770s Cowper and Newton were good friends, although Cowper was always aware of the harsh, strident side of Newton. As Cowper's literary ambition developed, he realized how far apart he and his old friend were on many fundamental issues. Newton's wife Mary was a quiet, unassuming, but firm person who endured ill health during most of her life. Cowper's letters contain many references to her father George (d. 1778), her niece Betsy (d. 1807), the daughter of her brother George, and her sister Elizabeth Cunningham (d. 1783). The Newtons acted as foster parents to Betsy and to Elizabeth's daughter Eliza (d. 1785).

POWLEY, SUSANNA, née UNWIN (1746–1835), and MATTHEW (1740–1806). Mrs Unwin's daughter and son-in-law, who married in 1774. They lived at Dewsbury, Yorkshire, where Powley was appointed vicar in 1777. Susanna was resentful of the devotion her mother lavished on Cowper, but her husband did not share his wife's hostility and sometimes turned to Cowper for advice.

PRICE, CHASE (1731–77), called 'Toby' by Cowper. He was the last boy (twentieth) in Cowper's sixth form at Westminster. He subsequently attended Christ Church and the Inner Temple before being called to the Bar. Later, he was a Member of Parliament (1759–77) and was constantly embroiled in schemes involving land grants, mines, and trade with India. A sometime poet and a patron of the theatre, he was a celebrated and ribald wit.

ROBERTS, SAMUEL (d. 1832). Cowper's servant. He had taken care of Cowper at Dr Cotton's and accompanied him when he left St Albans. He remained in Cowper's service until 1795. Ann or 'Nanny', Sam's wife, was also part of the Cowper–Unwin household at Olney, Weston, and, briefly, in Norfolk.

ROMNEY, GEORGE (1734–1802). Painter. At the zenith of his career his income was over £3,000 a year, and he was rivalled only by Reynolds as a portraitist. He immortalized Emma Hart, afterwards Lady Hamilton, in a series of portraits and sketches. The painter shared some of Hayley's radical political views. He was of a habitually melancholic cast of mind, and he and Cowper immediately sensed their similarity of spirits when they met at Eartham in 1792.

ROSE, SAMUEL (1767–1804). Rose graduated from the University of Glasgow in 1787, entered Lincoln's Inn, and was called to the Bar in 1796. While a student in Scotland, the overly excitable Rose lodged with William Richardson, a man of highly developed literary interests, and he, among others, inspired Rose to call upon Cowper in 1787. Cowper's enthusiastic response to the devotion of the younger man led to the beginning of a cordial friendship. His health was precarious from the time Cowper first met him, and there is a legend that he caught a cold from which he never recovered while defending William Blake in Chichester against the charge of sedition.

ROWLEY, CLOTWORTHY (1731–1805). Of a robust and unruly nature, Rowley lived in accordance with the adventurous spirit of his distinguished Admiralty family. Rowley and Cowper were neighbours at the Inner Temple, but Rowley withdrew from there in 1768, at which time he was called to the Irish Bar. He later became MP for Downpatrick (1771–1801).

SMITH, CHARLOTTE, née TURNER (1749–1806). Cowper met this celebrated novelist and poet at Eartham in 1792. Despite her position as an established writer, Mrs Smith was continually in financial difficulties. The principal causes of her monetary embarrassments were her improvident husband, from whom she had separated in 1786, and her twelve children. Her political sentiments were considered radical by many, but she and Cowper shared a bond of melancholia. In 1793, she dedicated her poem *The Emigrants* to the man whose own verse had given her 'infinite consolation'.

SMITH, ROBERT, afterwards Baron CARRINGTON (1752–1838). His family's fortune had been gained in banking, but he entered Parliament in 1779 as Member for Nottingham. He was generous with his money, and Cowper acted as his agent in distributing funds to the poor of Olney. He also provided Cowper and his friends with franks.

TEEDON, SAMUEL (d. 1798). He seems to have come to Olney from Bedford in 1775. He lived at a cottage at the junction of Dagnell Street and High Street, and was the Olney schoolmaster. In 1785 Cowper loathed him: 'He is the most obsequious, the most formal, the most pedantic of all creatures. So civil that it would be cruel to affront him, and so troublesome that it is impossible to bear him.' Cowper's attitude toward Teedon had softened considerably by 1787, and from about 1790 he allowed him a yearly allowance of £30, a great deal of money to Teedon. In turn, Teedon bestowed elaborate compliments and furnished spiritual prognostications. Although Cowper always kept his distance from Teedon, he increasingly relied on him as a confidant in spiritual matters. The extent of Cowper's psychic distress in 1792 and 1793 can be measured by his eager willingness to attend to Teedon's bizarre 'notices'.

THORNTON, JOHN (1720–90). A director of the Russia Company, who had extensive interests in foreign investments and affairs. He was a generous supporter of evangelical causes, and in 1779 he presented Newton to the rectory of St Mary Woolnoth. Frugal in his personal habits, somewhat of a recluse, and inclined towards eccentricity, he was a loyal friend to Cowper and a great admirer of his poetry.

THROCKMORTON, MARIA CATHERINE, afterwards Lady THROCKMORTON née GIFFARD (1762–1821), and JOHN, afterwards Sir JOHN (1753–1819). The Giffards, like the Throckmortons, were an old Catholic family. Maria and John married in 1782, and in 1791, when John succeeded to the estate and baronetcy of his grandfather Sir Robert, the couple went to live at Buckland House in Berkshire. The cultivation, breeding, friendliness, and youthfulness of the Throckmortons captivated Cowper, and he was especially involved in the activities of the family from 1786, when he moved to Weston and John Throckmorton became his landlord. Despite John's Catholicism, his membership of the Catholic Committee, and his friendship with Charles James Fox, Cowper responded warmly to him and to his wife, who was an eager copyist of the translation of Homer and who inspired three short poems. The Throckmortons as a family reminded Cowper of the cultivated society which he had known in London.

THURLOW, EDWARD, later first Baron THURLOW (1731–1806). Thurlow met Cowper when they were clerks in Mr Chapman's office. A man of unbridled ambition, he became Solicitor-General in 1770 and Attorney-General a year later. His support of George III's North American policy led to his elevation to Lord Chancellor and Baron Thurlow in 1778. Thurlow was often accused of vulgarity in his handling of legal cases and of duplicity in many of his administrative dealings. He was noted for being bold and rude, quick in his decisions, aloof, and lonely. He was sceptical of any religious beliefs. However, Cowper remembered Thurlow as a man interested in poetry and as a close friend who had promised to help him if he ever obtained power. The poet was disappointed by the rebuffs he later received from Thurlow, although the Lord Chancellor did write to him regarding his translation of Homer and, very reluctantly, assisted Hayley's scheme of gaining a royal pension for his old friend.

UNWIN, MARY (1724–96). Daughter of William Cawthorne, a

draper of Ely, and wife of the Revd Morley Unwin (1703–67), whom she married in 1742. On 11 November 1765 Cowper moved into the home of the Unwins. She in particular made Cowper feel immediately like a near relation, and he found in her what seemed to him a perfect combination of piety with a gentle, cheerful, intelligent character. Mrs Unwin—it was often said by Cowper and his friends—was like a mother to him. After Mr Unwin's death, they lived together at Olney, Weston, and in Norfolk.

UNWIN, WILLIAM (1744–86). Mary Unwin's son. He was educated at Charterhouse and at Christ's College, Cambridge. After a short ministry at Comberton, Cambridgeshire, where his evangelical sermons earned him a substantial reputation, he was instituted rector of Stock, Essex, in 1769. He was a gentle, highly intellectual, but very sensitive person, who quarrelled with his congregation at Stock regarding tithes. Unwin revered Cowper, whose letters to him often have the tone of the proud yet cautious parent offering advice to his offspring. Unwin married Anne Shuttleworth, by whom he had three children, John, William, and Marianne.

WILSON, HANNAH. Mary Unwin's niece. She was the daughter of Dick Coleman's wife Patty Wilson, who had previously been married to a Mr Wilson, but Patty was most likely the natural daughter of Mrs Unwin's father. As a young girl in the 1780s, Hannah acted as a servant at Orchard Side, and she moved with the household to Weston in 1786. When she was a child, she gave much pleasure to Cowper and Mrs Unwin; as she grew older, they found her high spirits displeasing.

To Walter Bagot

[The Cowper who wished to be one of the literati is much in evidence in his early letters. He speaks with considerable assurance of literary and amatory affairs. Supposedly engaged to the study of law, Cowper finds his attention continually wandering to more pressing matters, such as the latest play staged at Cambridge or the definition of a coxcomb.]

Grevile Street March 12th. 1749°

Dear Watty

In order to Vindicate Mr. Morgan's° Veracity & my own honour, I send you this. Does not this Sound well? I think there is something Theatrical in it; & the same Spirit kept up through a Tragedy might make a great Figure upon the English Stage.

Odd Enough! Two Friends corresponding by Letter at the Distance of a Mile & a half. An Indifferent person, would think we were afraid of seeing each other. No Rivers to interpose their Streams impassable; the Distance so Inconsiderable; the Weather fine, and both desirous of a Meeting: Why then says that Indifferent person, what a Devil should hinder you? Why don't you meet? Why thou Leaden-headed Puppy, says I, I'll tell thee why. This same Mr. Bagot is confined within the musty Walls of a nasty, stinking, abominable Prison;° and I myself am an humble Servant to old Father Antick the Law;° and Consequently have but very little time to myself. But Methinks, says he, you might find an hour or two some Evening, and that would be a little Satisfaction—Well thought on, faith Sir says I—& now Watty what say you to this honest Fellow's proposal? Will you appoint a time, I'll meet you at any place you shall name? Can you impose upon old Argus?° Or is the Dog more watchfull with 2 Eyes than his Grandfather was with a Hundred?

Morgan wanted me to come & shake Hands with you through the Door; but that was so like Pyramus & Thisbe that I could not bear the Thoughts of it.

Let me know in your Answer where Toby° is, when you heared from him & how I may direct to him. I writ to him at

Oxford & I hear he is in Whales; & though I have writ to him twice, would you think it! I have not heared from him once since I have been at Chapman's.°

I am Dear Watty, (thinking this long Enough for the Penny post)   yours sincerely
William Cowper

Direct to me at Mr Chapman's in Grevile Street near Holbourn.

To Chase Price

Grevile Street April 1st. 1752

Dear Toby

In return for your very agreeable favour I shall only present you with a few Lines which enter'd into my Pate as I was walking in the fields this Morning before Breakfast, and thinking what Compliment I should coin that might be worthy your Acceptance. In which you are to understand that with the Politeness of most Criticks I bestow much greater Commendation upon my own Judgment, than upon your Performance—However tho' I have Impudence enough to commend myself, I know you too well to shock your Modesty with an Encomium which tho' you really deserve, it would require more Eloquence than I am Master of, to make you think so. Ah! que Je suis bien poli—

> Trust me, the Meed of Praise dealt thriftily
> From the Nice Scale of Judgment, Honours more,
> Than does the lavish and o'erbearing Tide
> Of profuse Courtesy—& not all the Gems
> Of India's richest Soil at random spread
> O'er the gay Vesture of some glittering Dame,
> Give such bewitching Graces to the person,
> As the scant Lustre of a few, with choice
> And Comely guise of Ornament bestow'd.

I shall only observe how artfully you have ensur'd my Approbation by paying a Compliment to Celia at the same

time that you flatter my Vanity no less, by shewing that you
think my Nonsense worth a place in your Memory, & even in
your Performance. But I Question whether if you look in your
Common Place Book you will not find all this under Title,
Flummery° according to the Modern Expression, so it were best
to have done.

The very thing you say of Happiness I said t'other Day of
Content, which is only another Name for the same thing. It
will help to fill up this side so I will send it you.

O! ask not where Contentment may abide
  In whose still Mansion those true Joys abound
  That pour sweet Balm o'er Fortune's fest'ring Wound,
Whether she chuse sequester'd to reside
In the lone Hamlet on some Mountain wide,
  Whose rough top with brown Oaks or Pine Trees crown'd,
  Casts a dim Shade a settled gloom around:—
Or whether She amidst the glittering Tide
  Of Courtiers, pouring from the thick-throng'd Gate
Of Majesty, be seen: She nor assumes
  The high-swol'n Pomp of haughty-miened State,
Nor constant to the low-roof'd Cottage comes:
  On Honest Minds alone she deigns to wait.
There closes still her downy-feather'd Plumes;
  Nor wand'ring thence shifts her serene abode,
Pleas'd to possess the *Noblest Work of God.*

N:B: Pope says—

An Honest Man's the Noblest Work of God.°

I am sorry to find my Surmise was but too well grounded, I
hope the Rheumatism will not prevent your coming to Town
soon, 'till when I shall defer looking out for Chambers,° for I
shall be more likely to chose right and to my own Satisfaction
when you are here to *help chose.*

I hear from a good person that Watty Bagot is surpriz'd
that he hears not from me, I could tell him that I am no less
surpriz'd at his surprize, than he can be at my Silence. And so
you may tell him when you write to him next.

An Admirable thing is just publish'd by Mason of
Cambridge, which you shall read when you come to Town.

He calls it Elfrida° a Dramatick Poem: It is written upon the Greek Plan, like Samson Agonistes, & Comus—I do not find that it is much known in the World as yet, I picked it up accidentally at Brown's Coffee House,° & having read it there, recommended it to 2 or 3 who may be call'd sound & staunch Judges of all works of Genius. I need not tell you how they approved of it, *after having told you that it met with my Sov'reign Approbation.*

            I am Dear Toby | Your in & Sincere Friend
                                     W. Cowper.

Do prithee learn to write with your Mouth or your Toes, for your hands may probably be so often disabled for writing, that you may burst for want of communicating your Thoughts.

To Chase Price

                               Temple Feb: 21:1754.

Dear Toby

     I was just going to bestow the highest Encomiums upon you for having been so very punctual, when casting my Eyes upon your Postcript, it occurr'd to me, that you was not entirely disinterested in the Affair; yet I must in Justice to my *own Merit* allow it to be a very Laudable Motive, and wonder not that you who have been bless'd with a Specimen of my *Excellent Taste* in Poetry, are Impatient 'till you are in full Possession of all my Works. A certain Person° who is not at all Dear to me to speak of, has given herself the Air of calling me a *Coxcomb* often before now; I am willing to allow *her* the Privilege of *calling* me so, because I know she cannot in reality think me one, and Love me as she does. Now think not that because I have a *small Regard* for you, that therefore I shal dispense with your taking the same Liberty, for you may still entertain a Friendship for me and nevertheless be really & truly convinced that I am a Coxcomb, nay, you may like me the better for that Reason, Because—Simile agit in Simile.°

     And are you not a Coxcomb? Can you deny it? Is not your last Letter a Proof of it? Don't you there Brag of being better

Qualified to entertain the Fair Sex than my Worship? And don't you undervalue me as being Deficient in the most Essential point perhaps of good Breeding? Whatever Merit you are willing to ascribe to yourself from a more frequent Communication with the vicious part of the Sex, I am very ready to allow you—Only at the same time you must acknowledge that all the Advantages which arise from a Decent Familiarity with the worthiest part of it, are on my Side. The *Honest Impudence°* (as Ranger calls it) of a Libertine, will hardly defend him from Bashfullness in the Company of a Modest Woman; nay the very means he has made use of, whereby he has Acquir'd this Honest Impudence, disqualify him for the Entertainment of any, except those Women to whom he owes it. If this be the case, which is likely to make the best Figure in the best Company, He who cannot say a Rude thing, or he, who in order to avoid saying a Rude thing, must take care not to open his Lips! Come then, *Honest, Impudent* Toby, own for once, that it is not so wonderfull that I should have won the Affections of a Virtuous Woman, who saw that my Behaviour, various as it was, had no Mixture of Affectation in it: as it would have been; had you prevail'd in the same manner, who could not do it by appearing in your own undisguis'd Character, nor have affected to put on a Sedate Sober Appearance, without being discover'd for an Impostor. I beleive I have said rather more in my own Favour than there is Foundation for, and have somewhat Extenuated, or rather been Silent upon the Subject of the good Qualitys you are really Master of—But all this you must Impute to my *Modest assurance.* It is plain from your Letter, that you have a Heart susceptible of those sublime Enjoyments which you seem almost to Envy me. There is also some Appearance of Contrition towards the latter End of it; for which reason, if the Maxim be true that when a Man of Sense perceives & confesses his Error he is in a fair way to Amend it, I know not any Reason you have to Despair of succeeding in your Addresses to a Virtuous Woman. I wish you was once fairly taken in, for an affair of that sort would undoubtedly complete your Reformation; nothing else can—However I would advise you to wait 'till you are deeply smitten before you accost her as a Lover; your Reformation must be the Effect of your

Regard for her, and of your *very Sincere* Regard for her, otherwise it can never last. I think I know enough of you to pronounce, that any good Resolution you can make merely from a *Conviction* that it is Right, will be of no long Continuance; Your *Passions* must be strongly affected, so that what you Resolve upon, it shall become Delightfull to you to perform, or you are as far from the Performance of it as before you resolved.

I will answer your Question in your own Words—You must Amend, or Despair of finding in Honest Matrimony a sure Contentment.—Whatever means you think likely to work such a Reformation I would advise you to pursue; Neither the Single nor the Marry'd State afford any sure Contentment But to the Virtuous. A Vicious man in the Single State may perhaps find his Existence at the latter end of his Days barely tolerable, while he is young it may possibly be Agreeable rather than not, but this is very Hazardous: In the marry'd State his Case is Desperate, whether Young or Old he must be miserable.— For *Vicious* please to Read *Libertine* and you may apply all I have said to Yourself. I look upon you as one of the very best Species of Libertines otherwise I should not Subscribe myself your Affectionate Friend

W. Cowper.

PS: I You may remember that there was some small Difference between me and the Person I hinted at in the Beginning of my Letter; the Enclosed° was wrote upon that Subject since I saw you last. All is Comfortable & Happy between us at presant and I doubt not will continue so for ever. Indeed we had neither of us any great reason to be Dissatisfied, & perhaps Quarrel'd merely for the sake of the Reconciliation—which you may be sure made Ample Amends. Adieu!

To Joseph Hill

Mr. Hill—

If I write not to you
As I gladly would do
To a Man of your Mettle & Sense,
'Tis a Fault I must own
For which I'll attone
When I take my Departure from hence

To tell you the Truth,
I'm a queer kind of Youth
And I care not if all the World knows it;
Whether Sloven, or Beau,
In Square, Alley, or Row,
At Whitehall, in the Court, or the Closet.

Having written this much
In Honest high Dutch,
I must now take a Nobler Stile up:
Give my Fancy, a prick,
My Invention, a Kick,
And my Genius a pretty smart Fillip

For the Bus'ness in hand
You are to understand,
Is indeed neither trifling nor small:
But which you may transact
If your Scull is not crackt
As well as the best of them all.

And so may your *Dear Wife*
Be the Joy of your Life,
And of all our brave Troops the Commandress,
As you shall convey
What herein I say
To the very fair Lady, my Laundress.

That to Town I shall Trot
(No I Lie, I shall not,
For to Town I shall Jog in the Stage)

On October the Twentieth,
For my Father consenteth
To make me the Flower of the Age.

So bid her prepare°
Every Table & Chair,
And warm well my Bed by the Fire,
And if this be not done
I shall break her Back bone
As sure as I ever come nigh her.

I am Jovial & Merry,
Have writ till I'm weary.
And become, with a great deal of Talking, horse
So farewell—Sweet Lad!
Is all I shall add,
Except——

> your obedient *Stalking Horse*°
> W Cowper.

G Berk: | Octbr. 10th. 1755.

To John Duncombe

My dear Jacky,

I wish you had a more comfortable place° to end your days in, than that which I have so lately taken my leave of. For my own part, I believe no man ever quitted his Native place with less Regrett than myself, and were it not for the sake of a Friend or two° that I have left behind me, one of which small Number you will doubtless reckon yourself, I should never wish to see either the place or any thing that belongs to it again. Notwithstanding this Jack, you & I have spent many merry hours together in the Parsonage, my poor Father has often been the better for your Drollery, for you had the Knack, or the *Natural* Gift of making him Laugh, when no Creature else could have done it.

For this single reason, I should always have a regard, & a very Sincere one, for old Cicero, had I no other, and by the same rule, I shall continue to despise some certain persons, who treated him in a manner which did not indeed disgrace him, so much as it did themselves. It was hard upon him who did nothing to create him an Enemy, that he should find so few Friends; but it is the Lot of many others, and I hope as to myself, that the sort of men who professed themselves his Enemys, will everlastingly be mine.°

God bless you Jack, I can write no more at present, let me hear from you again & believe me in the mean time | Yours
                                                            Wm Cowper.

PS. | I have desired my Mother° to send you the Gold Sleeve buttons, which were my Father's, & imagine they will not be the less acceptable because they were his.

June 16. | 1757.

To John Duncombe

My Dear John,

The Old Proverb You mention may hold good with respect to most people but has nothing to do with You, who are not to be forgot by any man that has seen half so much of you as I have. And for This you are not more obliged to my Memory, than to your own Extraordinary Qualitys, which exist only in yourself.

My Brother told me that you entertained him sumptuously; I wish I could have partaken of the Treat, both because it is a singular Honour to be Entertained by You, who seldom make any Entertainments, and because I know no man at whose Table I should be more welcome. 'Tis true enough that I am not fond of the Law, but I am very fond of the Money that it produces, and have much too great a Value for my own Interest to be Remiss in my Application to it. I heartily wish I had an Opportunity of seeing you, because I believe you are Sincere when you say it would give you Pleasure to find yourself once more in my Company. It is long since our last Meeting Old Jack, and may be long before we meet again, but never Imagine, whether you hear from me or not, that I have so treacherous a Memory as to forget you. My Oldest Friends have the highest place in my Esteem, & you know very well that you are not a New one. Make my Compliments to Mrs. Essington,° and light your Pipe with This Epistle, unless you have immediate Occasion to make a different Use of it—

Yours Old Friend
Wm Cowper.

Temple | Nov: 21. 1758.

To John Duncombe

Dear Jack,

I have a great respect for your Virtues, notwithstanding that in your Letter to my Brother you talk Bawdy like an Old Midwife. You wonder I am not a more Punctual Correspondent; how the Devil should I be so, or what Subject can I possibly find to Entertain you upon? If I had a share in the Cabinet Councils of every Court in Europe, you would have no Pleasure in a Political Epistle; if I was a greater Philosopher than Sir Isaac Newton, you would think me a Fool if I should write to you upon the Subject of the Centripetal & Centrifugal Powers, the Solar System, and the Eccentrick Orbits of the Comets; And as great a Lawyer as I am, I dare not Indulge myself in the Pedantry of my Profession, lest you should not understand me, or I should not understand myself—In short I am afraid to tell you anything but that I am your most Obedient & Affectionate humble Servant

Wm C.

June 12. | 1759.

To the Nonsense Club°

[c.1760]

Letter from an owl to a bird of paradise.

Sir,

I have lately been under some uneasiness at your silence, and began to fear that our friends in Paradise were not so well as I could wish; but I was told yesterday that the pigeon you employed as a carrier, after having been long pursued by a hawk, found it necessary to drop your letter, in order to facilitate her escape. I send you this by the claws of a distant relation of mine, an eagle, who lives on the top of a neighbouring mountain. The nights being short at this time of the year, my epistle will probably be so too; and it strains my eyes not a little to write, when it is not as dark as pitch. I am likewise much distressed for ink: the blackberry juice which I had bottled up having been all exhausted, I am forced to dip my beak in the blood of a mouse, which I have just caught; and it is so very savoury, that I think in my heart I swallow more than I expend in writing. A monkey who lately arrived in these parts, is teaching me and my eldest daughter to dance. The motion was a little uneasy to us at first, as he taught us to stretch our wings wide, and to turn out our toes; but it is easier now. I, in particular, am a tolerable proficient in a horn-pipe, and can foot it very nimbly with a switch tucked under my left wing, considering my years and infirmities. As you are constantly gazing at the sun, it is no wonder that you complain of a weakness in your eyes; how should it be otherwise, when mine are none of the strongest, though I always draw the curtains over them as soon as he rises, in order to shut out as much of his light as possible? We have had a miserable dry season, and my ivy-bush is sadly out of repair. I shall be obliged to you if you will favour me with a shower or two, which you can easily do, by driving a few clouds together over the wood, and beating them about with your wings till they fall to pieces. I send you some of the largest berries the bush has produced, for your children to play withal. A neighbouring physician, who is a goat of great experience, says they will cure the worms; so if they should

chance to swallow them, you need not be frightened. I have
lately had a violent fit of the pip,° which festered my rump to a
prodigious degree. I have shed almost every feather in my tail,
and must not hope for a new pair of breeches till next spring;
so shall think myself very happy if I escape the chincough,°
which is generally very rife in moulting season.

I am, dear Sir, &c. &c.

Madge.°

P.S.—I hear my character as first minister° is a good deal
censured; but 'Let them censure; what care I?'

To Clotworthy Rowley

Dear Rowley,

Your Letter has taken me just in the Crisis, to:morrow I set
off for Brighthelmston,° and there I stay 'till the Winter brings
us all to Town again. This World is a shabby Fellow & uses us
ill, but a few years hence there will be no difference between
Us and our Fathers of the Tenth Generation upwards. I could
be as splenetick as you & with more reason if I thought proper
to indulge that Humour, but my Resolution is, & I would
advise you to adopt it, never to be melancholy while I have a
hundred pounds in the world to keep up my Spirits. God
knows how long that will be, but in the mean time, Iö
Triumphe.°—If a great Man struggling with Misfortunes is a
Noble Object, a little Man that despises them is no
contemptible one; And this is all the Philosophy I have in the
World at present; it savours pretty much of the Ancient Stoic,
but 'till the Stoics became Coxcombs they were in my Opinion
a very sensible Sect. If my Resolution to be a Great Man was
half so strong as it is to despise the Shame of being a little one,
I should not despair of a House in Lincoln's Inn Fields with
all its Appurtenances, for there is nothing more certain, & I
could prove it by a thousand Instances, than that every man
may be Rich if he will. What is the Industry of half the
Industrious Men in the World but Avarice, and call it by
which name you will, it almost always succeeds. But this

provokes me, that a Covetous Dog who will work by
Candle:light in a Winter Morning to get what he does not
want, shall be praised for his thriftiness, while a Gentleman
shall be abused for submitting to his Wants, rather than work
like an Ass to relieve them. Did you ever in your Life know a
man that was guided in the general Course of his Actions by
any thing but his natural Temper? And yet we blame each
other's Conduct as freely as if that Temper was the most
tractable Beast in the World, and we had nothing to do but to
twitch the Rein to the Right or the Left, and go just as we are
directed by others. All this is Nonsense, & nothing better.
There are some sensible Folks who having great Estates have
Wisdom enough too to spend them properly; there are others
who are not less Wise perhaps in knowing how to shift without
'em. Between these two degrees are they who spend their
Money dirtily, or get it so. If you ask me where they are to be
placed who amass much Wealth in an honest way, you must
be so good as to find them first and then I'll Answer the
Question. Upon the whole my dear Rowley, there is a degree
of Poverty that has no Disgrace belonging to it, that degree of
it I mean in which a man enjoys clean Linnen and good
Company, & if I never sink below this degree of it, I care not if
I never rise above it. This is a strange Epistle nor can I
imagine how the Devil I came to write it, but here it is such as
it is & much good may do you with it. I have no Estate as it
happens, so if it should fall into bad hands I shall be in no
danger of a Commission of Lunacy. Adieu! Carr° is well &
gives his Love to you.

Yours ever
Wm Cowper.

Sep. 2. 1762.

To Joseph Hill

[There are no surviving letters by Cowper from 9 Aug. 1763 until this one of 24 June 1765. After his breakdown in the Temple, hospitalization at Dr Cotton's, and conversion to evangelicalism, Cowper is totally changed and his vocabulary and sentiments are suffused with religious pieties.]

Huntingdon June 24. 1765.

Dear Joe,

The only Recompense I can make you for your friendly Attention to my Affairs, during my Illness, is to tell you that by the Mercy of God I am restored to perfect Health both of Mind and Body. This I beleive will give you Pleasure, and I would gladly do any thing from which you may receive it.

I left St. Albans on the 17th., arrived that day at Cambridge, spent some time there with my Brother, and came hither on the 22d. I have a Lodging that puts me continually in mind of our Summer Excursions; we have had many worse, and except the Size of it which however is sufficient for a single Man, but few better. I am not quite alone, having brought a Servant° with me from St. Albans, who is the very Mirrour of Fidelity and Affection for his Master. And whereas the Turkish Spy says° he kept no Servant because he would not have an Enemy in his House, I hired mine because I would have a Friend. Men do not usually bestow these Encomiums upon their Lacqueys, nor do they usually deserve them, but I have had Experience of mine both in Sickness and Health and never saw his Fellow.

The River Ouze, I forget how they spell it, is the most agreeable Circumstance in this part of the World. At This Town it is I beleive as wide as the Thames at Windsor; nor does the Silver Thames better deserve that Epithet, nor has it more Flowers upon its Banks, these being Attributes which in strict Truth belong to neither. Fluellin° would say they are as like as my Fingers to my Fingers, and there is Salmons in both. It is a noble Stream to bath in, and I shall make that use of it three times a Week, having introduced myself to it for the first time this Morning.

I beg you will remember me to all my Friends, which is a Task it will cost you no great Pains to execute. Parlicularly remember me to those of your own House, and beleive me your very Affectionate

Wm Cowper.

Direct to me at Mr. Martin's Grocer | at Huntingdon.

To Harriot Hesketh

Huntingdon, July 1, 1765.

My Dear Lady Hesketh,

Since the visit you were so kind as to pay me in the Temple (the only time I ever saw you without pleasure), what have I not suffered? And since it has pleased God to restore me to the use of my reason, what have I not enjoyed? You know by experience, how pleasant it is to feel the first approaches of health after a fever; but, Oh the fever of the brain! To feel the quenching of that fire is indeed a blessing which I think it impossible to receive without the most consummate gratitude. Terrible as this chastizement is, I acknowledge in it the hand of an infinite justice; nor is it at all more difficult for me to perceive in it the hand of an infinite mercy likewise, when I consider the effect it has had upon me. I am exceedingly thankful for it, and, without hypocrisy, esteem it the greatest blessing, next to life itself, I ever received from the divine bounty. I pray God that I may ever retain this sense of it, and then I am sure I shall continue to be as I am at present, really happy.

I write thus to you that you may not think me a forlorn and wretched creature; which you might be apt to do, considering my very distant removal from every friend I have in the world—a circumstance which, before this event befel me, would undoubtedly have made me so; but my affliction has taught me a road to happiness which without it I should never have found; and I know, and have experience of it every day, that the mercy of God, to him who believes himself the object of it, is more than sufficient to compensate for the loss of every other blessing.

You may now inform all those whom you think really interested in my welfare, that they have no need to be apprehensive on the score of my happiness at present. And you yourself will believe that my happiness is no dream, because I have told you the foundation on which it is built. What I have written would appear like enthusiasm to many, for we are apt to give that name to every warm affection of the mind in others, which we have not experienced in ourselves; but to you, who have so much to be thankful for, and a temper inclined to gratitude, it will not appear so.

I beg you will give my love to Sir Thomas, and believe that I am much obliged to you both, for enquiring after me at St. Albans.

Yours ever,
W.C.

To *Harriot Hesketh*

Huntingdon, July 4, 1765.

Being just emerged from the Ouze, I sit down to thank you, my dear Cousin, for your friendly and comfortable Letter. What could you think of my unaccountable behaviour to you in that visit I mentioned in my last? I remember I neither spoke to you, nor looked at you. The solution of the mystery indeed followed soon after, but at the same time it must have been inexplicable. The uproar within was even then begun, and my silence was only the sulkiness of a thunder-storm before it opens. I am glad however, that the only instance in which I knew not how to value your company was, when I was not in my senses. It was the first of the kind, and I trust in God it will be the last.

How naturally does affliction make us Christians! and how impossible is it when all human help is vain, and the whole earth too poor and trifling to furnish us with one moment's peace, how impossible is it then to avoid looking at the Gospel! It gives me some concern, though at the same time it increases my gratitude, to reflect that a convert made in Bedlam is more likely to be a stumbling-block to others, than to advance their faith. But if it has that effect upon any, it is owing to their reasoning amiss, and drawing their conclusions from false premises. He who can ascribe an amendment of life and manners, and a reformation of the heart itself, to madness, is guilty of an absurdity that in any other case would fasten the imputation of madness upon himself; for by so doing, he ascribes a reasonable effect to an unreasonable cause, and a positive effect to a negative. But when Christianity only is to be sacrificed, he that stabs deepest is always the wisest man. You, my dear Cousin, yourself, will be apt to think I carry the matter too far, and that in the present warmth of my heart, I make too ample a concession in saying that I am *only now* a convert. You think I always believed, and I thought so too, but you were deceived, and so was I. I called myself indeed a Christian, but he who knows my heart knows that I never did a right thing, nor abstained from a wrong one, because I was so. But if I did either, it was under the influence of some other motive. And it is such seeming Christians, such pretending believers, that do most mischief to the cause, and furnish the strongest arguments to support the infidelity of its enemies: unless profession and conduct go together, the man's life is a lie, and the validity of what he professes itself is called in question. The difference between a Christian and an Unbeliever would be so striking, if the treacherous allies of the Church would go over at once to the other side, that I am satisfied religion would be no loser by the bargain.

I reckon it one instance of the Providence that has attended me throughout this whole event, that instead of being delivered into the hands of one of the London physicians, who were so much nearer that I wonder I was not, I was carried to Doctor Cotton. I was not only treated by him with the greatest tenderness, while I was ill, and attended with the utmost diligence, but when my reason was restored to me, and I had so much need of a religious friend to converse with, to whom I could open my mind upon the subject without reserve, I could hardly have found a fitter person for the purpose. My eagerness and anxiety to settle my opinions upon that long neglected point, made it necessary that while my mind was yet weak, and my spirits uncertain, I should have some assistance. The Doctor was as ready to administer relief to me in this article likewise, and as well qualified to do it as in that which was more immediately his province. How many physicians would have thought this an irregular appetite, and a symptom of remaining madness! But if it were so, my friend was as mad as myself, and it is well for me that he was so.

My dear Cousin, you know not half the deliverances I have received; my Brother is the only one in the family who does. My recovery is indeed a signal one, but a greater if possible went before it. My future life must express my thankfulness, for by words I cannot do it.

I pray God bless you and my friend Sir Thomas.

Yours ever,
W.C.

To Joseph Hill

Dear Joe,

I am afraid the Month of October has proved rather unfavourable° to the belle Assemblée at Southampton; High Winds and continual Rains being bitter Enemies to that agreeable Lounge which you and I are equally fond of, I have very cordially betaken myself to my Book and my Fireside, and seldom leave them unless merely for Exercise. I have added another Family to the Number of those I was acquainted with when you was here. Their Name is Unwin— the most agreeable People imaginable; quite Sociable, and as free from the ceremonious Civility of Country Gentlefolks as any I ever met with. They treat me more like a near Relation than a Stranger, and their House is always open to me. The Old Gentleman carries me to Cambridge in his Chaise. He is a Man of Learning and good Sense, and as simple as Parson Adams.° His Wife, who is Young compared with her Husband, has a very uncommon Understanding, has read much to excellent purpose, and is more polite than a Dutchess. The Son, who belongs to Cambridge, is a most aimable Young Man, and the Daughter quite of a piece with the rest of the Family. They see but little Company which suits me exactly. Go when I will, I find the House full of Peace and Cordiality in all its parts, and am sure to hear no Scandal, but such Discourse instead of it, as we are all the better for. You remember Rousseau's Description of an English Morning;° such are the Mornings I spend with these Good People, and the Evenings differ from them in nothing, except that they are still more Snug and quieter. Now I know them, I wonder that I liked Huntingdon so well before I knew them, and am apt to think I should find every place disagreeable that had not an Unwin belonging to it.

This Incident convinces me of the Truth of an Observation I have often made, that when we circumscribe our Estimate of all that is clever within the Limits of our own Acquaintance, (which I at least have been always apt to do) we are guilty of a very uncharitable Censure upon the rest of the World, and of a Narrowness of Thinking disgracefull to ourselves. Wapping and Redriff° may contain some of the most Aimable Persons living, and such as one would go even to Wapping or Redriff to make an Acquaintance with. You remember Mr. Grey's Stanza°

> Full many a Gem of purest Ray Serene
> The deep unfathom'd Caves of Ocean bear,
> Full many a Rose is born to blush unseen,
> And waste its Fragrance on the Desart Air.

I have wrote to Eamonson,° and, as I expected have received no Answer. My Letter went the Day after You left Cambridge. I am afraid the Ten pounds you spoke of will grow mouldy if they lie at Child's° any longer. Shall be obliged to you therefore if you will remit them to Huntingdon.

My Love to all your Family, | Yours Dear Joe,
Wm Cowper.

Oct. 25. 1765

To Maria Cowper

Huntinn. Oct. 20. 1766.
My dear Cousin,
I am sorry for poor George's Illness,° and hope you will soon have Cause to thank God for his complete Recovery. We

have an Epidemical Fever in this Country likewise, which leaves behind it a continual Sighing almost to suffocation; not that I have seen any Instance of it, for Blessed be God our Family have hitherto escaped it, but such was the Account I heard of it this Morning.

I am obliged to you for the Interest you take in my Welfare, and for your enquiring so particularly after the manner in which my time passes here. As to Amusements, I mean what the World calls such, we have none: the Place indeed swarms with them, and Cards and Dancing are the professed Business of almost all the *Gentle* Inhabitants of Huntingdon. We refuse to take part in them, or to be Accessories to this way of Murthering our Time, and by so doing have acquired the Name of Methodists. Having told you how we *do not* spend our time, I will next say how we *do*. We Breakfast commonly between 8 and 9, 'till 11, we read either the Scripture, or the Sermons of some faithfull Preacher of those holy Mysteries: at 11 we attend divine Service which is performed here twice every day, and from 12 to 3 we separate and amuse ourselves as we please. During that Interval I either Read in my own Apartment, or Walk or Ride, or work in the Garden. We seldom sit an hour after Dinner, but if the Weather permits adjourn to the Garden, where with Mrs. Unwin and her Son I have generally the Pleasure of Religious Conversation 'till Tea time; if it Rains or is too windy for Walking, we either Converse within Doors, or sing some Hymns of Martin's Collection,° and by the Help of Mrs. Unwin's Harpsichord make up a tolerable Concert, in which however our Hearts I hope are the best and most musical Performers. After Tea we sally forth to walk in good earnest. Mrs. Unwin is a good Walker, and we have generally travel'd about 4 Miles before we see Home again. When the Days are short we make this Excursion in the former part of the Day, between Church time and Dinner. At Night we read and Converse as before 'till Supper, and commonly finish the Evening either with Hymns or a Sermon, and last of all the Family are called in to Prayers.—I need not tell *you* that such a Life as this is consistent with the utmost cheerfullness, accordingly we are all happy, and dwell together in Unity as Brethren. Mrs. Unwin has almost a maternal Affection for me, and I have something very like a filial one for her, and her Son and I are Brothers. Blessed be the God of my Salvation for such Companions, and for such a Life above all, for an Heart to like it.

I have had many anxious Thoughts about taking Orders: and I beleive every new Convert is apt to think himself called upon for that purpose; but it has pleased God, by means which there is no need to particularize, to give me full Satisfaction as to the Propriety of declining it. Indeed, they who have the least Idea of what I have suffered from the Dread of public Exhibitions, will readily excuse my never attempting them hereafter. In the mean time, if it please the Almighty, I may be an Instrument of turning many to the Truth, in a private way, & hope that my Endeavours in this Way have not been entirely unsuccessful. Had I the Zeal of Moses, I should want an Aaron to be my Spokesman.—Yours ever my Dear Cousin—

Wm Cowper.

I beg you will give my affectionate Respects to Mrs. Maitland° when you write to her, & to my Aunt Madan, whom now I *cannot* see her, I know how to value.—

To Maria Cowper

My dear Cousin,

The Newspaper° has told you the Truth. Poor Mr. Unwin being flung from his Horse as he was going to his Cure on Sunday Morning, received a dreadfull Fracture on the back part of his Scull, under which he languished 'till Thursday Evening and then died. This awful Dispensation has left an Impression upon our Spirits which will not presently be worn off. He died in a poor Cottage to which he was carried immediately after his Fall, about a Mile from home, and his Body could not be brought to his House, till the Spirit was gone to Him who gave it. May it be a Lesson to us to Watch, since we know not the Day nor the Hour when our Lord cometh.°

The Effect of it upon my Circumstances will only be a Change of the Place of my abode, for I shall still, by God's leave, continue with Mrs. Unwin, whose Behaviour to me has always been that of a Mother to a Son. By this afflictive Providence, it has pleased God, who always drops Comfort into the bitterest Cup, to open a Door for us out of an unevangelical Pasture, such as this is, into some better Ministry where we may hear the glad Tidings of Salvation, and be nourished by the Sincere Milk of the Word. We know not yet where we shall settle, but we trust that the Lord whom we seek, will go before us, and prepare a Rest for us. We have employed our Friend Haweis,° Dr. Conyers° of Helmsley in Yorkshire, and Mr. Newton of Olney to look out for us, but at present are entirely ignorant under which of the three we shall settle, or whether under either. I have wrote too to my Aunt Madan, to desire Martin to assist us with his Inquiries. It is probable we shall stay here 'till Michaelmas.

I beg my affectionate Respects to Mr. Cowper & all your Family, & am my Dear Cousin | Your Affectionate Friend & Servant

Wm Cowper.

July 13. 1767.

To Judith Madan

I wish, my dear Aunt, that any of my Letters may be made as effectual to your Consolation, as your last was to mine. I had for many days stood in great need of some spiritual Refreshment, having walked in Darkness, and found it a Trial of my utmost Strength to trust ever so little in the Lord, and stay upon my God. But his Mercy is ever watchfull over us, to pour Oil and Wine into our Wounds either with his own Hand, or by the Ministry of his faithfull Servants. I know he will recompense you for it, for though my Prayers are wretched things, and seem to myself generally to be little more than Lip:labour; yet he hears them graciously in my own behalf, and will not therefore turn away from them when they are preferred in yours. I may say safely that I *know* he hears them, because I know by the Gift of his free Mercy, that I have an allprevailing High:Priest and Intercessor at his Right Hand for ever, Jesus Christ the Righteous. Therefore though I am nothing and less than nothing & Vanity, yet the mighty God, the everlasting Lord, the Creator of the Ends of the Earth, will hear me. Oh! To what Privileges are Worms advanced, and how do the Extremes of Power & Weakness, Purity & Sinfullness meet together, by the Mediation of the Man Christ Jesus! The Lord give me some little Sense of his Goodness in this wonderfull Reconciliation!

I am afraid at present to put a Stop to the Enquiries of my Friends after a House for us, though I think I shall soon be able to do it with Security. Mr. Newton has sent us an Account of one, which seems by his Description to be the very thing we want, at a Village called Emberton, within about a Mile of his Church at Olney. He is in Treaty for us with the Owner of it, who lives it seems at a great Distance, so that we cannot have his definitive Answer in less than 10 days or a Fortnight. But there seems to be no Probability of any Objection to us on his part, nor are any Difficulties likely to arise on ours. It will be empty at Michaelmass.° Its Situation in this part of the World recommends it to Mrs. Unwin, who would wish to be near her Son,° and to me who would wish to be not altogether seperated from my Brother. The Lord will dispose of us according to his Goodness. Mr. Newton seems to have conceived a great Desire to have us for Neighbours, and I am sure we shall think ourselves highly favoured to be committed to the care of such a Pastor. May we be enabled to hold him in double Honour for his Work's sake, according to the Will of the great Shepherd of us All!

I have a great Regard for Lady Hesketh, a sincere Affection; and am therefore glad of Opportunities to lead her thoughts, as far as the Lord shall enable me, to the Things that belong to her Peace, so that I never write to her without attempting it. But there are wide Gaps in our Correspondence, which nevertheless proceeds after a Fashion. I received from her very lately a kind Invitation to Ealing, but Necessity is laid upon me, and I cannot accept those Offers. Though she is every thing that's Aimiable among men, yet I fear the Vail is upon her Heart, for I have never heard her speak Shibboleth plainly, nor does the Abundance of her poor Heart seem to be what it should be. Yet the Lord may have purposes of Grace toward her, which I beseech him to manifest in his own time. She sent me some time since the Stanzas° you mention, which I think are exceeding good. My dear Aunt! How lovely must be the Spirits of just men made perfect,° since Creatures so lovely in our Eyes, may yet have the Wrath of God abiding on them. The Lord avert it from Her, and number her with the glorious Assembly before his Throne for ever.

Your Affectionate Nephew
Wm Cowper.

July 18. 1767.

To Judith Madan

Dear Aunt,

I should not have suffered your last kind Letter to have laid by me so long unanswer'd, had it not been for many Hindrances and especially One, which has engaged much of my Attention. My dear Friend Mrs. Unwin, whom the Lord gave me to be a Comfort to me in that Wilderness from which he has just delivered me, has been for many Weeks past in so declining a way, and has suffered so many Attacks of the most excruciating Pain, that I have hardly been able to keep alive the faintest Hope of her Recovery. I know that our God heareth Prayer, and I know that he hath opened mine and many Hearts amongst this People to pray for her. Here lies my chief Support, without which I should look upon myself as already deprived of her. Again when I consider the great Meetness to which the Lord has wrought her for the Inheritance in Light, her most exemplary Patience under the sharpest Sufferings, her truly Christian Humility and Resignation, I am more than ever inclined to beleive that her Hour is come. Let me engage your Prayers for Her, and for Me. You know what I have most need of upon an Occasion like this: Pray that I may receive it at His Hands from whom every good and perfect Gift proceeds.° She is the chief Blessing I have met with in my Journey since the Lord was pleased to call me, and I hope the Influence of her edifying and Excellent Example will never leave me. Her Illness has been a sharp Trial to me—Oh that it may have a sanctified Effect, that I may rejoice to Surrender up to the Lord my dearest Comforts the Moment he shall require them. Oh! for no Will but the Will of my Heavenly Father! Doctor Cotton for whose advice we went together to St. Albans about a Month since, seemed to have so little Expectation that Medicine could help her, that he might be said to give her over. He prescribed however, but she has hardly been able to take his Medicines. Her Disorder is a Nervous Atrophy attended with violent Spasms of the Chest and Throat, and This is a bad Day with her; worse than common.

I return you many Thanks for the Verses you favor'd me with, which speak sweetly the Language of a Christian Soul. I wish I could pay you in kind, but must be contented to pay you in the best kind I can. I began to compose them Yesterday Morning before Daybreak, but fell asleep at the End of the two first Lines, when I awaked again the third and fourth were whisper'd to my Heart in a way which I have often experienced.

> Oh for a closer Walk with God,°
>   A calm & heav'nly Frame,
> *A Light to shine upon the Road*
>   *That leads me to the Lamb*!
>
> Where is the Blessedness I knew
>   When first I saw the Lord?
> Where is the Soul:refreshing View
>   Of Jesus in his Word?
>
> What peacefull Hours I then enjoy'd,
>   How sweet their Mem'ry still!
> But they have left an Aching Void
>   The World can never fill.
>
> Return, O Holy Dove, Return,
>   Sweet Messenger of Rest,
> I hate the Sins that made thee mourn
>   And drove thee from my Breast.

The dearest Idol I have known,
   Whate'er that Idol be,
Help me to tear it from Thy Throne,
   And worship Only Thee.

Then shall my Walk be close with God,
   Calm and serene my Frame,
Then purer Light shall mark the Road
   That leads me to the Lamb.

Yours my dear Aunt in the Bands of that Love which cannot be quenched

                             Wm Cowper.

Olney. Dece. 10. 67.

To Judith Madan

                                   [15 January 1768]

My dear Aunt

   I put off writing to you from day to day in hopes, that I shall find a subject in my own experience that may make it worth your while to hear from me. I would not always be complaining of barrenness and deadness, yet alas! I have little else to write about. The Lord has given me so many blessings in possession, and enabled me to hope assuredly for such unspeakable things when the great work of redemption shall be effectually completed in me that wheresoever I look, I see something that reminds me of ingratitude. If I look behind me, I see dangers, and precipices, and the bottomless pit, from whence He has plucked me with an outstretched arm, made bare for my deliverance. If I look forward, I see the sure portion of His people, an everlasting inheritance in light, and the covenant that secures it, sealed with the blood of Jesus. My present condition too is full of tokens of His love: the things which others may reckon in the number of their common mercies are not so to me, at least ought not to be such in my esteem. The breath I draw, and the free exercise of my senses, He has not only given to me, but restored them when I had deservedly forfeited both; and not only restored them to me, but accompanied them with such additional mercies, as can alone make them true and real blessings, faith in the Lord Jesus Christ as the only Saviour, and a desire to employ them, and every gift I receive from Him to the glory of His name. In the day of my first love I could not have enumerated those instances of His goodness without tears, but now, my reflections upon them serve rather to convince me of the dreadful obduracy of my nature, and afford me even a sensible proof that nothing less than the breath of the Almighty Spirit can soften it. But blessed be the Lord. Our anchor of hope is fastened on good ground, not in our own righteousness, but in that of Jesus: and every view of our own unworthiness is sanctified to us, and becomes a solid blessing if it drives us closer to our only refuge. Since I wrote the above, I have been taking a walk, and from my going out, to my coming in, I have been mourning over (I am afraid I ought to say repining at) my great insensibility. I began with these reflections soon after I rose this morning, and my attempt to write to you has furnished me with additional evidences of it. I profess myself a servant of God, I am writing to a servant of God, and about the things of God, and yet can hardly get forward so as to fill my paper. I can only tell you my dear Aunt that I love you, and I hope too for the Lord's sake; but I cannot *speak* any more than I can *do* the things that I would. I shall only add at this time that I am | dear aunt | Your Affectionate | &c. &c

To Maria Cowper

[In Sept. 1769, John Cowper became suddenly and violently ill. William went to Cambridge for about ten days to tend his brother, who quickly recovered his strength. Six months later, on 16 Feb. 1770, Cowper was again summoned to Cambridge. After a month— on 20 Mar.—John died. During that time, William had comforted his brother, who gradually became aware of the sufferings William had endured seven years earlier in the Temple. John also renounced his more worldly religion in favour of the gospel truths which William advocated.]

Dear Cousin,

My Brother continues much as he was. His Case is a very dangerous one. An Imposthume of the Liver, attended by an

Asthma & Dropsy. The Physician° has little Hope of his Recovery. I beleive I might say none at all, only, being a Friend, he does not formally give him over by ceasing to Visit him, lest it should sink his Spirits. For my own part I have no Expectation of his Recovery except by a signal Interposition of Providence in Answer to Prayer. His Case is clearly out of the Reach of Medicine, but I have seen many a Sickness heal'd where the Danger has been equally threatening, by the only Physician of Value. I doubt not he will have an Interest in your Prayers, as he has in the Prayers of many—may the Lord incline his Ear, and give an Answer of Peace!

I am much to be blamed for having so long neglected to write to you—I have as long neglected to write to my Aunt, but I hope that a fair Confession of my Fault, with a purpose of Amendment, will plead my Pardon with you both.

I know it is good to be afflicted—I trust that you have found it so, and that under the Teaching of God's own Spirit we shall both be purified by the many Furnaces into which he is pleased to cast us. The World is a Wilderness to Me, and I desire to find it such, 'till it shall please the Lord to release me from it. It is the Desire of my Soul to seek a better Country, where God shall wipe away all Tears from the Eyes of his People, and where, looking back upon the Ways by which he has led us, we shall be filled with everlasting Wonder, Love, & Praise.

My present Affliction is as great as most I have experienced: but

When I can hear my Saviour say,°
Strength shall be equal to thy Day,
Then I rejoice in deep Distress,
Leaning on All:sufficient Grace.

I beg you will present my affectionate Respects to the Family you are with. I often think of them, and when I do so, I think we shall meet no more 'till the great Trumpet brings us together. May we all appear at the Right Hand of that Blessed Emanuel, who has loved poor Sinners, & washed them from their Sins in his own most precious Blood.

My poor Brother is continually talking in a delirious way,

which makes it difficult for me to know what I write. I must add no more therefore, but that I am | my dear Cousin | Yours ever, with sincere Affection,

Wm Cowper.

Mar. 5. 1770.

To John Newton

Cambridge, 11 Mar: 1770

My dear Friend

I am in haste to make you a partaker of my Joy. Oh praise the Lord with me, and let us exalt his name together. My lamb that was lost is found, my child that was dead is alive again—The Lord has done it, he has given me the desire of my heart, my Brother is born of God.—My joy will not suffer me to sleep, and I have peace which cannot be expressed.

Yesterday in the afternoon he suddenly burst into tears, and said with a loud cry, 'O forsake me not!' I went to the bed-side when he grasped my hand, and I presently by his eyes and countenance found he was in prayer. Then turning to me, he said, 'Brother, I am full of what I could say to *You*.' The Nurse asked him if he would have any hartshorn or lavender.° He replied, 'none of these things will serve my purpose.' But I said, 'I know what would my dear, don't I?' He answered, 'you do, Brother.'

I left him for about an hour because I was afraid lest he should fatigue himself by too much talking, and because I wanted to praise the Lord for what I undertood to be clear evidence of a work begun. When I returned he said, 'Brother, if I live you and I shall be more like one another than we have been; whether I live or not all is well and will be so, I know it will, for I have felt that which I never felt before, and I am sure that God has visited me with this sickness to teach me what I was too proud to learn in health. I never had satisfaction 'till now. The doctrines I had been used to referred me to myself for the foundation of my hope, and then I could find nothing to rest upon. The sheet anchor of the soul was wanting.° I thought you wrong, yet wanted to believe as you did. I found myself unable to believe, yet always thought that one day I should be brought to do so. You suffered more than I have done before you believed these truths, but our sufferings though different in their kind & measure were directed to the same end. I hope he has taught me *that* which he teaches none but his own. I hope so. These things were foolishness to me once, I could not understand them, but now I have a solid foundation, and am satisfied.'

He spoke this with his arm about my neck, leaning his head against mine in the most composed manner.—When I went to bid him good night, he took hold of my hand, and resumed his discourse as follows.

'As empty and yet full, as having nothing and yet possessing all things. I see the rock upon which I once split, and I see the rock of my salvation. I have peace myself, and if I live I hope it will be that I may be made a messenger of the same peace to others. I have learned *that* in a moment which I could not have learned by reading many books in many years. I have often studied these points, and studied them with great attention, but was blinded by prejudice; and unless he who alone is worthy to unloose the seals,° had opened the book to me, I had been blinded still. Now they appear so plain, that though I am convinced no comment could ever have made me undertand them, I wonder I did not see them before—Yet my doubts and difficulties have only served to pave the way, and now they are solved, they make it plainer. The light I have received comes late, but it is a comfort to me that I never made the Gospel truths a subject of ridicule. Though I was averse to the persuasion and ways of God's people, I ever thought them respectable, and therefore not proper to be made a jest of.—I should delight to see the people of Olney, but am not worthy to appear amongst them. I should rejoice in an hour's conversation with Mr. Newton, but I am so weak in body that at present I could not bear it.'

I bid him good night, having talked with him so long as I thought it was safe to do so—and he tells me this morning, that the moment when he sent forth that cry, was the moment when light was darted into his soul.—He had thought much about these things in the course of his illness, but never 'till that instant was able to understand them.

It seems he has been in pursuit of the truth these five years, and tells me he believes he has read every author of note upon the subject. He has been long used to consider himself as appointed to instruct the people committed to his care in the most important concerns, and therefore accountable for his doctrine as well as his practice. He thinks he can say he never wilfully erred, but can make his appeal to the Lord, that in all that time, he was sincerely desirous of coming to the knowledge of the truth. I should be glad to fill my paper, but want of sleep and fatigue of spirits through the great emotions I have felt upon this occasion, oblige me to conclude. I will only add what he said to me this evening, as a wonderful proof of the power of God to build up a Soul and establish it in the truth in a few hours. His words were these: 'The evil I suffer is the consequence of my descent from the corrupt original stock and of my own transgressions. The Good I enjoy comes to me as the overflowing of his bounty; but the crown of all his mercies is this, that he has given me a Saviour, and not only the Saviour of Mankind, but my Saviour,

Yours my dear friend, you may imagine in much joy & peace & in the bonds of Gospel love

Wm. Cowper

To Judith Madan

Dear Aunt,

You may possibly by this time have heard of the Death of my dear Brother. I should not have left you to learn of it from any but myself, had I either spirits or opportunity to write sooner. He died on Tuesday last, the 20th. It was not judged proper that I should attend the Funeral. I therefore took leave of the melancholy scene as soon as possible, and returned to Olney on Thursday. He has left me to sing of Mercy and Judgment. Greater sufferings than he underwent are seldom seen, Greater Mercy than he received, I believe never. His views of Gospel Grace were as clear, and his sense of his Interest in Christ, as strong, as if he had been exercised in the Christian walk and warfare many years. This is my consolation,

and strong consolation I find it, that he is gone to his Father
and my Father, to his God and my God.°

He is to be buried at his Living° about seven miles from
Cambridge, by his own desire, this day. The Master° and
Fellows attend the Funeral.

I am, Dear Aunt, | Yours affectionately in the Lord
Wm Cowper

Olney | March 24th 1770

I shall be obliged to you, my Dear Aunt, if the next time you
write to dear Mrs Cowper at York,° you will be so good as to
inform her of this event.

To Joseph Hill

[There are no letters extant by Cowper from 14 Nov. 1772 to 18 May
1776. This is largely owing to the derangement he suffered in
early 1773 which lasted until the middle of 1774. During the winter of
1773, Cowper experienced a nightmare 'before the recollection of
which, all consolation vanishes'. In this dream, he heard the
dread words: 'Actum est de te, periisti' ('It is all over with you, you
have perished'). Cowper had become engaged to marry Mrs Unwin,
but this was broken off. In Apr. he moved to the Olney vicarage
under the care of the Newtons and did not return to his home,
Orchard Side, until 23 May 1774, over a year later. As he edged
slowly back to a semblance of normality, letter-writing became an
avocation to keep depression at bay. The letters to William Unwin
from 1779 to 1781 are particularly playful, displaying Cowper's
talents as mentor, raconteur, and wit.]

Dear Friend,

The very agreeable Contents of your last came safe to hand
in the Shape of two Notes for 30£.—I am to thank you
likewise for a Barrel of very good Oysters received about a
Fortnight ago.

One to whom Fish is so welcome as it is to me, can have no
great Occasion to distinguish the Sorts. In general therefore
whatever Fish are likely to think a Jaunt into the Country
agreeable, will be sure to find me ready to receive them; Butts,
Plaice, Flounder or any other. If Herrings are yet to be had, as
they cannot be bought at Olney 'till they are good for nothing,

they will be welcome too. We have seen none this year except a Parcel that Mrs. Unwin sent for, & the Fishmonger sent Stale ones, a Trick they are apt to put upon their Customers at a Distance.

Having suffer'd so much by Nervous Fevers myself, I know how to congratulate Ashley upon his Recovery. Other Distempers only Batter the Walls, but They creep silently into the Citadel & put the Garrison to the Sword.

You perceive I have not made a Squeamish Use of your obliging Offer. The Remembrance of past Years, & of the Sentiment formerly exchanged in our Evening Walks convinces me still that an unreserved Acceptance of what is generously offer'd, is the Handsomest way of dealing with one of your Character.

Beleive me Yours
Wm Cowper.

Nove. 12. 76.

The Willingborough Diligence passes our Door ev'ry Tuesday, Thursday & Saturday, & Inns at the Cross Keys St. John Street Smithfield.

As to the Frequency which you leave to my Choice too, you have no need to exceed the Number of your former Remittances.

To William Unwin

My dear Friend,

I hurry you into the Midst of things at once, which if it be not much in the Epistolary Stile, is acknowledg'd however to be very Sublime.—Mr. Morley, Videlicet the grocer, is guilty of such Neglect and Carelessness, and has lately so much disappointed your Mother, that she is at last obliged to leave him, and begs you will send her Mr. Rawlinson's Address,° that she may transfer her Custom to Him.—She adds moreover, that she was well aware of the Unseasonableness of Salmon at this time, & did not mean that you should order any to Olney till the Spring.

We are indebted to you for your Political Intelligence, but

have it not in our Power to pay you in kind. Proceed however
to give us such Information as cannot be learn'd from the
Newspaper, and when any thing arises at Olney that is not in
the threadbare Stile of daily Occurrences, you shall hear of it
in Return. Nothing of this sort has happen'd lately, except
that a Lion was imported here at the Fair,° Seventy Years of
Age, & as tame as a Goose. Your Mother and I saw him
embrace his Keeper with his Paws, and lick his Face. Others
saw him receive his Head in his Mouth, and restore it to him
again unhurt. A Sight we chose not to be favor'd with, but
rather advised the Honest Man to discontinue the Practise. A
Practise hardly reconcileable to Prudence, unless he had had a
Head to spare. The Beast however was a very Magnificent
one, and much more Royal in his Appearance, than those I
have seen in the Tower.°

The Paper tells us° that the Chancellor is frequently at the
Register Office, having conceived a Design to shorten the
Proceedings in his court. If he has indeed such a Purpose in
View, he is so Industrious and so Resolute, that he will never
let it drop unaccomplish'd. Perhaps the Practitioners will
have no reason to regret it, as they may gain in such an Event,
more by the Multiplicity of Suits, than they do at present by
the Length of them.

Your Mother joins me in affectionate Respects, I should
have said, in Love, to yourself, Mrs. Unwin, Miss Shuttleworth°
and Little John.° If you will accept this for a Letter, perhaps I
may be able to furnish more such upon Occasion.

Yours with Thanks for your last
Wm Cowper.—

July 18.–78.

To William Unwin

[July 1779]

My dear Friend,
    If you please you may give my Service to Mr. James
Martin, Glazier,° & tell him that I have furnish'd myself with
Glass from Bedford for just half the Money.

When I was at Margate it was an Excursion of Pleasure to go to see Ramsgate. The Pier, I remember, was accounted a most excellent Piece of Stonework, and such I found it. By this time I suppose it is finish'd, and surely it is no small advantage that you have an Opportunity of Observing how nicely those great Stones are put together, as often as you please, without either Trouble or Expence. But you think Margate more lively—So is a Cheshire Cheese full of Mites more Lively than a Sound one, but that very Liveliness only proves its Rottenness. I remember too that Margate tho' full of Company, was generally fill'd with such Company, as People who were Nice in the choice of their Company, were rather fearfull of keeping Company with. The Hoy° went to London every Week Loaded with Mackarel & Herrings, and return'd Loaded with Company. The Cheapness of the Conveyance made it equally commodious for Dead Fish and Lively Company. So Perhaps your Solitude at Ramsgate may turn out another Advantage, at least I should think it One.

There was not at that Time, much to be seen in the Isle of Thanet besides the Beauty of the Country & the fine Prospects of the Sea: which are no where surpass'd except in the Isle of Wight, & upon some Parts of the Coast of Hampshire. One Sight however, I remember engaged my Curiosity & I went to See it. A Fine Piece of Ruins, built by the late Lord Holland at a great Expence, which the Day after I saw it, Tumbled down for Nothing.° Perhaps therefore it is still a Ruin, and if it is I would advise you by all Means to Visit it, as it must have been much improved by this fortunate Incident. It is hardly possible to put Stones together with that Air of Wild & Magnificent Disorder which they are sure to acquire by falling of their own Accord.

We heartily wish that Mrs. Unwin may receive the utmost Benefit of Bathing. At the same time we caution *You* against the use of it, however the Heat of the Weather may seem to recommend it. It is not safe for thin Habits, Hectically inclin'd.

I remember (the fourth & last thing I mean to Remember upon this Occasion) that Sam: Cox the Council,° walking by the Sea Side as if absorb'd in deep Contemplation, was question'd about what He was Musing on. He replied, I was wondering that such an almost infinite and unwieldly Element, should produce a Sprat.

Our Love attends the Whole Party. | Yours Affectionately

Wm Cowper.

You are desired to Purchase 3 Pounds of Sixpenny White Worsted, at a Shop well recommended for that Commodity. The Isle of Thanet is famous for it beyond any other Place in the Kingdom.

To William Unwin

Amico Mio!

Be pleased to Buy me a Glazier's Diamond Pencil; I have Glazed the two Frames designed to receive my Pine Plants,° but I cannot mend the Kitchen Windows 'till by the Help of that Implement I can reduce the Glass to its proper Dimensions. If I were a Plumber I should be a complete Glazier, and possibly the happy time may come when I shall be seen trudging away to the Neighbouring Towns with a Shelf of Glass hanging at my Back. If Government should impose another Tax upon that Commodity,° I hardly know a Business in which a Gentleman might more successfully employ himself. A Chinese of ten times my Fortune would avail himself of such an Opportunity without Scruple, & why should not I, who want Money as much as any Mandarin in China. Rousseau would have been charmed to have seen me so occupied, & would have exclaimed with Rapture, that he had found the Emilius° who he supposed had subsisted only in his own Idea. I would recommend it to you to follow my Example, you will presently qualify yourself for the Task, and may not only amuse yourself at Home, but may even exercise your Skill in mending the Church Windows, which as it would save Money to the Parish, would conduce together with your other Ministerial Accomplishments to make you extremely popular in the Place.

I have 8 Pair of tame Pigeons—when I first Enter the Garden in a Morning, I find them Perched upon the Wall, waiting for their Breakfast, for I feed them always upon the

Gravel Walk. If your Wish should be accomplished, & you should find yourself furnish'd with the Wings of a Dove, I shall undoubtedly find you amongst them. Only be so good, if that should be the Case, as to announce yourself by some means or other, for I imagine, your Crop will require something better than Tares to fill it.

Your Mother and I, last Week made a Trip in a Post Chaise to Gayhurst, the Seat of Mr. Wright, about 4 Miles off. He understood that I did not much affect Strange Faces, and sent over his Servant on purpose to inform me that he was going into Leicestershire, & that if I chose to see the Gardens, I might gratify myself without Danger of seeing the Proprietor. I accepted the Invitation & was delighted with all I found there; the Situation is happy, the Gardens elegantly disposed, the Hot House in the most flourishing State, & the Orange Trees the most captivating Creatures of the kind I ever saw. A Man in short had need have the Talents of Cox or Langford the Auctioneers,° to do the whole Scene Justice.

> Our Love attends you all. | Yours
> Wm Cowper.

Sepr. 21, 79.
The Snuff Shop is Arnold's° in Newgate Street.

To William Unwin

My dear Friend,
I wrote my last Letter merely to inform you that I had nothing to say, in Answer to which you have said Nothing. I admire the Propriety of your Conduct, tho' I am a Loser by it. I will endeavour to Say something now, and shall hope for Something in return.

I have been well entertain'd with Johnson's Biography,° for which I thank you. With One Exception, and that a Swingeing one, I think he has acquitted himself with his usual Good Sense & Sufficiency. His Treatment of Milton is unmercifull to the last Degree. A Pensioner° is not likely to Spare a Republican, and the Doctor, in order I suppose, to convince his Royal Patron of the Sincerity of his Monarchical principles, has belabor'd that great Poet's Character with the most Industrious Cruelty. As a Man, he has hardly left him the shadow of one good Quality. Churlishness in his private Life, and a rancorous Hatred of every thing Royal in his Public, are the two Colours with which he has smear'd all the Canvass. If he had any Virtues, they are not to be found in the Doctor's Picture of him, and it is Well for Milton that some Sourness in his Temper is the only Vice with which his Memory has been charged. It is evident enough that if his Biographer could have discover'd more, he would not have spared him. As a Poet, he has treated him with Severity enough, and has pluck'd one or two of the most beautifull Feathers out of his Muse's Wing, & trampled them under his Great Foot. He has passed Sentence of Condemnation upon Lycidas;° & has taken Occasion from that charming Poem, to expose to Ridicule (what is indeed Ridiculous Enough) the childish Prattlement of Pastoral Compositions, as if Lycidas was the Prototype & Pattern of them all. The Liveliness of the Description, the Sweetness of the Numbers, the Classical Spirit of Antiquity that prevails in it, go for nothing. I am convinced by the way that he has no Ear for Poetical Numbers, or that it was stopp'd by Prejudice against the Harmony of Milton's. Was there ever any thing so delightfull as the Music of the Paradise Lost? It is like that of a fine Organ; has the fullest & the deepest Tones of Majesty, with all the Softness & Elegance of the Dorian Flute. Variety without End! & never equal'd unless perhaps by Virgil. Yet the Doctor has little or nothing to say upon this copious Theme, but talks something about the unfitness of the English Language for Blank Verse,° & how apt it is, in the Mouth of some Readers to degenerate into Declamation. Oh! I could thresh his old Jacket 'till I made his Pension Jingle in his Pocket.

I could talk a good while longer but I have no Room. Our Love attends yourself, Mrs. Unwin, & Miss Shuttleworth, not forgetting the two Miniature Pictures at your Elbow.

Yours affectionately
Wm Cowper.

Octr. 31. 79.

To Joseph Hill

Mon Ami!

By this time I suppose you have ventured to take your Fingers out of your Ears, being deliver'd from the Deafening Shouts of the most Zealous Mob that ever Strain'd their Lungs in the Cause of Religion.° I congratulate you upon a gentle Relapse into the customary Sounds of a great City, which, though we Rustics abhorr them as Noisy & dissonant, are a Musical & sweet Murmur compared with what you have lately heard. The Tinkling of a Kennel may be distinguished now, where the Roaring of a Cascade would have been sunk and lost. I never suspected 'till the Newspaper inform'd me of it a few Days since, that the barbarous Uproar had reached Great Queen Street°—I hope Mrs. Hill was in the Country— You I know, are more apt to be Angry than terrified but had more Prudence, I trust, than to Oppose your little Person to such a furious Torrent. I shall rejoice to hear you are in Health, and that as I am sure you did not take up the Protestant Cudgels upon this Harebrain'd Occasion, so you have not been pull'd in pieces as a Papist.

If you ever take the Tip of the Chancellor's Ear between your Finger and Thumb, you can hardly improve the Opportunity to better Purpose, than if you should Whisper into it the Voice of Compassion & Lenity to the Lace Makers. I am an Eye Witness of their Poverty, and do know, that Hundreds in this little Town, are upon the Point of Starving, & that the most unremitting Industry is but barely sufficient to keep them from it. I know that the Bill by which they would have been so fatally affected is thrown out, but Lord Stormont threatens them with another, and if another like it should pass, they are undone.° We lately sent a Petition from hence to Lord Dartmouth,° I signed it, and am sure the Contents are true.—The Purport of it was to inform him that there are very near 1200 Lace Makers in this Beggarly Town, the most of whom had Reason enough while the Bill was in Agitation, to look upon every Loaf they bought as the last they should ever be able to Earn.—I can never think it good Policy to incur the Certain Inconvenience of Ruining 300,000, in order to prevent a remote and possible Damage though to a much greater Number. The Measure is like a Scythe, and the poor Lacemakers are the Sickly Crop that trembles before the Edge of it. The Prospect of peace with America is like the Streak of Dawn in their Horizon, but this Bill is like a Black Cloud behind it, that threatens their Hope of a comfortable Day with utter Extinction. I did not perceive 'till this Moment that I had tack'd two Similes together, a Practise, which though warranted by the Example of Homer and allowable in an Epic Poem, is rather Luxuriant & Licentious in a Letter; lest I should add a third, I conclude myself with my best Respects to Mrs. Hill, Your Affectionate

Wm Cowper.

July 8. 1780.

To Maria Cowper

My dear Cousin,

Mr. Newton having desired me to be of the Party,° I am come to meet him. You see me Sixteen years Older at the least than when I saw You last, but the Effects of Time seem to have taken Place rather on the Outside of my Head, than Within it. What was Brown is become Grey, but what was Foolish remains Foolish still. Green Fruit must Rot before it Ripens, if the Season is such as to afford it nothing but Cold Winds and dark Clouds that intercept every Ray of Sunshine. My Days steal away Silently and March on (as poor Mad King Lear would have made his Soldiers March) as if they were Shod with Felt.° Not so Silently but that I hear them, yet were it not that I am always Listening to their Flight, having no Infirmity that I had not when I was much Younger, I should deceive myself with an Imagination that I am still Young.

I am fond of Writing, as an Amusement, but I do not always find it one. Being rather scantily furnished with Subjects that are good for any thing, and Corresponding only with those who have no Relish for such as are good for

Nothing, I often find myself reduced to the Necessity, the disagreeable Necessity of Writing about Myself. This does not mend the Matter much, for though in a Description of my own Condition, I discover abundant Materials to Employ my Pen upon, yet as the Task is not very agreeable to *me*, so I am Sufficiently aware that it is likely to prove Irksome to others. A Painter who should confine himself in the Exercise of his Art to the Drawing of his own Picture, must be a Wonderfull Coxcomb if he did not soon grow Sick of his Occupation, and be peculiarly fortunate, if he did not make others as Sick as Himself.

Remote as your Dwelling is from the late Scene° of Riot and Confusion, I hope that though you could not but hear the Report of it, you heard no more, and that the Roarings of the mad Multitude did not reach you. That was a Day of Terror to the Innocent, and the Present is a Day of still greater Terror to the Guilty. The Law was for a few Moments like an Arrow in the Quiver, seemed to be of no Use, and did no Execution, now it is an Arrow upon the String, and many who despised it lately, are trembling as they Stand before the Point of it.

I have talked more already than I have formerly done in three Visits. You remember my Taciturnity, never to be forgotten by those who knew me. Not to depart entirely from what might be for aught I know, the most shining Part of my character, I here Shut my Mouth, make my Bow, & return to Olney.

My Love attends your Family—Mrs. Unwin presents her Affectionate Respects, & desires me to add for the Satisfaction of Mr. & Mrs. Newton, who have heard she was Indisposed, that she is better.

Yours my Dear Cousin—
Wm Cowper .

July 20. 1780.

To William Unwin

[Although Unwin responded warmly to the whimsical, inventive side of Cowper's imagination, Cowper kept *Poems, by William Cowper of the Inner Temple, Esq.* a secret from him until it had been accepted for publication by Joseph Johnson. Instead, Cowper had relied on John Newton, whose proposed Preface the publisher thought unseemly. As Cowper's literary ambitions increased, he turned to Unwin, rather than Newton, as his 'Authorship's Go-between' with his publisher.]

My dear friend,

I believe I never give trouble without feeling more than I give; so much by way of preface, and Apology.

Thus stands the case. Johnson has begun to print, and Mr. Newton has already corrected the first Sheet. This unexpected dispatch makes it necessary for Me to furnish myself with the means of Communication, viz: the franks, as soon as may be. There are reasons, (I believe I mention'd them in my last) why I chuse to revise the proof myself. Nevertheless if your Delicacy must suffer the puncture of a pin's point in procuring the franks for me, I release you entirely from the Task. You are as free as if I had never mention'd them. But you will oblige me by a speedy Answer upon this Subject, because it is expedient that the Printer should know to whom he is to send his Copy; and when the press is once set, those humble Servants of the poets are rather impatient of delay, because the types are wanted for the works of other Authors who are all equally in haste to be born.

This fine weather I suppose sets you on horseback, and allures the Ladies into the Garden. If I was at Stock, I should be of their party. And while they sat knotting or Netting° in the Shade, should comfort myself with the thought that I had not a beast under me, whose walk would seem tedious, whose Trot would Jumble me, and whose gallop might throw me into a Ditch. What Nature expressly design'd me for, I have never been able to conjecture, I seem to myself so universally disqualified for the common and customary Occupations and Amusements of Mankind. When I was a Boy, I excell'd at cricket and Football, but the fame I acquir'd by Atchievements

in that way, is long since forgotten, and I do not know that I
have made a figure in any thing since. I am sure however that
she did not design me for a Horseman, and that if all men
were of my Kind, there would be an end of all Jockeyship for
ever.

I am rather straiten'd in time, and not very rich in
materials, therefore with our joint Love to you all, I conclude
myself yours Ever.

Wm C.

May. 1781

To John Newton

My dear friend—
I might date my letter from the Green-house, which we
have converted into a summer parlour. The Walls hung with
garden mats, and the floor covered with a carpet, the Sun too
in a great measure excluded by an awning of mats which
forbids him to shine any where except upon the carpet, it
affords us by far the pleasantest retreat in Olney. We eat,
drink and sleep where we always did, but here we spend all
the rest of our time, and find that the sound of the wind in the
trees, and the singing of birds, are much more agreeable to our
Ears, than the incessant barking of dogs and screaming of
children, not to mention the exchange of a sweet-smelling
garden for the putrid exhalations of Silver End. It is an
Observation that naturally occurrs upon the Occasion, and
which many other Occasions furnish an Opportunity to make,
that people long for what they have not, and overlook the good
in their possession. This is so true in the present instance, that
for years past I should have thought myself happy to enjoy a
retirement even less flattering to my natural taste than this in
which I am now writing, and have often looked wistfully at a
snug cottage, which on account of its situation at a distance
from noise and disagreeable objects, seemed to promise me all
I could wish or expect, so far as happiness may be said to be
local, never once adverting to this comfortable nook, which

affords me all that could be found in the most sequester'd hermitage, with the advantage of having all those accommodations near at hand, which no hermitage could possibly afford me. People imagine they should be happy in circumstances which they would find insupportably burthensome in less than a week. A man that has been cloathed in fine linen and fared sumptuously ev'ry day, envies the peasant under a thatched hovel, who in return envies Him as much his palace and his pleasure-ground. Could they change situations the fine gentleman would find his ceilings were too low, and that his casements admitted too much wind, that he had no cellar for his wine, and no wine to put in his cellar. These with a thousand other mortifying deficiencies, would shatter his romantic project into innumerable fragments in a moment. The Clown at the same time would find the accession of so much unwieldy treasure an incumbrance quite incompatible with an hour's ease. His choice would be puzzled by variety, he would drink to excess because he would foresee no end of his abundance, and he would eat himself sick for the same reason. He would have no idea of any other happiness than sensual gratification, would make himself a beast, and die of his good fortune. The rich gentleman had perhaps, or might have had if he pleased, at the shortest notice, just such a recess as this, but if he had it he overlooked it, or if he had it not, forgot that he might command it whenever he would. The rustic too was actually in possession of some blessings which he was a fool to relinquish, but which he could neither see nor feel because he had the daily and constant use of them; such as good health, bodily strength, a head and a heart that never ached, and temperance, to the practise of which he was bound by necessity, that humanly speaking, was a pledge and a Security for the continuance of them all.

Thus I have sent you a School-boy's theme. When I write to you, I do not write without thinking, but always without premeditation, the consequence is that such thoughts as pass through my head when I am not writing, make the Subject of my letters to you.

Johnson sent me lately a sort of Apology for his printer's negligence, with his promise of greater diligence for the future. There was need enough of both. I have received but one sheet since you left us. Still indeed I see that there is time enough before us, but I see like wise that no length of time can be sufficient for the accomplishment of a work that does not go forward. I know not yet whether he will add Conversation° to those poems already in his hands, nor do I care much. No man ever wrote such quantities of verse as I have written this last year, with so much indifference about the Event, or rather with so little ambition of public praise. My pieces are such as may possibly be made usefull. The more they are approved, the more likely they are to spread, and consequently the more likely to attain the end of usefullness, which as I said once before, except my present amusement, is the only end I propose. And even in the pursuit of this purpose, commendable as it is in itself, I have not the spur I should once have had, my labor must go unrewarded, and as Mr. Raban° once said, I am raising a scaffold before a house that others are to live in, and not I.

I have left myself no room for politics, which I thought when I began would have been my principal theme.

Mr. Symonds's° letters certainly are not here. Our servants never touch a paper without leave, and are so observant of our Injunction, in this particular, that unless I burn the covers of the News, they accumulate till they make a litter in the parlour. They cannot therefore have been destroyed through carelessness, and consequently if they were with us we should be able to find them.

Our love to you both. | Yours my dear Sir
Wm Cowper.

Augt. 16. 1781.

To William Unwin

My dear friend,
What a world are you daily conversant with, which I have not seen these twenty Years and shall never see again. The arts of dissipation I suppose are nowhere practised with more refinement or success than at the place of your present

residence; by your account of it, it seems to be just what it was when I visited it, a scene of Idleness and Luxury, music, dancing, cards, walking, riding, bathing, eating, drinking, coffee, tea, scandal, dressing, yawning, sleeping. The rooms perhaps more magnificent, because the proprietors are grown richer, but the manners and occupations of the company just the same. Though my life has long been like that of a Recluse, I have not the temper of one, nor am I in the least an Enemy to cheerfullness and good humor; but I cannot envy you your situation; I even feel myself constrained to prefer the Silence of this nook, and the snug fire-side in our diminutive parlour to all the splendor and gaiety of Brighthelmstone.

You ask me how I feel on the occasion of my approaching publication—perfectly at my ease; if I had not been pretty well assured beforehand that my tranquillity would be but little endanger'd by such a measure, I would never have engaged in it, for I cannot bear disturbance. I have had in view two principal objects, first, to amuse myself, and secondly to compass that point in such a manner as that others might possibly be the better for my amusement. If I have succeeded, it will give me pleasure, but if I have failed, I shall not be mortified to the degree that might perhaps be expected. I remember an old adage (though not where it is to be found) bene vixit qui bene latuit°—and if I had recollected it at the right time, it should have been the motto to my Book.° By the way it will make an excellent one for Retirement° if you can but tell me whom to quote for it. The Critics cannot deprive me of the pleasure I have in reflecting that so far as my leisure has been employed in writing for the public, it has been conscientiously employed, and with a view to their advantage. There is nothing agreeable to be sure in being chronicled for a dunce, but I beleive there lives not a man upon earth who would be less affected by it than myself. With all this Indifference to Fame, which you know me too well to suppose me capable of affecting, I have taken the utmost pains to deserve it. This may appear a mystery or a paradox in practise, but it is true. I consider'd that the taste of the day is refined and delicate to excess, and that to disgust that delicacy of taste by a slovenly inattention to it, would be to forfiet at once all hope of being usefull; and for this reason, though I have written more verse this last year than perhaps any man in England, have finished and polished and touched and retouched with the utmost care. If after all I should be converted into waste paper, it may be my misfortune, but it will not be my fault, & I shall bear it with the most perfect Serenity.

I do not mean to give Quarme° a Copy. He is a good natured little man, and crows exactly like a Cock, but knows no more of verse than the Cock he imitates.

Whoever supposes that Lady Austen's fortune is precarious, is mistaken. I can assure you upon the ground of the most circumstantial and authentic Information, that it is both genteel and perfectly safe.

Your Mother adds her Love, mine accompanies hers, and our united wishes for your prosperity in every respect desire to be of the party.

Yours
Wm Cowper.

Octr. 6. 1781.

To William Unwin

[22–4 December 1781]

My dear Friend—

I write under the Impression of a Difficulty not easily Surmounted, the Want of Something to Say. Letter:Spinning is generally more Entertaining to the Writer than the Reader, for your sake therefore I would avoid it; but a dearth of Materials is very apt to betray one into a Trifling Strain, in spite of all one's Endeavours to be Serious.

What have you done with your perverse Parishioner? Perhaps when he has put a Lock upon his Pew, he may shut up himself in it oftener than he used to do; you remember a certain Story about the Boy & his Trunk.° The Consciousness that the Seat is become his own so Emphatically that he can Exclude every body else, may make him fond of it. I beleive many a Man that keeps a Carriage, Rides in it because he keeps one, tho' sometimes he would otherwise prefer a Walk.

I lay by my Paper for the present—I really can go on no further.

I left off Saturday, this present being Monday Morning, I renew the Attempt, in hopes that I may possibly Catch some Subject by the End, and be more Successfull.

> So have I seen the Maids in vain
> Tumble & teaze a tangled Skein,
> They Bite the Lip, they Scratch the Head,
> And cry—the deuce is in the Thread,
> They torture it & Jerk it round,
> 'Till the right End at last is found,
> Then Wind & Wind & Wind away,
> And what was Work, is changed to Play.

When I wrote the 2 first Lines, I thought I had engaged in a hazardous Enterprize. For thought I, should my Poetical Vein be as dry as my Prosaic, I shall spoil the Sheet, & send Nothing at all, for I could upon no Account endure the Thought of beginning again. But I think I have succeeded to Admiration, & am willing to flatter myself that I have even seen a Worse Impromptû in the Newspaper.

Though we Live in a Nook, and the World is quite unconscious that there are any such Beings in it as ourselves, yet we are not unconcern'd about what passes in it. The present awfull Crisis,° Big with the Fate of England, engages much of our Attention. The Action is probably over by this time, and tho' *We* know it not, the grand Question is decided, whether the War shall Roar in our own once peacefull Fields, or whether we shall still only hear of it at a Distance. I can compare the Nation to no Similitude more apt, than that of an Ancient Castle that had been for Days assaulted by the Battering Ram. It was long before the Stroke of that Engine made any sensible Impression, but the continual Repetition at length communicated a slight Tremor to the Wall, the next and the next & the next Blow encreased it. Another Shock puts the whole Mass in Motion, from the Top to the Foundation it bends forward, & is every Moment driven farther from the Perpendicular; 'till at last the decisive Blow is given, & down it comes. Every Million that has been raised with the last Century, has had an Effect upon the Constitution like that of a Blow from the aforesaid Ram upon the aforesaid Wall. The Impulse becomes more & more important, & the Impression it makes is continually augmented; unless therefore something Extraordinary Intervenes to prevent it, you will find the Consequence, at the End of my Simile. Yours & Theirs.

W.C.

To William Unwin

Jan. 17. 1782

My dear William,

I am glad we agree in our Opinion of King Critic° and the Writers on whom he has bestowed his Animadversions. It is a matter of Indifference to me whether I think with the World at large or not, but I wish my friends to be of my mind.—The same Work will wear a different appearance in the eyes of the same man according to the different views with which he reads it; if merely for his Amusement, his Candour being in less danger of a twist from Interest or prejudice, he is pleased with what is really pleasing, and is not overcurious to discover a blemish, because the exercise of a minute exactness is not consistent with his purpose. But if once he becomes a Critic by trade, the case is altered. He must then at any rate establish if he can an Opinion in every mind, of his uncommon discernment, and his exquisite Taste. This great end he can never accomplish by thinking in the track that has been beaten under the hoof of public Judgment. He must endeavor to convince the world that their favorite Authors have more faults than they are aware of, and such as they have never suspected, having marked out a Writer universally esteemed, whom he finds it for that very reason convenient to depreciate and traduce, he will overlook some of his beauties, he will faintly praise others, and in such a manner as to make thousands more modest though quite as judicious as himself, question whether they are beauties at all. Can there be a stronger illustration of all that I have said, than the Severity of

Johnson's remarks upon Prior?° I might have said the Injustice? His Reputation as an Author who with much Labor indeed but with admirable success, has embellished all his poems with the most charming Ease, stood unshaken 'till Johnson thrust his head against it. And how does he attack him in this his principal fort? I cannot recollect his very words, but I am much mistaken indeed if my Memory fails me with respect to the purport of them. His Words, he says, appear to be forced into their proper places. There indeed we find them, but find likewise that their arrangement has been the effect of constraint, and that without violence they would certainly have stood in a different order.° By your leave most learned Doctor, this is the most disingenuous remark I have ever met with, and would have come with a better grace from Curl or Dennis.° Every man conversant with Verse-writing knows, and knows by painfull experience, that the familiar stile, is of all stiles the most difficult to succeed in. To make verse speak the language of prose without being prosaic, to marshal the words of it in such order as they might naturally take in falling from the lips of an extemporary speaker, yet without meanness; harmoniously, elegantly, and without seeming to displace a syllable for the sake of the rhime, is one of the most arduous tasks a poet can undertake. He that could accomplish this task was Prior; many have imitated his excellence in this particular, but the best Copies have fallen far short of the Original. And now to tell us, after we and our Fathers have admired him for it so long, that he is an Easy Writer indeed, but that his Ease has an Air of stiffness in it, in short that his Ease is not Ease but only something like it, what is it but a self contradiction, an Observation that grants what it is just going to deny and denies what it has just granted, in the same Sentence and in the same breath?—But I have filled the greatest part of my Sheet with a very uninteresting Subject. I will only say, that as a Nation we are not much indebted in point of poetical Credit, to this too sagacious and unmercifull Judge; and that for myself in particular, I have reason to rejoice that he enter'd upon and exhausted the labors of his Office, before my poor volume could possibly become an Object of them. By the way you cannot have a book at the time you mention. I have lived a Fortnight and

more in Expectation of the last sheet which is not yet arrived.
I hope however that for his own sake my Publisher will take
care to catch the Season and secure a Market, if possible.

You have already furnished John's Memory with by far the
greatest part of what a Parent would wish to store it with. If
all that is merely trivial and all that has an immoral tendency
were expunged from our English poets, how would they
shrink, and how would some of them completely vanish? I
believe there are some of Dryden's Fables° which he would
find very entertaining. They are for the most part fine
Compositions, and not above his Apprehension, but Dryden
has written few things that are not blotted here and there with
an unchaste allusion, so that you must pick his way for him,
lest he should tread in the dirt. You did not mention Milton's
Allegro and Penseroso, which I remember being so charmed
with when I was a boy, that I was never weary of them. There
are even passages in the paradisaical part of Paradise lost,
which he might study with advantage and to teach him, as
you can, to deliver some of the fine Orations made in the
Pandæmonïum, and those between Satan, Ithuriel and
Zephon° with emphasis, dignity and propriety, might be of
great use to him hereafter. The sooner the Ear is formed and
the Organs of speech are accustomed to the various inflexions
of the Voice which the rehearsal of those passages demands,
the better. I should think too that Thomson's Seasons° might
afford him some usefull Lessons. At least they would have a
tendency to give his mind an observing and a Philosophical
turn. I do not forget that he is but a child, but I remember
that he is a child favour'd with talents superior to his years.—
We were much pleased with his Remark on your Almsgiving,
and doubt not but it will be verified with respect to the 2
Guineas you sent us, which have made 4 Christian people
happy.—Ships I have none,° nor have touched a pencil these
three years. If ever I take it up again, (which I rather suspect I
shall not, the Employment requiring stronger Eyes than mine)
it shall be at John's Service.—We congratulate all the parties
concerned on the happy recovery of your three Unwinnikins
from the Small Pox.
Our united love attends all the Family. | Yours my dear friend
                                        Wm Cowper.

To William Unwin

My dear friend,

Nothing has given me so much pleasure since the publication of my volume, as your favorable opinion of it. It may possibly meet with acceptance from hundreds, whose commendation would afford me no other satisfaction than what I should find in the hope that it might do them good. I have some neighbors in this place who say they like it—doubtless I had rather they should than they they should not—but I know them to be persons of no more Taste in poetry than skill in the Mathematics, their applause therefore is a sound that has no music in it for me. But my vanity was not so entirely quiescent when I read your friendly account of the manner in which it had affected *you*; it was tickled and pleased and told me in a pretty loud whisper, that others perhaps of whose taste and judgment I had an high opinion, would approve it too. As a Giver of good counsel, I wish to please all—as an Author, I am perfectly indifferent to the Judgment of all except the few who are indeed judicious. The circumstance however in your letter which pleased me most, was that you wrote in high spirits, and though you said much, suppressed more, lest you should hurt my delicacy. My delicacy is obliged to you, but you observe it is not so squeamish, but that after it has feasted upon praise expressed, it can find a comfortable dessert in the contemplation of praise implied.—I now feel as if I should be glad to begin another, but from the will to the power is a step too wide for me to take at present, and the season of the year brings with it so many avocations into the garden, where I am my own fac totum, that I have little or no leisure for the quill. I should do myself much wrong were I to omitt mentioning the great complacency with which I read your narrative of Mrs. Unwin's Smiles and tears. Persons of much sensibility are always persons of taste, a taste for poetry depends indeed upon that very article more than upon any other. If she had Aristotle by heart, I should not esteem her judgment so highly, were she defective in point of feeling, as I do and must esteem it, knowing her to have such feelings as Aristotle could not communicate, and as half the Readers in the world are destitute of. This it is that makes me set so high a price upon your mother's opinion. She is a Critic by nature and not by Rule, and has a perception of what is good or bad in composition that I never knew deceive her. Insomuch that when two sorts of expression have pleaded equally for the preference in my own esteem, and I have referred, as in such cases I always did, the decision of the point to Her, I never knew her at a loss for a just one.

Whether I shall receive any answer from his Chancellorship° or not, is at present in ambiguo, and will probably continue in the same state of ambiguity much longer. He is so busy a man, and at this time, if the papers may be credited, so particularly busy, that I am forced to mortify myself with the thought that both my Book and my Letter may be thrown into a corner as too insignificant for a Statesman's notice, and never found 'till his Executor finds them. This affair however is neither ad my libitum nor his. I have sent him the Truth, and the Truth which I know he is ignorant of. He that put it into the heart of a certain Eastern Monarch° to amuse himself one sleepless night with listening to the records of his Kingdom, is able to give birth to such another occasion in Lord Thurlow's instance, and inspire him with a curiosity to know what he has received from a friend he once loved and valued. If an answer comes however, you shall not long be a stranger to the Contents of it.

I have read your Letter to their Worships° and much approve of it. May it have the Effect it ought! If not, still you have acted an humane and becoming part, and the poor aching toes and fingers of the prisoners will not appear in judgment against you. I have made a slight alteration in the last sentence which perhaps you will not disapprove.

Our Love is with you and your Family.

Yours ever
Wm Cowper.

Mar. 18. | 1782.

I shall beg you to be the carrier of a Copy to Mrs. Powley.°
We expect your arrival here with much eagerness.

To William Unwin

My dear friend,

Entertaining some hope that Mr. Newton's next Letter would furnish me with the means of satisfying your enquiry on the subject of Dr. Johnson's opinion,° I have 'till now delay'd my answer to your last. But the information is not yet come, Mr. Newton having intermitted a week more than usual since his last writing. When I receive it, favorable or not, it shall be communicated to you. But I am not very sanguine in my expectations from that quarter, very learned and very critical heads are hard to please. He may perhaps treat me with lenity for the sake of my subject and design, but the composition, I think, will hardly escape his censure. But though all Doctors may not be of the same mind, there is one Doctor at least, whom I have lately discovered, my professed admirer. He too like Johnson was with difficulty persuaded to read, having an aversion to all poetry except the Night Thoughts,° which on a certain occasion, when being confined on board a ship he had no other employment, he got by heart. He was however prevailed upon, and read me several times over, so that if my volume had sailed with him instead of Dr. Young's, I perhaps might have occupied that shelf in his memory which he then allotted to the Doctor. His name is Renny° and he lives at Newport pagnel.

It is a sort of paradox but it is true.—We are never more in danger than when we think ourselves most secure, nor in reality more secure than when we seem perhaps to be most in danger. Both sides of this apparent contradiction were lately verified in my experience. Passing from the greenhouse to the barn I saw three Kittens, (for we have so many in our retinue) looking with a fixt attention at something which lay on the threshold of a door nailed up. I took but little notice of them at first, but a loud hiss engaged me to attend more closely, when behold! a Viper, the largest I remember to have seen, rearing itself, darting its forked tongue, and ejaculating the afore-mentioned hiss at the nose of a Kitten almost in contact with his lips. I ran into the Hall for a hoe with a long handle with which I intended to assail him, and returning in a few seconds, missed him. He was gone, and I feared had escaped me. Still however the Kittens sat watching immoveably upon the same spot. I concluded therefore that sliding between the door and the threshold he had found his way out of the garden into the yard. I went round immediately, and there found him in close conversation with the Old Cat, whose curiosity being excited by so novel an appearance, inclined her to pat his head repeatedly with her forefoot, with her claws however sheathed, and not in anger, but in the way of philosophical enquiry and examination. To prevent her falling a victim to so laudable an exercise of her talents, I interposed in a moment with the hoe, and performed upon him an act of decapitation, which though not immediately mortal, proved so in the end.° Had he slid into the passages, where it is dark, or had he when in the yard met with no interruption from the cat, and secreted himself in any of the Outhouses, it is hardly possible but that some of the family must have been bitten. He might have been trodden upon without being perceived, and have slipp'd away before the sufferer could have well distinguished what foe had wounded him. Three years ago we discovered one in the same place, which the barber slew with a trowel.

Our proposed removal to Mr. Small's,° was as you suppose a jest, or rather a joco-serious matter. We never looked upon it as entirely feasible, yet we saw in it something so like practicability that we did not esteem it altogether unworthy of our attention. It was one of those projects which people of lively imaginations play with and admire for a few days, and then break in pieces. Lady Austen returned on Thursday from London, where she spent the last fortnight, and whither she was called by an unexpected opportunity to dispose of the remainder of her Lease. She has now therefore no longer any connexion with the great City, she has none on earth whom she calls friends but us, and no Home but at Olney. Her abode is to be at the Vicarage where she has hired as much room as she wants, which she will embellish with her own furniture, and which she will occupy as soon as Mrs. Scot has produced another child,° which is expected to make its entry in October.

Mr. Bull, a dissenting Minister of Newport, a learned, ingenious, good-natured, pious friend of ours, who sometimes visits us, and whom we visited last week, has put into my hands three volumes of French poetry composed by Madame Guion.—A Quietist say you and a Fanatic, I will have nothing to do with her. 'Tis very well, you are welcome to have nothing to do with her, but in the mean time her verse is the only French verse I ever read that I found agreeable. There is a neatness in it equal to that which we applaud with so much reason in the compositions of Prior. I have translated several of them, and shall proceed in my translations 'till I have filled a Lilliputian paper-book I happen to have by me, which when filled I shall present to Mr. Bull. He is her passionate admirer, rode 20 miles to see her picture in the house of a stranger, which stranger politely insisted on his acceptance of it, and it now hangs over his parlour chimney. It is a striking pourtrait, too characteristic not to be a strong resemblance, and were it encompassed with a glory instead of being dress'd in a Nun's hood, might pass for the face of an Angel.

Our meadows are covered with a Winter flood in August. The rushes with which our bottomless chairs were to have been bottom'd, and much Hay which was not carried, are gone down the river on a voyage to Ely, and it is even uncertain whether they will ever return. Sic transit gloria mundi! I am glad you have found a Curate, may he answer. Am happy in Mrs. Bouverie's° continued approbation, it is worth while to write for such a Reader.

Yours, with our united Love to all at Stock
William Cowper.

Next time you write shall be glad of a frank to your Sister.
Augt. 3. 1782.

To William Unwin

[At about the same time as Unwin assumed the role of Cowper's principal literary advisor, he became his intermediary with Lady Austen, with whom the poet and Mrs Unwin had just been reconciled.]

[27 August 1782]

The last four days have been days of adventure, teeming with incidents in which the opposite ingredients of pain and pleasure have been plentifully mingled, and of the most interesting kind. Lady Austen's behaviour° to us ever since her return to Clifton has been such as to engage our affections to her more than ever. A flood indeed has sometimes parted us for many days, but though it has often been impossible for us who never ride to visit *Her*, as soon as the water has become fordable by an Ass, she has mounted one & visited *Us*. On Thursday last, in the Evening, she came down with her Sister to the Evening Lecture. She had not been long seated in her pew, before she was attacked by the most excruciating pains of a bilious Cholic. Having much resolution however, and being determined not to alarm her Sister, the congregation, or the Minister, she bore it without discovering much of what she felt even to Mrs. Jones, 'till the service was over.—It is a Disorder to which she has lately been very subject.—We were just sitting down to supper when a hasty rap alarmed us. I ran to the Hall Window, for the Hares° being loose it was impossible to open the door. The Evening had been a dismal one, raining almost continually, but just at that time it held up. I entreated Mrs. Jones to go round to the gate, and understanding by her tremulous voice that something distressfull was at hand, made haste to meet her. I had no sooner reached the yard door and opened it, than Lady Austen appeared leaning upon Mr. Scott.° She could not speak, but thrusting her other arm under mine, with much difficulty made shift to attain the great chair by the fireside in the parlour. There she suffer'd unutterable anguish for a considerable time, 'till at length by your mother's application and assistance being a little relieved she contrived to climb the stair case, and after about 3 hours agony was put to bed. At eleven at night we sent off a messenger to Northampton who returned at 7 the next morning, and brought a Physician° with him. He prescribed and she was better. Friday night she slept tolerably, rose cheerfull, and entertained us all Saturday with much agreeable conversation as usual. But her Spirits being too great for her strength, the consequence was a frightfull Hysteric fit which seized her just when she was going to bed. She was alone, for her Sister had been obliged to go home, and thinking there was no need of such a precaution, she would have nobody else to sleep with her. The appointed signal was that she should knock if she wanted any thing. She did so, Your mother hasten'd to the chamber, and I after her to know if I could be of any use. She had not begun to undress, so I was admitted, and soon after, her Disorder became quite convulsive, accompanied with most of the symptoms of the most violent fits of that sort I have ever seen. In about an hour she grew better, rested tolerably, was in good spirits on Sunday, and last night, well enough to return to Clifton upon the Ass. To-day we dine there.

Are you curious to know her sentiments of *you*? The question has no doubt excited your curiosity if you had none before; suppose however I postpone the gratification of it and make it part of my next letter, finishing this with something more important? No—you must be satisfied this moment; no man that merits the good opinion of others, can be indifferent to it.—You shall then—

She would have known you for your Mother's son the moment she saw you had you not been announced by name. This is some praise let me tell you, especially from her, who thinks that mother the best of Women, and loves her at least as much as if she were her own. Your figure the most elegant she ever saw—no longer complain of calveless legs, and a belly with nothing in it. Your countenance quite handsome— no longer be ashamed of a nose you have sometimes thought too long. Every motion of your limbs, your action, your attitude bespeak the Gentleman—added to all this, your Vivacity and your good sense, together with an amiable disposition which she is sure you possess though she has but an hour's knowledge of you, have placed you so high in her esteem, that had you an opportunity to cultivate an interest there you would soon be without a rival. 14 years ago I would not have made you this relation, such a stripling as you was at that time would have been spoil'd by so much praise, and through the mere hunger after more would have lost what he had acquired already. But being the Father of a Family and the Minister of three parishes,° I am not afraid to trust you with it. I beg Mrs. Unwin will add a short Postcript to your next, just to inform me whether when you perused this picture of yourself, you blushed and how often. I had almost forgot what she desired me to insert, that she wishes as much for a Mr. Unwin here, as you can possibly for a Lady Austen at Stock.

Notwithstanding the uncommon rigour of the Season, much of our Wheat is carried and in good condition. It does not appear that the murmurings of the Farmers were with any reason, the corn has suffered much less by the mildew than was reported, and if it is at all injured (in this part of the world at least) it must be ascribed to their foolish impatience who *would* cut it down too soon. It is so cold this 27th. of August that I shake in the Greenhouse where I am writing.

Our united Love attends you all—your Letter is gone to Dewsbury.

Yours my dear William
Wm C

To William Unwin

[c.October 1782]

My dear William,

The modest terms in which you express yourself on the subject of Lady Austen's commendation, embolden me to add my Suffrage to hers, and to confirm it by assuring you that I think her just and well-founded in her opinion of you. The Compliment indeed glances at myself, for were you less than she accounts you, I ought not to afford you that place in my esteem which you have held so long. My own sagacity therefore and discernment are not a little concerned upon the occasion, for either you resemble the picture, or I have mistaken my man and formed an erroneous judgment of his character. With respect to your face and figure indeed, there I leave the Ladies to determine, as being naturally best qualified to decide the point; but whether you are perfectly the man of sense and the Gentleman, is a question in which I am as much interested as they, and which, you being my friend, I am of course prepared to settle in your Favor.

That Lady, whom when you know her as well, you will love as much as we do, is and has been during the last fortnight as part of our family. Before she was perfectly restored to health, she returned to Clifton. Soon after her return Mr. Jones had occasion to go to London. No sooner was he gone, than the chateau being left without a Garrison, was beseiged as regularly as the night came on. Vilains were both heard and seen in the garden and at the doors and windows. The Kitchen window in particular was attempted, from which they took a complete pane of glass exactly opposite to the iron by which it was fasten'd, but providentially the window had been nail'd to the wood work in order to keep it close and that the air might be excluded. Thus they were disappointed and being discover'd by the maid, withdrew. The Ladies being worn out with continual watching and repeated alarms, were at last prevailed upon to take refuge with us. Men furnished with fire arms were put into the house, and the rascals having intelligence of this circumstance, beat a retreat. Mr. Jones return'd, Mrs. Jones and Miss Green,° her daughter, left us, but Lady Austen's Spirits having been too much disturbed to be capable of repose in a place where she had been so much terrified, she was left behind. She remains with us, 'till her lodgings at the vicarage can be made ready for her reception, which cannot be till Mrs. Scott's delivery,° who is in daily expectation of her puerperium. I have now sent you what has occurred of most moment in our history, since my last.

I say Amen with all my heart to your observation on religious characters. Men who profess themselves adepts in mathematical knowledge, in astronomy or jurisprudence, are generally as well qualified as they would appear. The reason may be, that they are always liable to detection, should they attempt to impose upon mankind, and therefore take care to be what they pretend. In Religion alone, a profession is often slightly taken up and slovenly carried on, because forsooth candor and charity require us to hope the best and to judge favorably of our neighbor, and because it is easy to deceive the ignorant who are a great majority upon this subject. Let a man attach himself to a particular party, contend furiously for what are properly called evangelical doctrines, and enlist himself under the banner of some popular preacher, and the business is done. Behold a Christian, a Saint, a Phœnix! In the mean time perhaps his heart and his temper, and even his conduct are unsanctified, possibly less exemplary than those of some avowed Infidels. No matter—he can talk—he has the Shibboleth of the true Church—the Bible in his pocket and a head well stored with notions. But the quiet, humble, modest and peaceable person, who is in his practise what the other is only in his profession, who hates a noise and therefore makes none, who knowing the snares that are in the world keeps himself as much out of it as he can, never enters it but when Duty calls, and even then with fear and trembling, is the Christian that will always stand highest in the estimation of those, who bring all characters to the test of true Wisdom, and judge of the tree by its fruit.

You are desirous of visiting the prisoners,° you wish to administer to their necessities, and to give them instruction. This Task you will undertake, though you expect to encounter many things in the performance of it that will give you pain. Now *This* I can understand—you will not listen to the sensibilities that distress yourself, but to the distresses of others. Therefore when I meet with one of the specious praters above mention'd, I will send him to Stock, that by your diffidence he may be taught a lesson of modesty, by your generosity a little feeling for others, and by your general conduct in short, to chatter less and to do more.

We pity Mrs. Unwin and her sufferings from the Tooth-ach. Our best love to her and to her Sister. Your little ones with John the Great at their head, have always an affectionate share of our remembrance!

Yours my dear friend.
Wm C

To Mary Newton

My dear Madam,

The Soals° with which you favor'd us were remarkably fine. Accept our Thanks for them. Thanks likewise for the trouble you take in vending my poems, and still more for the interest you take in their success. My Authorship is undoubtedly pleased when I hear that they are approved either by the great or the small, but to be approved by the Great, as Horace observed° many years ago, is Fame indeed. Having met with encouragement, I consequently wish to write again, but wishes are a very small part of the qualifications necessary for such a purpose. Many a man who has succeeded tolerably well in his first attempt has spoiled all by the second. But it just occurs to me that I told you so once before, and if my Memory had served me with the Intelligence a minute sooner, I would not have repeated the observation now.

The Winter sets in with great Severity. The rigor of the season and the advanced price of grain are very threat'ning to the poor. It is well with those that can feed upon a promise and wrap themselves up warm in the robe of Salvation. A good fire-side and a well-spread table are but very indifferent substitutes for these better accommodations; so very indifferent, that I would gladly exchange them both for the rags and the unsatisfied hunger of the poorest creature that looks forward with hope to a better world & weeps tears of joy in the midst of penury and distress.—What a world is this! how mysteriously govern'd, and in appearance left to itself. One Man,° having squander'd thousands at a gaming table, finds it convenient to travel, gives his Estate to somebody to manage for him, amuses himself a few years in France and Italy, returns perhaps wiser than he went having acquired Knowledge which but for his follies he would never have acquired, again makes a splendid figure at home, shines in the Senate, governs his country as its Minister, is admired for his abilities, and if successfull, adored at least by a party. When he dies, he is praised as a Demigod, and his monument records every thing but his vices. The exact contrast of such a picture is to be found in many cottages at Olney. I have no need to describe them, you know the characters I mean. They Love God, they trust him, they pray to him in secret, and though he means to reward them openly, the day of recompense is delay'd. In the mean time they suffer every thing that infirmity and poverty can inflict upon them. Who would suspect that has not a spiritual eye to discern it, that the fine gentleman was one whom his Maker held in abhorrence, and the Wretch last mentioned, dear to him as the apple of his eye?° It is no wonder that the World who are not in the secret, find themselves obliged, some of them to doubt a Providence, and others absolutely to deny it, when almost all the real virtue there is in it, is to be found living and dying in a state of neglected obscurity, and all the vices of others cannot exclude them from the privilege of worship and honor! But behind the curtain the matter is explained, very little however to the satisfaction of the Great.

If you ask me why I have written thus, and to you especially to whom there was no need to write thus, I can only reply, that having a Letter to write and no News to communicate, I pick'd up the first subject I found, and pursued it as far as was convenient for my purpose.

Mr. Newton and I are of one mind on the subject of Patriotism. Our dispute was no sooner begun than it ended. It would be well perhaps if when two Disputants began to engage, their friends would hurry each into a seperate chaise, and order them to opposite points of the compass. Let one travel 20 miles East, the other as many West, then let them write their opinions by the Post. Much altercation and chafing of the Spirit would be prevented, they would sooner come to a right understanding, and running away from each other, would carry on the combat more judiciously in exact proportion to the distance.

My Love to that Gentleman if you please, and tell him that like Him, though I Love my Country I hate its follies and its Sins, and had rather see it scourged in mercy, than judiciously harden'd by prosperity.

Mrs. Unwin not very well, but better than she has been. She adds her Love to both.

Yours my Dear Madam as ever

Nove. 23. 82.   Wm Cowper.

To Joseph Hill

My dear friend—

At 7 o'clock this Evening, being the 7th. of December, I imagine I see you in your box° at the Coffee house. No doubt the Waiter, as ingenious and adroit as his predecessors were before him, raises the teapot to the cieling with his right hand, while in his left hand the tea cup descending almost to the floor, receives a limpid stream; limpid in its descent, but no sooner has it reached its destination, than frothing and foaming to the view it becomes a roaring syllabub. This is the 19th. winter since I saw you in this situation, and if 19 more pass over me before I die I shall still remember a circumstance we have often laugh'd at.

How different is the complexion of your Evenings and mine! Yours spent amid the ceaseless Hum that proceeds from the inside of 50 noisy and busy periwigs,° mine by a domestic fireside, in a retreat as silent as retirement can make it, where no noise is made but what we make for our own amusement. For instance, here are two Ladies and your humble Servant in company; one of the Ladies has been playing on the Harpsichord, while I with the other have been playing at Battledore and Shuttlecock. A little dog in the mean time howling under the chair of the former, performed in the Vocal way to admiration. This Entertainment over, I began my letter, and having nothing more important to communicate, have given you an account of it. I know you love dearly to be idle when you can find an opportunity to be so. But as such opportunities are rare with you, I thought it possible that a short description of the Idleness I enjoy might give you pleasure. The happiness we cannot call our own, we yet seem to possess, while we sympathize with our friends who can.

The papers tell me that peace is at hand,° and that it is at a great distance, that the Siege of Gibraltar is abandoned, and that it is to be still continued. It is happy for me that though I love my country I have but little curiosity. There was a time when these contradictories would have distress'd me, but I have learned by experience that it is best for little people like myself to be patient, and to wait 'till time affords the Intelligence which no speculations of theirs can ever furnish.

I thank you for a fine Cod with Oysters, and hope that e'er long I shall have to thank you for procuring me Elliott's medicines.° Every time I feel the least uneasiness in either eye, I tremble, lest my Æsculapius° being departed my infallible remedy should be lost for ever. Adieu! my respects to Mrs. Hill.

Yours faithfully
Wm Cowper.

To William Unwin

My dear friend,

The Sturgeon was incomparable, the best we ever had. We like both Sturgeon and Salmon, but chuse the former, as the more durable commodity of the two—; thanking you at the same time for your bounty.

To dispatch your questions first, which are of more importance than any subject that is likely to occurr at present, will be both the civilest and the wisest course. Wallnut shells skillfully perforated, and bound over the eyes are esteemed a good remedy for squinting. The pupil naturally seeking its light at the aperture, becomes at length habituated to a just position. But to alleviate your anxiety upon this subject, I have heard good judges of beauty declare that they thought a slight distortion of the eye in a pretty face, rather advantageous.

The figure however cannot be good if the legs do not stand perpendicular to the person. Knock-knees therefore must be corrected if they can. It is, I suppose, a case of weakness. I should therefore recommend the Cold bath as a strengthener, and riding on horse-back as soon as the boy is capable of it, as a mean of forcing the knees into their proper line. Their pressure against the saddle will naturally push them outward, and accordingly you may frequently observe the legs of persons habituated from their infancy to this sort of exercise, curved almost into an arch. Witness half the jockeys and postillions in the Kingdom. The more the little man is made to turn the point of his toe inward when he is riding, I suppose, the better.

You ask me how I like the Peace. When a Country is exhausted, Peace is always preferable to war, and so far I like it, but no farther. Bad however as it is, it might be attended with some benefits, which the jarring interests of irreconcileable parties, will not suffer us to reap at present. The papers inform me that Lord Bute is at the bottom of all this mischief.° No matter—if the Country is to be visited for its iniquities, there would be discord and anarchy, though Lord Bute were mouldering in the tomb of his ancestors. The Chancellor too is blamed, and perhaps with reason. The Nation stands much in need of a political reform, to which he is an Enemy, and consequently to all who advise one. A man of his abilities must have great influence, must either do much good or much evil. Though wise, he is not infallible, and the Errors of wise men are the most pernicious of all. I have procured the Etching you recommended,° and admire it as the express image of a face with which I was once familiar. But his great Hat and his long band give him the air of an awkward Country parson.

One of my Hares is dead—behold his

Epitaph

Here lies, whom hound did ne'er pursue,
 Nor swifter Grey:hound follow,
Whose foot ne'er tainted morning dew,
 Nor Ear heard Huntsman's hollow,

Tiney, the surliest of his kind,
 Who, nurs'd with tender care,
And to domestic bounds confin'd,
 Was still a wild Jack Hare.

Though duely from my hand he took
 His pittance ev'ry night,
He did it with a jealous look,
 And when he could, would bite.

His diet was of wheaten bread,
   And milk and Oats and straw,
Thistles, or Lettuces instead,
   With sand to scow'r his maw.

———

On twigs of hawthorn he regaled,
   Or pippins russet peel,
And when his juicey sallads fail'd,
   Sliced carrot pleas'd him well.

———

A Turkey carpet was his lawn
   On which he loved to bound,
To skip and gambol like a fawn
   And swing his rump around.

———

His frisking was at evening hours,
   For then he lost his fear,
But most before approaching show'rs,
   Or when a storm drew near.

———

Eight years and 5 round rolling moons
   He thus saw steal away,
Slumbr'ing out all his idle noons,
   And ev'ry night at play.

———

I kept him for old service sake
   For he would oft beguile
My heart of thoughts that made it ach,
   And force me to a smile.

———

But now beneath this Wallnut shade
   He finds his long, last home,
And waits in snug concealment laid,
   'Till gentler Puss shall come.

———

She still more antient, feels the shocks
From which no care can save,
And partner once of Tiney's box,
Must soon partake his grave.

———

We shall be happy to see you and Mrs. U. with you, or any part of your family. I hope to be able to send a Melon or two.

Yours ever, with our united Love
Wm C.

Mar. 30. 1783.

To William Bull

My dear friend,

My Greenhouse fronted with Myrtles, and where I hear nothing but the pattering of a fine shower and the sound of distant thunder, wants only the fumes of your pipe to make it perfectly delightfull. Tobacco was not known in the Golden age. So much the worse for the Golden age. This age of Iron or Lead would be insupportable without it, and therefore we may reasonably suppose that the Happiness of those better days would have been much improved by the Use of it.—We hope that you and your Son are perfectly recover'd. The season has been most unfavorable to animal life, and I, who am merely Animal, have suffer'd much by it.

Though I should be glad to write, I write little or nothing. The time for such fruit is not yet come, but I expect it, and wish for it. I want Amusement, and deprived of that, have none to supply the place of it. I send you however, according to my promise to send you every thing, 2 Stanzas composed at the request of Lady Austen. She wanted words to a tune° she much admired and I gave her the following.

On Peace.

No longer I follow a sound,
No longer a dream I pursue,
Oh Happiness, not to be found,
Unattainable treasure, Adieu!
I have sought thee in splendor and dress,
In the regions of pleasure and taste,
I have sought thee, and seem'd to possess,
But have prov'd thee a Vision at last.

———————

An humbler ambition and Hope
The voice of true Wisdom inspires,
'Tis sufficient if Peace be the scope
And the summit of all our desires:
Peace may be the lot of the mind
That asks it in meekness and love,
But Rapture and Bliss are confin'd
To the glorified Spirits above.

———————

                                        Yours
                                        W.C.

June 3. 1783.

To William Unwin

My dear William,

Our severest Winter, commonly called the Spring, is now over, and I find myself seated in my favorite recess, the Greenhouse. In such a situation, so silent, so shady, where no human foot is heard, and where only my Myrtles presume to peep in at the window, you may suppose I have no interruption to complain of, and that my thoughts are perfectly at my command. But the beauties of the spot are themselves an interruption; my attention is continually called upon by those very myrtles, by a double row of Grass pinks just beginning to blossom, and by a bed of Beans already in bloom. And you are to consider it, if you please, as no small proof of my regard that though you have so many powerfull Rivals, I disengage myself from them all, and devote this hour entirely to you.

You are not acquainted with the Revd. Mr. Bull of Newport. Perhaps it is as well for you that you are not. You would regret still more than you do, that there are so many Miles interposed between us. He spends part of the day with us to-morrow. A Dissenter, but a liberal one; a man of Letters and of Genius, master of a fine imagination, or rather *not* master of it; an imagination, which when he finds himself in the company he loves and can confide in, runs away with him into such fields of speculation as amuse and enliven every other imagination that has the happiness to be of the party. At other times he has a tender and delicate sort of melancholy in his disposition, not less agreeable in its way. No men are better qualified for companions in such a world as this, than men of such a temperament. Every scene of life has two sides, a dark and a bright one, and the mind that has an equal mixture of melancholy and vivacity, is best of all qualified for the contemplation of either. It can be lively without levity, and pensive without dejection. Such a man is Mr. Bull. But he smokes tobacco—nothing is perfect—nihil est ab omni parte beatum.°

I find that your friend Mr. Fytche° has lost his cause; and more mortifying still, has lost it by a single voice. Had I been a Peer, he should have been secure of mine. For I am persuaded that if conditional Presentations were in fashion, and if every Minister held his benefice, as the Judges their Office, upon the terms of Quamdiu se bene gesserit,° it would be better for the cause of Religion, and more for the honor of the Establishment. There ought to be discipline somewhere, and if the Bishops will not exercise it, I do not see why Lay Patrons should have their hands tied. If I remember your state of the case, (and I never heard it stated but by you) my reflections upon it are pertinent. It is however long since we talked about it and I may possibly misconceive it at present—if so—they go for nothing. I understand that he presented upon condition that if the Parson proved immoral or negligent, he should have

liberty to call upon him either for his Resignation or the
penalty. If I am wrong correct me.

On the other side I send you a something, a song if you
please, composed last Thursday. The Incident happen'd the
day before.

> The Rose had been wash'd (just wash'd in a show'r)
> Which Mary to Anna° convey'd,
> The plentifull moisture incumber'd the flow'r,
> And weigh'd down its beautifull head.

> ————

> The Cup was all fill'd, and the leaves were all wet,
> And it seem'd to a fancifull view,
> To weep for the buds it had left with regret
> On the flourishing bush where it grew.

> ————

> I hastily seiz'd it, unfit as it was
> For a nosegay, so dripping and drown'd,
> And swinging it rudely, too rudely alas!,
> I snapt it—it fell to the ground.

> ————

> And such, I exclaim'd, is the pitiless part
> Some act by the delicate mind,
> Regardless of wringing and breaking a heart
> Already to sorrow resign'd.

> ————

> This elegant Rose, had I shaken it less,
> Might have bloom'd with its Owner awhile,
> And the Tear that is wiped with a little Address,
> May be follow'd perhaps by a Smile.

> ————

> The Muslin is found, the gown is admired
> Procure us some franks—adieu—I am tir'd.

>   W.C.

June 8. | 1783.

To William Unwin

My dear William,

I feel myself sensibly obliged by the interest you take in the success of my productions. Your feelings upon the subject are such as I should have myself, had I an opportunity of calling Johnson aside to make the enquiry you purpose.° But I am pretty well prepared for the worst; and so long as I have the opinion of a few capable judges in my favor, and am thereby convinced that I have neither disgraced myself nor my subject, shall not feel myself disposed to any extreme anxiety about the sale. To aim with success at the spiritual good of mankind, and to become popular by writing on scriptural subjects, were an unreasonable ambition even for a Poet to entertain in days like these. Verse may have many charms, but has none powerfull enough to conquer the aversion of a dissipated age to such instruction. Ask the question therefore boldly, and be not mortified even though he should shake his head and drop his chin, for it is no more than we have reason to expect. We will lay the fault upon the vice of the times, and we will acquitt the Poet.

I am glad you were pleased with my Latin Ode, and indeed with my English dirge° as much as I was myself. The tune laid me under a disadvantage, obliging me to write in Alexandrines, which I suppose would suit no ear but a French one. Neither did I intend any thing more than that the subject and the words should be sufficiently accommodated to the Music. The Ballad is a species of poetry, I beleive, peculiar to this country, equally adapted to the drollest and the most tragical subjects. Simplicity and Ease are its proper characteristics; our forefathers excelled in it, but we moderns have lost the art. It is observed that we have few good English Odes, but to make amends we have many excellent ballads, not inferior perhaps in true poetical merit to some of the very best Odes that the Greek or Latin languages have to boast of. It is a sort of composition I was ever fond of, and if graver matters had not called me another way, should have addicted myself to it more than to any other. I inherit a taste for it from my Father who succeeded well in it himself, and who lived at a time when the best pieces in that way were produced. What can be prettier than Gay's Ballad,° (or rather Swift's, Arbuthnot's, Pope's, & Gay's) in the What d'ye call it? 'Twas when the seas were roaring. I have been well informed that they all contributed, and that the most celebrated association of clever fellows this country ever saw, did not think it beneath them to unite their strength and abilities in the composition of a song. The success however answer'd their wishes, and our puny days will never produce such another. The Ballads that Bourne has translated,° beautifull in themselves are still more beautifull in his version of them, infinitely surpassing in my judgment, all that Ovid or Tibullus° have left behind them. They are quite as elegant, and far more touching and pathetic than the tenderest strokes of either.

So much for Ballads and Ballad writers. A worthy subject you will say for a man whose head might be filled with better things. And *it is* filled with better things, but to so ill a purpose that I thrust into it all manner of topics that may prove more amusing. As for instance—I have two Goldfinches which in the summer occupy the Greenhouse. A few days since being employed in cleaning out their cages, I placed that which I had in hand upon the table, while the other hung against the wall. The windows and the door stood wide open. I went to fill the fountain at the pump, and on my return was not a little surprised to find a gold-finch sitting on the top of the cage I had been cleaning, and singing to and kissing the gold-finch within. I approached him and he discover'd no fear. Still nearer, and he discover'd none. I advanced my hand towards him, and he took no notice of it. I siezed him, and supposed I had caught a new bird. But casting my eye upon the other cage, perceived my mistake. Its inhabitant during my absence had contrived to find an opening where the wire had been a little bent, and made no other use of the escape it afforded him than to salute his friend and converse with him more intimately than he had done before. I returned him to his proper mansion, but in vain. In less than a minute he had thrust his little person through the aperture again, and again perched upon his neighbor's cage, kissing him as at the first, and singing as if transported with the fortunate adventure. I could not but respect such friendship as for the sake of its gratification had twice declined an opportunity to be free, and consenting to their union, resolved that for the future one cage should hold them. I am glad of such incidents, for at a pinch and when I need entertainment, the versification of them serves to divert me.°

I hope you will receive a very fine melon which we send according to your last direction; it will leave this place on Wednesday. Accept my Love and present it to all your family. Your mother is well and adds hers. I transcribe for you a piece of Mme. Guion,° not as the best, but as being shorter than many and as good as most of them. It will give you an idea of her manner. When you write to or see Mr. Smith° I beseech you remember me to him as one that esteems him highly.

Yours ever
Wm C.

Augt. 4. 83.

To John Newton

My dear friend

My time is Short and my opportunity not the most favorable. My letter will consequently be short likewise, and perhaps not very intelligible. I find it no very easy matter to bring my mind into that degree of composure which is neessary to the arrangement either of words or matter. You will naturally expect to receive some account of this confusion that I describe; some reason given for it. On Saturday night at eleven o'clock, when I had not been in bed 5 minutes, and when Mrs. Unwin was but just laid down, we were alarmed by a cry of fire, announced by two or three Shill° screams upon our stair-case. Our maids who were going to bed saw it from their windows, and in appearance so near that they thought our own house in danger. I immediately rose, and putting by the curtain, saw sheets of fire rising above the ridge of Mr. Palmer's House° opposite to ours. The deception was such that I had no doubt it had begun with *him*, but soon found that it was rather farther off. In fact it was at three places, in the

Outhouses belonging to George Griggs, Lucy and Abigail Tyrrel.° Having broke out in three different parts, it is supposed to have been maliciously kindled. A tar-barrel and a quantity of Tallow made a most tremendous blaze, and the buildings it had seized upon being all thatched, the appearance became every moment more formidable. Providentially the night was perfectly calm, so calm that candles without lanterns of which there were multitudes in the street, burnt as steadily as in a house. By 4 in the morning it was so far reduced that all danger seemed to be over, but the confusion it had occasioned was almost infinite. Every man who supposed his dwelling house in jeopardy, emptied it as fast as he could, and conveyed his moveables to the house of some neighbor supposed to be more secure. Ours, in the space of two hours, was so filled with all sorts of lumber that we had not even room for a chair by the fireside. George Griggs is the principal sufferer. He gave 18 Guineas or nearly that Sum to a woman whom in his hurry he mistook for his wife, but the supposed wife walked off with the money and he will probably never recover it. He has likewise lost 40 pounds worth of wool. London never exhibited a scene of greater depredation, drunkenness and riot. Every thing was stolen that could be got at, and every drop of liquor drunk that was not guarded. Only one thief has yet been detected; a woman of the name of Jackson,° who was stopp'd by young Henshman° with an apron full of plunder. He was forced to strike her down before he could wrest it from her. Could you visit the place, you would see a most striking proof of a providence interposing to stop the progress of the flames. They had almost reached, that is to say, within 6 yards of Daniel Raban's° wood pile, in which there were 50 pounds worth of faggots and furze; and exactly there, they were extinguished. Otherwise, especially if a breath of air had happen'd to move, all that side of the town must probably have been consumed. After all this dreadfull conflagration we find nothing burnt but the Outhouses, and the dwellings to which they belong'd have suffer'd only the damage of being unroofed on that side next the fire. No lives were lost nor any limbs broken. Mrs. Unwin whose spirits served her while the hubbub lasted and the day after, begins to feel the effect of it now. But I hope she will be releived from it soon, being better this evening than I expected. As for me, I am impregnable to all such assaults.—I have nothing however but this subject in my mind, and it is in vain that I invite any other into it. Having therefore exhausted this, I finish. Assuring you of our united love, and hoping to find myself in a frame of mind more suited to my employment when I write next.

I just add that Mr. Bull dined with us on Thursday (I should have said called upon us just after dinner) and in the course of his conversation discovered that he was grieved at not having heard from you.

Yours my dear friend
Wm Cowper.

Mond. Nove. 3. 1783.

The books have been forgot in the bustle but will send them by the next opportunity.

To John Newton

My dear friend—A parcel arrived last night the contents of which shall be disposed of according to order. We thank Mrs. Newton (not from the Teeth outwards) for the tooth brushes.

The Country around us is much alarm'd with apprehensions of fire. Two have happen'd since That of Olney. One at Hitchin,° where the damage is said to amount to 11,000£, and another at a place not far from Hitchin of which I have not learnt the name. Letters have been dropt at Bedford threat'ning to burn the Town, and the Inhabitants have been so intimidated as to have placed a guard in many parts of it, several nights past. Some Madman or some Devil has broke loose, who it is to be hoped will pay dear for these effusions of his Malignity.—Since our Conflagration here, we have sent two Women and a Boy to the Justice for depredation. Sue Riviss° for stealing a piece of Beef, which, in her excuse, she said she intended to take care of. This Lady, whom you well remember, escaped for want of evidence. Not that evidence was indeed wanting, but Our men of Goatham° judged it unnecessary to send it. With her, went the woman I mention'd before,° who it seems has made some sort of profession, but upon this occasion allowed herself a latitude of conduct rather inconsistent with it, having filled her apron with wearing apparel, which she likewise intended to take care of. She would have gone to the County Gaol, had Billy Raban, the Baker's son,° who prosecuted, insisted upon it. But He, good natur'dly, though I think weakly, interposed in her favor and begg'd her off. The young Gentleman who accompanied these fair ones, is the Junior Son of Molly Boswell.° He had stolen some Iron work the property of Griggs the Butcher. Being convicted he was order'd to be whipt, which operation he underwent at the Cart's tail° from the Stone house to the High Arch and back again.° He seem'd to show great fortitude but it was all an imposition upon the public. The Beedle who perform'd it had filled his left hand with red Ocre, through which after every stroke he drew the lash of his whip, leaving the appearance of a wound upon the skin, but in reality not hurting him at all. This being perceived by Mr. Constable Henshcomb° who followed the beedle, he applied his cane without any such management or precaution to the shoulders of the too mercifull Executioner. The scene immediately became more interesting, the Beedle could by no means be prevailed upon to strike hard, which provoked the Constable to strike harder, and this double flogging continued, 'till a Lass of Silver End, pitying the pitiful Beedle thus suffering under the hands of the pitiless Constable, joined the procession, and placing herself immediately behind the latter, seized him by his capillary Club and pulling him backward by the same, slapt his face with a most Amazonian fury. This Concatenation of events has taken up more of my paper than I intended it should, but I could not forbear to inform you how the Beedle thresh'd the thief, the Constable the Beedle, and the Lady the Constable, and how the thief was the only person concern'd, who suffer'd nothing.—Mr. Teedon has been here and is gone again. He came to thank me for an old pair of Breeches. In answer to our enquiries after his health, he replied that he had a slow fever, which made him take all possible care not to inflame his blood. I admired his prudence, but in his particular instance, could not very clearly discern the need of it. Pumpwater will not heat him much, and to speak a little in his own stile, more inebriating fluids are to Him I fancy, not very attainable. He brought us news, the Truth of which however I do not vouch for, that the Town of Bedford was actually on fire yesterday and the flames not extinguish'd when the bearer of the tidings left it.

Swift observes,° when he is giving his reasons why the Preacher is elevated always above his hearers, that let the crowd be as great as it will below, there is always room enough over head. If the French Philosophers° can carry their Art of flying to the perfection they desire, the observation may be reversed, the Crowd will be over head, and they will have most room who stay below. I can assure you however upon my own experience that this way of travelling is very delightfull. I dreamt a night or two since that I drove myself through the upper regions in a Balloon and pair, with the greatest ease and security; having finish'd the Tour I intended, I made a short turn, and with one flourish of my whip, descended; my horses prancing and curvetting with an infinite share of Spirit, but without the least danger either to me or my Vehicle. The time we may suppose is at hand, and seems to be prognosticated by my dream, when these airy excursions will be universal, when Judges will fly the Circuit, and Bishops their Visitations, and when the Tour of Europe will be perform'd with much greater speed and with equal advantage by all who travel merely for the sake of having it to say, that they have made it.

I beg you will accept for yourself and yours our unfeigned Love, and remember me affectionately to Mr. Bacon when you see him.

Yours my dear friend
Wm Cowper.

Novr. 17. 1783.

———

Mrs. U. will speak for herself.

To John Newton

My dear friend—I too have taken leave of the old year and parted from it just when you did; but with very different sentiments and feelings upon the occasion. I looked back upon all the passages and occurrences of it, as a traveller looks back upon a wilderness through which he has passed with weariness and sorrow of heart, reaping no other fruit of his labor than the poor consolation, that dreary as the desert was, he has left it all behind him. The traveller would find even this comfort considerably lessened, if as soon as he had passed one wilderness, another of equal length, and equally desolate should expect him. In this particular, His experience and mine would exactly tally. I should rejoice indeed that the old year is over and gone, if I had not every reason to prophecy a new one similar to it. The new one is already old in my account. I am not indeed sufficiently second-sighted to be able to boast by anticipation an acquaintance with the events of it yet unborn, but rest convinced that be they what they may, not one of them comes a messenger of good to Me. If even death itself should be of the number, he is no friend of mine. It is an alleviation of the woes even of an unenlightened man, that he can wish for death, and indulge a hope at least, that in death he shall find deliverance. But loaded as my life is with despair, I have no such comfort as would result from a supposed probability of better things to come, were it once ended. For more unhappy than the traveller with whom I set out, pass through what difficulties I may, through whatever dangers and afflictions, I am not a whit the nearer home, unless a dungeon may be called so. This is no very agreeable theme; but in so great a dearth of subjects to write upon, and especially impressed as I am at this moment with a sense of my own condition, I could chuse no other. The weather is an exact emblem of my mind in its present state. A thick fog invelops every thing, and at the same time it freezes intensely. You will tell me that this cold gloom will be succeeded by a cheerful spring, and endeavor to encourage me to hope for a spiritual change resembling it. But it will be lost labor: Nature revives again, but a soul once slain, lives no more. The hedge that has been apparently dead, is not so, it will burst into leaf and blossom at the appointed time; but no such time is appointed for the stake that stands in it. It is as dead as it seems, and will prove itself no dissembler. The latter end of next month will complete a period of eleven years in which I have spoke no other language. It is a long time for a man whose eyes were once opened to spend in darkness, long enough to make despair an inveterate habit, and such it is in me. My friends I know expect that I shall see yet again, they think it necessary to the existence of divine truth, that he who once had possession of it should never finally lose it. I admitt the solidity of this reasoning in every case but my own. And why not in my own? For causes which to them it appears madness to alledge, but which rest upon my mind with a weight of immoveable conviction. If I am recoverable, why am I thus? Why crippled and made useless in the church just at that time of life when my judgment and experience being matured, I might be most usefull. Why cashiered and turn'd out of service, 'till according to the course of nature there is not life enough left in me, to make amends for the years I have lost. 'Till there is no reasonable hope left that the fruit can ever pay the expence of the fallow? I forestall the Answer. God's ways are mysterious, and he giveth no account of his matters. An answer that would serve my purpose as well as theirs that use it. There is a mystery in my destruction, and in time it shall be explained.

We are glad you have found so much hidden treasure. And Mrs. U. desires me to tell you that you did her no more than justice in beleiving that she would rejoice in it. It is not easy to surmise the reason why the Revd. Doctor your predecessor° concealed it. Being a subject of a free Government, and I suppose full of the divinity most in fashion, he could not bear lest his great riches should expose him to persecution. Nor can I suppose that he held it any disgrace for a dignitary of the Church to be wealthy, at a time when Churchmen in general spare no pains to become so. But the Wisdom of some men has a droll sort of Knavishness in it much like that of the Magpie, who hides what he finds with a deal of contrivance merely for the pleasure of doing it.

Mrs. Unwin is tolerably well. She wishes me to add that she

shall be obliged to Mrs. Newton, if when an opportunity offers, she will give the Worsted merchant a Jog. We congratulate you that Eliza° does not grow worse, which I know you expected would be the case in the course of the Winter. Present our love to her. Remember us to Sally Johnson,° and assure yourself that we remain as warmly as ever | Yours
                                     WC. | M.U.

Jan. 13. 1784.

To John Newton

                                  Feb. 10, 1784
My dear Friend,
   The morning is my writing time, and in the morning I have no spirits. So much the worse for my correspondents. Sleep, that refreshes my body, seems to cripple me in every other respect. As the evening approaches, I grow more alert, and when I am retiring to bed, am more fit for mental occupation than at any other time. So it fares with us, whom they call nervous. By a strange inversion of the animal œconomy, we are ready to sleep when we have most need to be awake, and go to bed when we might sit up to some purpose. The watch is irregularly wound up, it goes in the night when it is not wanted, and in the day stands still. In many respects we have the advantage of our forefathers, the Picts. We sleep in a whole skin, and are not obliged to submit to the painful operation of punctuating ourselves from head to foot, in order that we may be decently dressed and fit to appear abroad. But on the other hand, we have reason enough to envy them their tone of nerves, and that flow of spirits, which effectually secured them from all uncomfortable impressions of a gloomy atmosphere, and from every shade of melancholy from every other cause. They understood (I suppose) the use of vulnerary herbs, having frequent occasion for some skill in surgery, but physicians (I presume) they had none, having no need of any. Is it possible, that a creature like myself, can be descended

from such progenitors, in whom there appears not a single
trace of family resemblance? What an alteration have a few
ages made! They, without cloathing, would defy the severest
season, and I, with all the accommodations that art has since
invented, am hardly secure even in the mildest. If the wind
blows upon me when my pores are open, I catch cold. A cough
is the consequence. I suppose if such a disorder could have
seized a Pict, his friends would have concluded that a bone
had stuck in his throat, and that he was in some danger of
choking. They would perhaps have addressed themselves to
the cure of his cough, by thrusting their fingers into his gullet,
which would only have exasperated the case. But they would
never have thought of administering Laudanum, my only
remedy. For this difference however, that has obtained
between me and my ancestors, I am indebted to the luxurious
practices and enfeebling self-indulgence, of a long line of
grandsires, who from generation to generation have been
employed in deteriorating the breed, 'till at last the collected
effects of all their follies have centered in my puny self.—A
man indeed, but not in the image of those that went before me.
A man, who sighs and groans, who wears out life in dejection
and oppression of spirits, and who never thinks of the
Aborigines of the country to which I belong, without wishing
that I had been born among them. The evil is without a
remedy, unless the ages that are passed could be recalled, my
whole pedigree be permitted to live again, and being properly
admonished to beware of enervating sloth and refinement,
would preserve their hardiness of nature unimpaired, and
transmit the desirable quality to their posterity. I once saw
Adam in a dream. We sometimes say of a picture, that we
doubt not its likeness to the original, though we never saw
him, a judgment we have some reason to form, when the face
is strongly charactered, and the features full of expression. So
I think of my visionary Adam, and for a similar reason. His
figure was aukward indeed in the extreme. It was evident, that
he had never been taught by a Frenchman to hold his head
erect, or to turn out his toes; to dispose gracefully of his arms,
or to simper without a meaning. But if Mr. Bacon° was called
upon to produce a statue of Hercules, he need not wish for a
juster pattern. He stood like a rock; the size of his limbs, the

prominence of his muscles, and the height of his stature, all conspired to bespeak him a creature whose strength had suffered no diminution; and who, being the first of his race, did not come into the world under a necessity of sustaining a load of infirmities, derived to him from the intemperance of others. He was as much stouter than a Pict, as I suppose a Pict to have been than I. Upon my hypothesis therefore, there has been a gradual declension in point of bodily vigor from Adam down to me, at least if my dream were a just representation of that gentleman, and deserve the credit I cannot help giving it, such must have been the case.

Mary Guthrie° is dead, & I need not tell you gone to heaven. James Abraham's wife° died yesterday. George Knight° about a fortnight since. Two women have died of the small pox, and two children that had it have recovered. It does not spread.

Mrs. Unwin who is well joins me in the most affectionate remembrance of you and yours. Many thanks for an excellent quarter of Lamb, which, if we know your hand-writing, came from Hoxton.°

Yours my dear friend truely
Wm. Cowper.

To John Newton

My dear friend—

It being his Majesty's pleasure that I should yet have another opportunity to write, before he dissolves the parliament,° I avail myself of it with all possible alacrity. I thank you for your last, which was not the less welcome for coming like an Extraordinary Gazette, at a time when it was not expected. As when the sea is uncommonly agitated, the water finds its way into creeks and holes of rocks, which in its calmer state it never reaches, in like manner the effect of these turbulent times is felt even at Orchard side, where in general we live as undisturbed by the political element, as shrimps or cockles that have been accidentally deposited in some hollow beyond the watermark, by the usual dashing of the waves. We

were sitting yesterday after dinner, the two Ladies and myself,
very composedly and without the least apprehension of any
such intrusion, in our snug parlour, one Lady knitting, the
other netting, and the Gentleman winding worsted, when to
our unspeakable surprize, a mob appeared before the window,
a smart rap was heard at the door, the boys hallowed, and the
maid announced Mr. Grenville.° Puss was unfortunately let
out of her box, so that the Candidate with all his good friends
at his heels was refused admittance at the grand Entry, and
referred to the Back door as the only possible way of
approach. Candidates are creatures not very susceptible of
affronts, and would rather I suppose climb in at a window
than be absolutely excluded. In a minute, the yard, the
Kitchen and the parlour were filled. Mr. Grenville advancing
toward me, shook me by the hand with a degree or cordiality
that was extremely seducing. As soon as He and as many as
could find chairs were seated, he began to open the intent of
his visit. I told him I had no vote, for which he readily gave
me credit. I assured him I had no influence; which he was not
equally inclined to believe, and the less no doubt, because Mr.
Ashburner the Drapier° addressing himself to me at that
moment, informed me that I had a great deal. Supposing that
I could not be possessed of such a treasure without knowing it,
I ventured to confirm my first assertion by saying that if I had
any, I was utterly at a loss to imagine where it could be or
wherein it consisted. Thus ended the conference. Mr. Grenville
squeezed me by the hand again, kissed the Ladies, and
withdrew. He kissed likewise the Maid in the kitchen, and
seemed upon the whole a most loving, kissing, kind-hearted
gentleman. He is very young, genteel and handsome. He has a
pair of very good eyes in his head, which not being sufficient
as it should seem for the many nice and difficult purposes of a
Senator, he had a third also which he wore suspended by a
ribband from his Button-hole. The boys halloo'd, the dogs
bark'd, puss scamper'd, the heroe with his long train of
obsequious followers withdrew, we made ourselves very merry
with the adventure, and in a short time settled into our former
tranquillity, never probably to be thus interrupted more. I
thought myself however happy in being able to affirm truely
that I had not that influence for which he sued, and which,

had I been possessed of it, with my present views of the dispute between the Crown and the Commons,° I must have refused him. For he is on the side of the former. It is comfortable to be of no consequence in a world where one cannot exercise any without disobliging somebody. The Town however seems to be much at his service, and if he be equally successful throughout the County, he will undoubtedly carry his Election. Mr. Ashburner perhaps was a little mortified, because it was evident that I owed the honor of this visit to his misrepresentation of my importance. But had he thought proper to assure Mr. Grenville that I had three heads, I should not I suppose have been bound to produce them.

Mr. Scott° who you say was so much admired in your pulpit, would be equally admired in his own, at least by all capable judges, were he not so apt to be angry with his congregation. This hurts him, and had he the understanding and eloquence of Paul himself, would still hurt him. He seldom, hardly ever indeed preaches a gentle, well temper'd sermon but I hear it highly commended. But warmth of temper indulged to a degree that may be called scolding, defeats the end of preaching; it is a misapplication of his powers which it also cripples, and teizes away his hearers. But he is a good man, and may perhaps out grow it.

Many thanks for the worsted which is excellent. We are as well as a Spring hardly less severe than the severest Winter, will give us leave to be. With our united Love we conclude ourselves yours and Mrs. Newton's affectionate and faithfull

W.C. | M.U.

Mar. 29. 84.

To John Newton

April 26. 1784.

My dear friend.

We are truely sorry that you have been indisposed. It is well however to have passed through such a season and to have fared no worse. A cold and a sore throat are troublesome things, but in general an ague is more troublesome; and in this part of the world few have escaped one. I have lately been an invalid myself, and am just recover'd from a rheumatic pain in my back, the most excruciating of the sort I ever felt. There was talk of bleeding and blistering, but I escaped with only an embrocation and a box of pills. Mr. Grindon attended me, who though he fidgets about the world as usual, is, I think a dying man,° having had some time since a stroke of apoplexy, and lately a paralytic one. His loss will be felt in this country. Though I do not think him absolutely an Æsculapius, I beleive him to be as skillfull as most of his fraternity in the neighborhood; besides which, he has the merit of being extremely cautious, a very necessary quality in a practitioner upon the constitutions of others.

We are glad that your book° runs. It will not indeed satisfy those whom nothing *could* satisfy but your accession to their party, but the liberal will say you do well. & it is in the opinion of such men only that you can feel yourself interested.

I have lately been employed in reading Beattie's and Blair's Lectures.° The latter I have not yet finished. I find the former the most agreeable of the two: indeed the most entertaining writer upon dry subjects that I ever met with. His imagination is highly poetical, his language easy and elegant, and his manner so familiar that we seem to be conversing with an old friend upon terms of the most sociable intercourse while we read him. Blair is, on the contrary, rather stiff. Not that his stile is pedantic, but that his air is formal. He is a sensible man and understands his subjects, but too conscious that he is addressing the public, and too sollicitous about his success, to indulge himself for a moment in that play of fancy which makes the other so agreeable. In Blair we find a Scholar. In Beattie both a scholar and an amiable man, indeed so amiable that I have wished for his acquaintance ever since I read his book. Having never in my life perused a page of Aristotle, I am glad to have had an opportunity of learning more than I suppose he would have taught me, from the writings of two modern Critics. I felt myself too a little disposed to compliment my own acumen upon the occasion. For though the Art of Writing and composing was never much my study, I did not find that they had any great news to tell me. They have

assisted me in putting my own observations into some
method, but have not suggested many of which I was not by
some means or other, previously apprized. In fact, Critics did
not originally beget authors, but Authors made Critics.
Common sense dictated to Writers the necessity of method,
connexion, and thoughts congruous to the nature of their
subject, Genius prompted them with embellishments, and
then came the Critics. Observing the good effects of an
attention to these Items, they enacted laws for the observance
of them in time to come, and having drawn their rules for good
writing from what was actually well written, boasted themselves the Inventors of an Art, which yet the Authors of the
day had already exemplified. They are however usefull in
their way, giving us at one view a Map of the boundaries
which propriety sets to fancy, and serving as Judges to whom
the public may at once appeal when pester'd with the vagaries
of those who have had the hardiness to transgress them.

The candidates for this County° have set an example of
Œconomy which other candidates would do well to follow,
having come to an agreement on both sides to defray the
expences to their Voters, but to open no House, for the
entertainment of the rabble. A reform however which the
rabble did not at all approve of, and testified their dislike of it
by a riot. A stage was built from which the Orators had
designed to harrangue the Electors. This became the first
victim of their fury. Having very little curiosity to hear what
Gentlemen could say who would give them nothing better
than words, they broke it in pieces and threw the fragments
upon the hustings. The Sheriff, the Members, the Lawyers,
the Voters were instantly put to flight. They rallied, but were
again routed by a second assault like the former. They then
proceeded to break the windows of the Inn to which they had
fled, and a fear prevailing that at night they would fire the
town, a proposal was made by the freeholders to face about,
and endeavour to secure them. At that instant a Rioter dress'd
in a Merry Andrew's jacket,° stepp'd forward and challenged
the best man among them. Olney sent the Hero to the field
who made him repent him of his presumption. Mr. Ashburner°
was He. Seizing him by the throat he shook him, he threw him
to the Earth, he made the hollowness of his scull resound by

the application of his fists, and dragg'd him into custody without sustaining the least damage to his person. Animated by this example, the other freeholders followed it, and in five minutes 28 out of 30 ragamuffins were lodged in gaol.

Adieu my dear friend, Writing makes my back ache and my paper is full. We love you and are Yours

W. and M.

To William Unwin

My dear William—

The Subject of face-painting may be consider'd I think in two points of view. First there is room for dispute with respect to the consistency of the practise with good morals, and secondly, whether it be on the whole convenient or not may be a matter worthy of agitation. I set out with all the formality of logical disquisition, but do not promise to observe the same regularity any farther than it may comport with my purpose of writing as fast as I can. As to the Immorality of the custom, were I in France I should see none. On the contrary, it seems in that country to be a symptom of modest consciousness, and a tacit confession of what all know to be true, that French faces have in fact neither red nor white of their own. This humble acknowledgment of a defect looks the more like a virtue, being found among a people not remarkable for Humility. Again, before we can prove the practise to be immoral, we must prove immorality in the *design* of those who use it. Either that they intend a deception, or to kindle unlawfull desires in the beholders. But the French ladies so far as their purpose comes in question, must be acquitted of both these charges. Nobody supposes their color to be natural for a moment, any more than he would if it were blue or green. And this unambiguous judgment of the matter is owing to two causes. First to the universal knowledge we have that French women are naturally either brown or yellow with very few exceptions; and secondly to the inartificial manner in which they paint. For they do not, as I am most satisfactorily informed, even attempt an imitation of nature, but besmear themselves hastily and at a venture, anxious only to lay on enough. Where, therefore, there is no wanton intention nor a wish to deceive, I can discover no immorality. But in England I am afraid our painted ladies are not clearly entitled to the same apology. They even imitate nature with such exactness, that the whole Public is sometimes divided into parties who litigate with great warmth the question, whether painted or not? This was remarkably the case with a Miss Bunkham° whom I well remember; her roses and lilies were never discover'd to be spurious, 'till she attained an age that made the supposition of their being natural, impossible. This anxiety to be not merely red and white, which is all they aim at in France, but to be thought very beautifull, and much more beautifull than nature has made them, is a symptom not very favorable to the idea we would wish to entertain of the chastity, purity and modesty of our Countrywomen. That they are guilty of a design to deceive, is certain. Otherwise, why so much Art? And if to deceive, wherefore and with what purpose? Certainly either to gratify Vanity of the silliest kind, or which is still more criminal, to decoy and inveigle and carry on more successfully, the business of Temptation. Here therefore my opinion splits itself into two opposite sides upon the same question. I can suppose a French woman though painted an inch deep to be a virtuous, discreet, excellent character, and in no instance should I think the worse of one because she was painted. But an English Belle must pardon me if I have not the same charity for Her. She is at least an Impostor whether she cheats me or not, because she means to do so; and it is well if that be all the censure she deserves. This brings me to my second class of ideas upon this topic, and here I feel that I should be fearfully puzzled were I called upon to recommend the practise on the score of convenience. If a Husband chose that his Wife should paint, perhaps it might be her duty as well as her interest to comply, but I think he would not much consult his own for reasons that will follow. In the first place she would admire herself the more, and in the next, if she managed the matter well, she might be more admired by others. An acquisition that might bring her virtue under trials to which otherwise it might never have been exposed. In no other case however can I imagine the practise in this country to be either expedient or convenient. As a general one it certainly is not expedient, because in general English women have no occasion for it. A swarthy complexion is a rarity here. And the Sex, especially since Innoculation has been so much in use, have very little cause to complain that Nature has not been kind to them in the article of complexion. They may hide and spoil a good one, but they cannot, at least they hardly can give themselves a better. But even if they could, there is yet a tragedy in the sequel which should make them tremble. I understand that in France though the use of Rouge be general the use of White paint is far from being so. In England She that uses one commonly uses both.. Now all white paints or lotions or whatever they be called, are Mercurial, consequently poisonous, consequently ruinous in time to the constitution. The Miss Bunkham abovemention'd was a miserable Witness of this truth, it being certain that her flesh fell from her bones before she died. Lady Coventry° was hardly a less melancholy proof of it. And a London Physician perhaps were he at liberty to blab, could publish a Bill of female Mortality of a length that would astonish us. For these reasons I utterly condemn the practise as it obtains in England. And for a reason superior to all these I must disapprove it. I cannot indeed discover that Scripture forbids it in so many words, but That anxious sollicitude about the person which such an Artifice evidently betrays, is I am sure contrary to the Tenour and Spirit of it throughout. Show me a Woman with a painted face, and I will show you a woman whose heart is set on things of the earth and not on things above. But this observation of mine applies to it only when it is an imitative art, for in the use of French women I think it as innocent as in the use of a Wild Indian, who draws a circle round her face, and makes two spots perhaps blue perhaps white in the middle of it.—Such are my thoughts upon the matter.

Your Mother gives you her true love. Her respects and mine attend all the party. She wishes you to bring her a pound of the best pins. Thanks for the books, cloth, and brushes.

Vive valeque.° Yours ever
Wm C.

May 3d. 1784.

To William Unwin

[*c.*20 May 1784]

My dear William—

It is hard upon us Striplings who have uncles still living (N.B. I myself have an Uncle still alive°) that those venerable gentlemen should stand in our way even when the Ladies are in question. That I for instance, should find in one page of your letter a hope that Miss Shuttleworth would be of your party, and be told in the next that she is engaged to your uncle.° Well—we may perhaps never be Uncles, but we may reasonably hope that the time is coming when others as young as we are now, shall envy us the privileges of Old Age, and see us engross that share in the attention of the Ladies to which their Youth must aspire in vain. Make our Compliments if you please to your Sister Elizabeth, and tell her that we are both mortified at having missed the pleasure of seeing her.

Balloons° are so much the mode, that even in this Country we have attempted a Balloon. You may possibly remember that at a place call'd Weston, little more than a mile from Olney, there lives a family whose name is Throckmorton. The present possessor of the Estate is a young man whom I remember a boy. He has a Wife, who is young, genteel and handsome. They are papists, but much more amiable than many protestants. We never had any intercourse with the family, though ever since we lived here we have enjoyed the range of their pleasure grounds, having been favor'd with a key that admitts us into all. When this man succeeded to the Estate on the death of his elder Brother,° and come to settle at Weston, I sent him a complimentary card requesting the continuance of that privilege, having till then enjoyed it by the favor of his Mother,° who on that occasion went to finish her days at Bath. You may conclude that he granted it, and for about 2 years nothing more passed between us. A fortnight ago I received an Invitation in the civillest terms, in which he told me that the next day he should attempt to fill a Balloon, and if it would be any pleasure to me to be present, should be happy to see me. Your Mother and I went. The whole Country were there, but the Balloon could not be filled. The endeavour was I believe very philosophically made, but such a process depends for its success upon such niceties as make it very precarious. Our reception was however flattering to a great degree insomuch that more notice seemed to be taken of us than we could possibly have expected, indeed rather more than of any of his other guests. They even seemed anxious to recommend themselves to our regards. We drank chocolate and were asked to dine, but were engaged. A day or two after Mrs. U. and I walked that way and were overtaken in a shower. I found a tree that I thought could shelter us both, a large Elm in a grove that fronts the Mansion. Mrs. T. observed us, and running towards us in the rain, insisted on our walking in. He was gone out. We sat chatting with her till the weather cleared up, and then, at her instance took a walk with her in the garden. The Garden is almost their only walk, and is certainly their only retreat in which they are not liable to interruption. She offer'd us a Key of it in a manner that made it impossible not to accept it, and said that she would send us one. A few days after, in the cool of the Evening we walked that way again. We saw them going toward the house, and exchanged bows & curtsies at a little distance, but did not join them. In a few minutes, when we had passed the house, and had almost reached the gate that opens out of the Park into the adjoining field, I heard the Iron Gate belonging to the Court yard ring, and saw Mr. T. advancing toward us. We made equal haste to meet him. He presented to us the Key, which I told him I esteemed a singular favor, and after a few such speeches as are made upon such occasions, we parted. This happen'd about a week ago. I concluded nothing less than that all this civility and attention was designed on their part as the prelude to a nearer acquaintance. But here at present the matter rests. I should like exceedingly to be on an easy footing there, to give a Morning call and now and then to receive one, but nothing more. For though he is one of the most agreeable men I ever saw, I could not wish to visit him in any other way, neither our house, furniture, servants or income being such as qualify us to make entertainments. Nor would I on any account be introduced to the neighbouring Gentry, which must be the consequence of our dining there; there not being a man in the country except himself with whom I could endure to associate. They are Squires. Merely such. Purseproud and Sportsmen. But Mr. T. is altogether a man of fashion, and respectable on every account.

I have told you a long Story. Farewell. We number the days as they pass, and are glad that we shall see you and your Sister soon.

Yours
WC.

To the Gentleman's Magazine

May 28. [1784]

Mr. Urban,

Convinced that you despise no communications that may gratify curiosity, amuse rationally, or add, though but a little, to the stock of public knowledge, I send you a circumstantial account of an animal, which, though its general properties are pretty well known, is for the most part such a stranger to man, that we are but little aware of its peculiarities. We know indeed that the hare is good to hunt and good to eat, but in all other respects poor Puss° is a neglected subject.

In the year 1774, being much indisposed both in mind and body, incapable of diverting myself either with company or books, and yet in a condition that made some diversion necessary, I was glad of any thing that would engage my attention without fatiguing it. The children of a neighbour of mine had a leveret given them for a plaything; it was at that time about three months old. Understanding better how to tease the poor creature than to feed it, and soon becoming weary of their charge, they readily consented that their father, who saw it pining and growing leaner every day, should offer it to my acceptance. I was willing enough to take the prisoner under my protection, perceiving that in the management of such an animal, and in the attempt to tame it, I should find just that sort of employment which my case required. It was soon known among the neighbours that I was pleased with the present; and the consequence was, that in a short time I had as many leverets offered to me as would have stocked a paddock. I undertook the care of three, which it is necessary that I should here distinguish by the names I gave them, Puss, Tiney, and Bess.° Notwithstanding the two feminine appellatives, I must inform you that they were all males. Immediately commencing carpenter, I built them homes to sleep in; each had a separate apartment so contrived that their ordure would pass thro' the bottom of it; an earthen pan placed under each received whatsoever fell, which being duly emptied and washed, they were thus kept perfectly sweet and clean. In the daytime they had the range of a hall, and at night retired each to his own bed, never intruding into that of another.

Puss grew presently familiar, would leap into my lap, raise himself upon his hinder feet, and bite the hair from my temples. He would suffer me to take him up and to carry him about in my arms, and has more then once fallen asleep upon my knee. He was ill three days, during which time I nursed him, kept him apart from his fellows that they might not molest him (for, like many other wild animals, they persecute one of their own species that is sick), and, by constant care and trying him with a variety of herbs, restored him to perfect health. No creature could be more grateful than my patient after his recovery; a sentiment which he most significantly expressed, by licking my hand, first the back of it, then the palm, then every finger separately, then between all the fingers, as if anxious to leave no part of it unsaluted, a ceremony which he never performed but once again upon a similar occasion. Finding him extremely tractable, I made it my custom to carry him always after breakfast into the garden, where he hid himself generally under the leaves of a cucumber vine, sleeping or chewing the cud till evening; in the leaves also of that vine he found a favourite repast. I had not long habituated him to this taste of liberty, before he began to be impatient for the return of the time when he might enjoy it. He would invite me to the garden by drumming upon my knee, and by a look of such expression as it was not possible to misinterpret. If this rhetoric did not immediately succeed, he would take the skirt of my coat between his teeth, and pull at it with all his force. Thus Puss might be said to be perfectly tamed, the shyness of his nature was done away, and on the whole it was visible, by many symptoms which I have not room to enumerate, that he was happier in human society than when shut up with his natural companions.

Not so Tiney. Upon him the kindest treatment had not the least effect. He too was sick, and in his sickness had an equal share of my attention; but if, after his recovery I took the liberty to stroke him, he would grunt, strike with his fore feet, spring forward and bite. He was, however, very entertaining in his way, even his surliness was matter of mirth, and in his play he preserved such an air of gravity, and performed his feats with such a solemnity of manner, that in him too I had an agreeable companion.

Bess, who died soon after he was full grown, and whose death was occasioned by his being turned into his box which had been washed, while it was yet damp, was a hare of great humour and drollery. Puss was tamed by gentle usage; Tiney was not to be tamed at all; and Bess had a courage and confidence that made him tame from the beginning. I always admitted them into the parlour after supper, when the carpet affording their feet a firm hold, they would frisk and bound and play a thousand gambols, in which, Bess, being remarkably strong and fearless, was always superior to the rest, and proved himself the Vestris° of the party. One evening the cat being in the room had the hardiness to pat Bess upon the cheek, an indignity which he resented by drumming upon her back with such violence, that the cat was happy to escape from under his paws and hide herself.

You observe, Sir, that I describe these animals as having each a character of his own. Such they were in fact, and their countenances were so expressive of that character, that, when I looked only on the face of either, I immediately knew which it was. It is said, that a shepherd, however numerous his flock, soon becomes so familiar with their features, that he can by that indication only distinguish each from all the rest, and yet to a common observer the difference is hardly perceptible. I doubt not that the same discrimination in the cast of countenances would be discoverable in hares, and am persuaded that among a thousand of them no two could be found exactly similar; a circumstance little suspected by those who have not had opportunity to observe it. These creatures have a singular sagacity in discovering the minutest alteration that is made in the place to which they are accustomed, and instantly apply their nose to the examination of a new object. A small hole being burnt in the carpet, it was mended with a patch, and that patch in a moment underwent the strictest scrutiny. They seem too to be very much directed by the smell in the choice of their favourites; so some persons, though they saw them daily, they could never be reconciled, and would even scream when they attempted to touch them; but a miller coming in, engaged their affections at once; his powdered coat had charms that were irresistible. You will not wonder, Sir, that my intimate acquaintance with these specimens of the kind has taught me to hold the sportsman's amusement in abhorrence; he little knows what amiable creatures he persecutes, of what gratitude they are capable, how cheerful they are in their spirits, what enjoyment they have of life, and that, impressed as they seem with a peculiar dread of man, it is only because man gives them peculiar cause for it.

That I may not be tedious, I will just give you a short summary of those articles of diet that suit them best, and then retire to make room for some more important correspondent.

I take it to be a general opinion that they graze, but it is an erroneous one, at least grass is not their staple; they seem rather to use it medicinally, soon quitting it for leaves of almost any kind. Sowthistle, dent-de-lion, and lettuce are their favourite vegetables, especially the last. I discovered by accident that fine white sand is in great estimation with them; I suppose as a digestive. It happened that I was cleaning a bird-cage while the hares were with me; I placed a pot filled with such sand upon the floor, to which being at once directed by a strong instinct, they devoured it voraciously; since that time I have generally taken care to see them well supplied with it. They account green corn a delicacy, both blade and stalk, but the ear they seldom eat; straw of any kind, especially wheat-straw, is another of their dainties; they will feed greedily upon oats, but if furnished with clean straw never want them; it serves them also for a bed, and, if shaken up daily, will keep sweet and dry for a considerable time. They do not indeed require aromatic herbs, but will eat a small quantity of them with great relish, and are particularly fond of the plant called musk; they seem to resemble sheep in this, that, if their pasture be too succulent, they are very subject to the rot; to prevent which, I always made bread their principal nourishment, and, filling a pan with it cut into small squares, placed it every evening in their chambers, for they feed only at evening and in the night; during the winter, when vegetables are not to be got, I mingled this mess of bread with shreds of carrot, adding to it the rind of apples cut extremely thin; for tho' they are fond of the paring, the apple itself disgusts them. These, however, not being a sufficient substitute for the juice of summer herbs, they must at this time be supplied with water; but so placed, that they cannot overset it into their beds. I must not omit that occasionally they are much pleased with twigs of hawthorn and of the common briar, eating even the very wood when it is of considerable thickness.

Bess, I have said, died young; Tiney lived to be nine years old, and died at last, I have reason to think, of some hurt in his loins by a fall. Puss is still living, and has just completed his tenth year, discovering no signs of decay nor even of age, except that he is grown more discreet and less frolicksome than he was. I cannot conclude, Sir, without informing you that I have lately introduced a dog to his acquaintance, a spaniel that had never seen a hare to a hare that had never seen a spaniel. I did it with great caution, but there was no real need of it. Puss discovered no token of fear, nor Marquis° the least symptom of hostility. There is therefore, it should seem, no natural antipathy between dog and hare, but the pursuit of the one occasions the flight of the other, and the dog pursues because he is trained to it: they eat bread at the same time out of the same hand, and are in all respects sociable and friendly. Yours, &c.

W.C.

PS. I should not do complete justice to my subject, did I not add, that they have no ill scent belonging to them, that they are indefatigably nice in keeping themselves clean, for which purpose nature has furnished them with a brush under each foot; and that they are never infested by any vermin.

To John Newton

Sepr. 18. 1784.

My dear friend—

Following your good example I lay before me a sheet of my largest paper. It was this moment fair and unblemished, but I have begun to blot it, and having begun, am not likely to cease 'till I have spoil'd it. I have sent you many a sheet that in my judgment of it, has been very unworthy of your acceptance, but my conscience was in some measure satisfied by reflecting that it if were good for nothing, at the same time it cost you nothing except the trouble of reading it. But the case is altered now. You must pay a solid price for frothy matter, and though I do not absolutely pick your pocket, yet you lose your money and as the saying is, are never the wiser. A Saying literally fulfilled to the Reader of my Epistles.

My Greenhouse is never so pleasant as when we are just upon the point of being turned out of it. The gentleness of Autumnal suns and the calmness of this latter season make it a much more agreeable retreat than we ever find it in summer; when the winds being generally brisk we cannot cool it by admitting a sufficient quantity of air without being at the same time incommoded by it. But now I sit with all the windows and the door wide open, and am regaled with the scent of every flower in a garden as full of flowers as I have known how to make it. We keep no bees, but if I lived in a Hive I should hardly hear more of their music. All the bees in the neighborhood resort to a bed of mignonette opposite to the window, and pay me for the honey they get out of it by a Hum which though rather monotonous is as agreeable to my ear as the whistling of my linnets. All the sounds that Nature utters are delightfull; at least in this country. I should not perhaps find the roaring of lions in Africa, or of Bears in Russia very pleasing, but I know no beast in England whose voice I do not account musical, save and except always the braying of an ass. The notes of all our birds and fowls please me without one exception. I should not indeed think of Keeping a goose in a cage that I might hang him up in the parlour for the sake of his melody, but a goose upon a Common or in a farm yard is no bad performer. And as to insects, if the black beetle and beetles indeed of all hues will keep out of my way, I have no objection to any of the rest. On the contrary in whatever key they sing, from the Gnat's fine treble to the Base of the Humble bee I admire them all. Seriously however, it strikes me as a very observable instance of providential Kindness to Man, that such an exact accord has been contrived between the Ear and the sounds with which, at least in a rural situation, it is almost every moment visited. All the world is sensible of the uncomfortable effect that certain sounds have upon the nerves and consequently upon the Spirits. And if a sinfull world had been filled with such as would have curdled the blood, and have made the sense of hearing a perpetual inconvenience, I do not know that we should have had a right to complain. But now, the fields, the woods, the gardens, have each their concerts, and the ear of man is for ever regaled by creatures who mean only to please themselves. Even the ears that are deaf to the gospel, are continually entertained, though without knowing it, by sounds for which they are solely indebted to its Author. There is somewhere in infinite space, a world that does not roll within the precincts of mercy. And as it is reasonable and even scriptural to suppose that there is music in heaven, in those dismal regions perhaps the Reverse of it is found. Tones so dismal as to make woe itself more insupportable, and to acuminate even despair. But my paper admonishes me in good time to draw the reins and to check the descent of my fancy into deeps with which she is but too familiar.

Our best Love attends you both with Yours. | Sum, ut sempter, Tui studiosissimus°

W.C.

To William Unwin

Olney Nove. 29 1784.

My dear William—

I am happy that you are pleased, and accept it as an earnest that I shall not at least disgust the public. For though I know your partiality to me, I know at the same time with what laudable tenderness you feel for your own reputation, and that for the sake of that most delicate part of your property, though you would not criticize me with an unfriendly and undue severity, you would however beware of being satisfied too hastily and with no warrantable cause for being so.—I called you the Tutour of your *two* sons, in contemplation of the certainty of that event, and accounting it no violation of truth to assert *that* as true to-day which will be so to-morrow. It is a fact in suspense, not a fiction.

My principal Errand to you now, is to give you information on the following subject. The moment Mr. Newton knew (and I took care that he should learn it first from me) that I had communicated to you what I had concealed form him, and that you were my Authorship's Go-between with Johnson upon this occasion, he sent me, a most friendly letter indeed, but one in every line of which I could hear the soft murmurs of something like mortification, that could not be entirely suppressed. It contained nothing however that you yourself would have blamed, or that I had not every reason to consider as evidence of his regard to me. He concluded the subject with desiring to know something of my plan, to be favor'd with an extract by way of specimen, or (which he should like better still) with wishing me to order Johnson to send him a proof as fast as they were printed off. Determining not to accede to this last request for many reasons, but especially because I would no more show my poem piece-meal, than I would my house if I had one, the merits of the structure in either case being equally liable to suffer by such a partial view of it, I have endeavor'd to compromise the difference between us, and to satisfy Him without disgracing myself. The proof-sheets I have absolutely, though civilly, refused. But I have sent him a copy of the arguments of each book, more dilated and circumstantial than those inserted in the work. And to these I have added an Extract as he desired, selecting, as most suited his taste, the View of the Restoration of all things, which you recollect to have seen near the End of the last book.° I held it necessary to tell you this, lest if you should call upon him, he should startle you by discovering a degree of Information upon the subject, which you would not otherwise know how to reconcile or to account for.

You have executed your commissions *á merveille*.° We not only approve but admire. No apology was wanting for the balance struck at the bottom, which we accounted rather a beauty than a deformity. Pardon a poor poet, who cannot speak even of Pounds, Shillings and Pence but in his own way. Your Uncle has three pounds in his hands which you will be so good as to appropriate.

I have read Lunardi° with pleasure. He is a lively sensible young fellow, and I suppose a very favorable sample of the Italians. When I look at his picture, I can fancy that I see in him that good sense and courage that no doubt were legible in the face of a young Roman 2000 years ago. I hope that you *have*, or that you *will* remember to thank Miss Unwin° for me. I congratulate you, (we both do so) on the successfull administration of your Trust respecting that Lady, and doubt not but she will handsomely express her sense of your merits as a Guardian.

In the Epistle to Mr. Hill, if the Copy be still with you, be pleased to substitute Hill for Joe—°

To John Newton

[22 April 1785]

My dear friend,

When I received your account of the great Celebrity of John Gilpin,° I felt myself both flattered and grieved. Being man, and having in my composition all the ingredients of which other men are made, and Vanity among the rest, it pleased me to reflect that I was on a sudden become so famous and that all the world was busy enquiring after me. But the next moment, recollecting my former self, and that thirteen years ago, as harmless as John's history is I should not then have written it, my spirits rather sunk and I was ashamed of my success. Your letter was followed the next post by one from

Mr. Unwin. You tell me that I am rivalled by Mrs. Bellamy,° and he that I have a competitor for fame not less formidable in the learned Pig.° Alas! what is an author's popularity worth, in a world that can Suffer a prostitute on one side, and a pig on the other to ecclipse his brightest glories? I am therefore sufficiently humbled by these considerations, and unless I should hereafter be ordained to engross the public attention by means more magnificent than a song, am persuaded that I shall suffer no real detriment by their applause. I have produced many things under the influence of despair, which Hope would not have permitted to spring. But if the soil of that melancholy in which I have walked so long has thrown up here and there an unprofitable fungus, it is well at least that it is not chargeable with having brought forth poison. Like you I see, or think I can see, that Gilpin may have his use. Causes in appearance trivial produce often the most beneficial consequences, and perhaps my volumes may now travel to a distance, which if they had not been ushered into the world by that notable horseman, they would never have reached. I hope that neither the Master of St. Paul's° or any other school, who may have commenced my admirer on John's account, will write to me for such a reason. Yet a little while, and if they have laughed with me, their note will be changed, and perhaps they will revile me. Tirocinium° is no friend of theirs, on the contrary, if it have the effect I wish it to have, it will prove much their enemy; for it gives no quarter to modern pædagogues, but finding them all alike guilty of supineness and neglect in the affair of Morals, condemns them, both School Masters and Heads of Colleges, without distinction. Our temper differs somewhat from that of the antient Jews. They would neither dance nor weep.° We indeed weep not if a man mourn unto us, but I must need say that if he pipe we seem disposed to dance with the greatest alacrity. I ought to tell you that this remark has a reference to John Gilpin, otherwise having been jumbled a little out of its place you might be at a loss for the application.

Johnson has not pleased me. He has been now five Months in possession of the Copy and has printed little more than half of it. I wrote to him lately to accelerate his progress. The consequence is that instead of receiving two sheets in a°

To Joseph Hill

My dear friend

I write in a nook that I call my Bouderie; It is a Summer house not much bigger than a Sedan chair, the door of which opens into the garden that is now crowded with pinks, roses and honey-suckles, and the window into my neighbour's orchard. It formerly served an Apothecary, now dead,° as a smoking room, and under my feet is a trapdoor which once cover'd a hole in the ground where he kept his bottles. At present however it is dedicated to sublimer uses. Having lined it with garden-mats, and furnished it with a table and two chairs, here I write all that I write in summer-time, whether to the Public or to my friends. It is secure from all noise, and a refuge from all intrusion; for intrusions sometimes trouble me even at Olney. I have never lived, I believe it is impossible to live where they can be altogether evaded. At Berkhamsted I was haunted by the younger Harcourt,° in the Temple by T. White° Esqre., at Weymouth by Mr. Foy,° and at Olney I have a Mr. Teedon° to dread, who in his most single person includes the disagreeables of them all. He is the most obsequious, the most formal, the most pedantic of all creatures. So civil that it would be cruel to affront him, and so troublesome that it is impossible to bear him. Being possessed of a little Latin, he seldom uses a word that is not derived from that language, and being a bigot to propriety of pronunciation, studiously and constantly lays the accent upon the wrong syllable. I think that Sheridan would adore him.° He has formed his stile (he told me so himself) by the pattern that Mr. Hervey has furnish'd him with in his Theron and Aspasio,° accordingly he never says that my garden is gay, but that the flowery tribe are finely variegated and extremely fragrant. The weather with him is never fine, but genial, never cold and uncomfortable, but rigorous and frowning. If he cannot recollect a thing, he tells me that it is not within his recognizance, convincing me at the same time that the Orthography of the word is quite familiar to him, by laying a particular stress upon the g. In short he surfeits me whenever I am so unhappy as to encounter him, which is too often my lot in the Winter, but thanks to my Bouderie, I can hide myself from him now. A poet's retreat is sacred. He acknowledges the truth of that proposition, and never presumes to violate it.

The last sentence puts me in mind to tell you that I have order'd my volume to your door. My Bookseller is the most dilatory of all his fraternity, or you would have received it long since. It is more than a month since I returned him the last proof, and consequently since the Printing was finished. I sent him the Manuscript at the beginning of last November that he might publish while the Town is full, and he will hit the exact moment when it is entirely empty. Patience, you percieve is in no situation exempted from the severest trials; a remark that may serve to comfort you under the numberless troubles of your own.

I have to thank you for two baskets of very large and very fine Mackarel, since I thank'd you for the first. Adieu! my friend. Assure yourself that your many friendly offices and favors, though poorly return'd, are not thrown away upon the ungratefull, and believe me | with my respects to Mrs. Hill |

Your Affectionate
Wm Cowper.

June 29. 1785.

To John Newton

Sepr. 24. 1785

My dear friend

I am sorry that an excursion which you would otherwise have found so agreeable, was attended with so great a Drawback upon its pleasures as Miss Cunningham's illness° must needs have been. Had she been able to bathe in the sea, it might have been of service to her, but I knew her weakness and delicacy of habit to be such, as did not encourage any very sanguine hopes that the regimen would suit her. I remember Southampton well,° having spent much time there; but though I was young, and had no objections on the score of conscience either to Dancing or Cards, I never was in the assembly room in my life. I never was fond of company, and especially disliked it in the country. A walk to Nettley Abbey° or to Freemantle° or to Redbridge,° or a book by the fire-side, had always more charms for me than any other amusement that the place afforded. I was also a Sailor, and being of Sir Thomas Hesketh's party, who was himself born one, was often press'd into the service. But though I gave myself an air and wore trowsers, had no genuine right to that honour, disliking much to be occupied in great waters unless in the finest weather. How they contrive to elude the wearisomeness that attends a sea-life who take long voyages, you know better than I, but for my own part I seldom have sailed so far as from Hampton river to Portsmouth without feeling the confinement irksome, and sometimes to a degree that was almost insupportable. There is a certain perverseness of which I believe all men have a share, but of which no man has a larger share than I. I mean that temper or humour or whatever it is to be called, that indisposes us to a situation though not unpleasant in itself, merely because we cannot get out of it. I could not endure the room in which I now write, were I conscious that the doors were lock'd; in less than 5 minutes I should feel myself a prisoner, though I can spend hours in it under an assurance that I may leave it when I please, without experiencing any tædium at all. It was for this reason I suppose that the Yacht was always disagreeable to me. Could I have stepp'd out of it into a corn field or a garden I should have liked it well enough, but being surrounded with water I was as much confined in it as if I had been surrounded by fire, and did not find that it made me any adequate compensation for such an abridgment of my liberty. I make little doubt but Noah was glad when he was enlarged from the ark, and we are sure that Jonah was when he came out of the fish, and so was I to escape from the good sloop the Harriot.

In my last I wrote you word that Mr. Perry° was given over by his friends, and pronounced a dead man by his physician. Just when I had reached the end of the foregoing paragraph, he came in. His errand hither was to bring two letters which I enclose, one is to yourself, in which he will give you I doubt not such an account both of his body and mind, as will make all that I might say upon those subjects superfluous. The only consequences of his illness seem to be that he looks a little pale, and that, though always a most excellent man, he is still more angelic than he was. Illness sanctified is better than health. But I know a man who has been a sufferer by a worse Illness than his almost these 14 Years, and who at present is only the worse for it.

Mr. Scott° called upon us yesterday. He is much inclined to set up a Sunday School if he can raise a fund for the purpose. Mr. Jones° has had one some time at Clifton, and Mr. Unwin writes me word that he has been thinking of nothing else day and night for a fortnight. It is a wholesome measure that seems to bid fair to be pretty generally adopted, and for the good effects that it promises, deserves well to be so. I know not indeed, while the spread of the Gospel continues so limited as it is, how a reformation of manners in the lower class of mankind, can otherwise be brought to pass, or by what other means the utter abolition of all principle among them, Moral as well as Religious, can possibly be prevented. Heathenish parents can only bring up Heathenish children, an assertion nowhere oftener or more clearly illustrated than at Olney, where children 7 years of age infest the streets every evening with curses and with songs to which it would be unseemly to give their proper Epithet. Such urchins as these, could not be so diabolically accomplish'd unless by the connivance of their parents. It is well indeed if in some instances their parents be not themselves their instructors; judging by their proficiency one can hardly suppose any other. It is therefore doubtless an act of the greatest charity to snatch them out of such hands, before the inveteracy of the Evil shall have made it desperate. Mr. Teedon° I should imagine will be employed as a Teacher should this expedient be carried into effect; I know not at least that we have any other person among us so well qualified for the service. He is indisputably a Christian man, and miserably poor, whose revenues need improvement as much as any children in the world can possibly need instruction.

I understand that Mr. Jones is in London; it is possible that you may have seen him, and if you have, are better acquainted with his present intentions respecting Lord P.° than myself. We saw him not long since, when he talked of resigning his office immediately, but I hear that he was afterwards otherwise advised and repented of his purpose. I think it great pity that he did. A thing that a man had better never have touched cannot be too soon relinquished. While his Principal kept himself at a distance, his connexion with him was less offensive; but now, to all who interest themselves in his conduct as a Minister of the Gospel, it is an offence indeed. He seems aware of it, and we hope therefore will soon abandon it.

Mrs. Unwin hopes that a Hare which she sent before Mrs. Newton went her journey, arrived safe. By this Week's Coach she also sent three fowls and a Ham with cabbages, of whose safe arrival she will likewise be glad to hear. She has long been troubled with a pain in her side, which we take to be of the spasmodic kind, but is otherwise well. She joins with me in love to yourself and to Mrs. Newton, and to the young Ladies. Neither do we forget Sally Johnson.°

Believe me my dear friend | With true Affection Yours
                                          Wm. Cowper.

Hannah° desires me to give her Duty to Miss Cunningham° and to Miss Catlett.°

To Harriot Hesketh

[Beneath the postmark, Lady Hesketh wrote: 'First letter in answer to one [10 Oct. 1785] I sent him after some years Silence.' The cousins had exchanged letters last in 1767, eighteen years earlier.]

My dear Cousin—

It is no new thing with you to give pleasure, but I will venture to say that you do not often give more than you gave me this morning. When I came down to breakfast and found upon the table a Letter frank'd by my Uncle,° and when opening that frank I found that it contained a letter from you, I said within myself, this is just as it should be; We are all grown young again, and the days that I thought I should see no more, are actually return'd. You perceive therefore that you judged well when you conjectured that a line from you would not be disagreeable to me. It could not be otherwise, than as in fact it proved, a most agreeable surprize, for I can truely boast of an affection for you that neither years nor interrupted intercourse have at all abated. I need only recollect how much I valued you once, and with how much cause, immediately to feel a revival of the same value; if that can be said to revive, which at the most has only been dormant for want of employment. But I slander it when I say that it has slept. A thousand times have I recollected a thousand scenes in which our two selves have formed the whole of the Drama, with the greatest pleasure; at times too when I had no reason to suppose that I should ever hear from you again. I have laugh'd with you at the Arabian Nights' Entertainment,° which afforded us, as you well know, a fund of merriment that deserves never to be forgot. I have walk'd with you to Nettley Abbey, and have scrambled with you over hedges in every direction, and many other feats we have performed together, upon the field of my remembrance, and all within these few years; should I say within this twelve-month I should not transgress the truth. The hours that I have spent with you were among the pleasantest of my former days, and are therefore chronicled in my mind so deeply as to fear no erasure. Neither do I forget my poor friend Sir Thomas. I should remember him indeed at any rate on account of his personal kindnesses to myself, but the last testimony that he gave of his regard for you,° endears him to me still more. With his uncommon understanding (for with many peculiarities he had more sense than any of his acquaintance) and with his generous sensibilities, it was hardly possible that he should not distinguish you as he has done. As it was the last, so it was the best proof that he could give of a judgement that never deceived him when he would allow himself leisure to consult it.

You say that you have often heard of me. That puzzles me. I cannot imagine from what quarter. But it is no matter. I must tell you however, my Cousin, that your information has been a little defective. That I am happy in my situation is true. I live and have lived these 20 years with Mrs. Unwin, to whose affectionate care of me during the far greater part of that time, it is under Providence owing, that I live at all. But I do not account myself happy in having been for 13 of those years° in a state of mind that has made all that care and attention necessary. An Attention and a care, that have injured her health, and which, had she not been uncommonly supported, must have brought her to her grave. But I will pass to another subject; it would be cruel to particularize only to give pain, neither would I by any means give a sable hue to the first letter of a Correspondence so unexpectedly renew'd.

I am delighted with what you tell me of my Uncle's good health. To enjoy any measure of cheerfullness at so late a day is much, but to have that late day enliven'd with the vivacity of youth, is much more, and in these post-diluvian times a rarity indeed. Happy for the most part, are parents who have daughters. Daughters are not apt to outlive their natural affections, which a Son has generally survived even before his boyish years are expired. I rejoice particularly in my Uncle's felicity who has three female descendents° from his little person, who leave him nothing to wish for upon that head.

My dear Cousin, Dejection of Spirits, which I suppose may have prevented many a man from becoming an Author, made me one. I find constant employment necessary, and therefore take care to be constantly employ'd. Manual occupations° do not engage the mind sufficiently, as I know by experience, having tried many. But Composition, especially of verse, absorbs it wholly. I write therefore generally three hours in a Morning, and in an Evening I Transcribe. I read also; but less than I write, for I must have bodily exercise, and therefore never pass a day without it. I have read the Mirror,° and many of the papers I admired, but not all. Dr. Beattie° is so great a fav'rite of mine, that where he shines I seem to have no eyes for the beauties of others, and I think that all the best papers are his.

You ask me where I have been this Summer—I answer at Olney. Should you ask me where I spent the last 17 Summers I should still answer at Olney. Ay— and the Winters also. I have seldom left it, and except when I attended my Brother in his last Illness, never I believe a fortnight together.

My book is called the Task. I would order you one from the Booksellers, were the publication now my own. But being rather, as you know, of the least opulent of those who may be called Gentlemen Rhimers, I cannot afford to print at my own expence, and am therefore forced to make a present of the Copy.°

Adieu my beloved Cousin, I shall not always be thus nimble in reply, but shall always have great pleasure in answering you when I can. I have several small matters° in the Gentleman's Magazines for the last year or two, but I do not take it in, and therefore cannot refer you to them.

My poor Puss is in good health, except a Cough which never troubled her 'till this day. Herself, a House dog and a small Spaniel, were just now basking in the beams of our fireside, very comfortably in a group, but the great beast Mungo° desired to be let into the Kitchen just before I could tell you so. He is very fond of Puss, often salutes her with his black muzzle, and licks her face. The bread that she happens to leave is his constant perquisite, so that he may not be altogether disinterested in his attachment.

To me at Olney is Direction enough. Mr. Newton is now Minister of St. Mary Woolnoth, and has been several years.

Yours, my friend and Cousin!
Wm Cowper.

Octr. 12. | 1785.

To Harriot Hesketh

[Cowper had begun work on his translation of the *Iliad* late in 1784. The letters of the next five years demonstrate how obsessed he had become with every aspect of his work on Homer—the metrics, historical accuracy, and his subscription list.]

Olney Novr. 9. 1785

My dearest Cousin,

Whose last most affectionate letter has run in my head ever since I received it, and which I now sit down to answer two days sooner than the Post will serve me, I thank you for it; and with a warmth for which I am sure you will give me credit, though I do not spend many words in desribing it. I do not seek *new* friends, not being altogether sure that I should find them, but have unspeakable pleasure in being still beloved by an old one.—I hope that now our correspondence has suffer'd its *last* interruption, and that we shall go down together to the grave, chatting and chirping as merrily as such a scene of things as this, will permitt.

I am happy that my poems have pleased you. My volume has afforded me no such pleasure at any time, either while I was writing it or since its publication, as I have derived from yours and my Uncle's opinion of it. I make certain allowances for partiality, and for that peculiar quickness of taste with which you both relish what you like, and after all draw-backs upon those accounts duley made, find myself rich in the measure of your approbation that still remains. But above all I honour John Gilpin, since it was He who first encouraged you to write. I made him on purpose to laugh at, and he served his purpose well; but I am now indebted to him for a more valuable acquisition than all the laughter in the world amounts to, the recovery of my intercourse with you, which is to me inestimable.

My benevolent and generous Cousin; when I was once ask'd if I wanted any thing and given delicately enough to understand that the Enquirer was ready to supply all my occasions, I thankfully and civilly, but positively declined the favour. I neither suffer, nor have suffer'd any such inconveniences as I had not much rather endure, than come under obligations of that sort, to a person comparatively with yourself, a Stranger to me. But to you I answer otherwise. I know you thoroughly and the liberality of your disposition; and have that consummate confidence in the sincerity of your wish to serve me, that delivers me from all aukward constraint, and from all fear of trespassing by acceptance. To you therefore I reply, Yes. Whensoever, and Whatsoever, and in what manner soever you please; and add moreover, that my affection for the Giver is such, as will encrease to me tenfold the satisfaction that I shall have in receiving. It is necessary however that I should let you a little into the state of my finances, that you may not suppose them more narrowly circumscribed than they are. Since Mrs. Unwin and I have lived at Olney, we have had but one purse; although during the whole of that time, 'till lately, her income was nearly double mine. Her revenues indeed are now in some measure reduced, and do not much exceed my own;° the worst consequence of this, is, that we are forced to deny ourselves some things which hitherto we have been better able to afford, but they are such things as neither Life nor the Well-being of Life depend upon. My own income has been better than it is, but when it was best, it would not have enabled me to live as my connexions demanded that I should, had it not been combined with a better than itself. At least at this end of the Kingdom. Of this I had full proof during three months that I spent in Lodgings at Huntingdon. In which time by the help of good management and a clear notion of oeconomical matters, I contrived to spend the income of a twelvemonth. Now, my beloved Cousin, you are in possession of the whole case as it stands. Strain no points to your own inconvenience or hurt, for there is no need of it; but indulge yourself in communicating, no matter what, that you can spare without missing it, since by so doing you will be sure to add to the comforts of my life one of the sweetest that I can enjoy, a token and proof of your affection.

In the affair of my next publication, toward which you also offer me so kindly your assistance, there will be no need that you should help me in the manner that you propose. It will be a large work consisting, I should imagine, of Six volumes at the least. The 21st. of this Month I shall have spent a year upon it, and it will cost me more than another. I do not love the Booksellers well enough to make them a Present of such a labour, but intend to publish by Subscription. Your Vote and Interest therefore my dear Cousin upon the occasion if you please, but nothing more. I will trouble you with some papers of Proposals when the time shall come, and am sure that you will circulate as many for me as you can. Now my Dear, I am going to tell you a secret. It is a great Secret, that you must not whisper even to your Cat. No creature is at this moment apprized of it, but Mrs. Unwin and her son. I am making a new Translation of Homer, and am upon the point of finishing the twenty first book of the Iliad. The reasons upon which I undertake this Herculean labour, and by which I justify an enterprize in which I seem to be so effectually anticipated by Pope, although in fact, he has not anticipated me at all, I may possibly give you if you wish for them, when I can find nothing more interesting to say. A period which I do not conceive to be very near.

I have not answer'd many things in your Letter, nor can do it at present for want of room. I cannot believe but that I should know you, notwithstanding all that Time may have done. There is not a feature in your face, could I meet it upon the road by itself, that I should not instantly recollect. I should say, That is my Cousin's nose, or those are her lips and chin, and no woman upon earth can claim them but herself. As for me, I am a very smart youth of my years. I am not indeed grown grey so much as I am grown bald. No matter. There was more Hair in the world than ever had the honour to belong to me. Accordingly having found just enough to curl a little at my ears, and to intermix with a little of my own that still hangs behind, I appear if you see me in an afternoon, to have a very decent head-dress, not easily distinguish'd from my natural growth; which being worn with a small bag and a black-ribband about my neck, continues to me the charms of my Youth, even on the verge of Age.

Yours my dearest Cousin
Wm Cowper.

Away with the fear of writing too often.
P.S.—That the view I give you of myself may be complete, I add the 2 following Items.—That I am in debt to nobody, and that I grow fat.

To Harriot Hesketh

Novr. 17 [1785]

My dearest Cousin,
    I am glad that I always loved you as I did. It releases me from any occasion to suspect that my present affection for you is indebted for its existence to any selfish considerations. No. I am sure that I love you disinterestedly and for your own sake, because I never thought of you with any other sentiments than those of the truest affection, even while I was under the

influence of a persuasion that I should never hear from you again. But with my present feelings superadded to those that I always had for you, I find it no easy matter to do justice to my sensations. I perceive myself in a state of mind similar to that of the traveller described in Pope's Messiah,° who as he passes through a sandy desart, starts at the sudden and unexpected sound of a waterfall. You have placed me in a situation new to me, and in which I feel myself somewhat puzzled to know how I ought to behave. At the same time that I would not grieve you by putting a check upon your bounty, I would be as carefull not to abuse it, as if I were a Miser and the question were not about your money but my own. In the first place I thank you for your Note.° I should have taken it excessively ill of any body but yourself who had called it a trifle. To me I assure you it is no such matter, whatever it may appear to you. Secondly, as to the Writing-desk.° It is certain that I have not one, and it is equally certain that I have gone on notably well these many years without one. Why therefore should I put you to expence for an article that I cannot be said to want My Dear, we live you must know in a house that has two small parlours. The Hare has entirely occupied one these 12 years, and has made it unfit to be the receptacle of any thing better than the box in which she sleeps. The other which we ourselves occupy is already so filled with chairs, tables, &c, not forgetting our own proper persons as absolutely to forbid the importation of any thing more. I have indeed a small Summer house in our farthest garden (for we have two) that just affords room to myself, two chairs and a table. There I always write in Summer, and there also in Winter when the day is bright. Upon that table indeed such a desk might stand, but then this Sejour° is at such a distance from the house, and thieves are so numerous in the town, that in all probability it would be stolen. You know now, my Dear, the whole state of the matter, therefore judge for yourself. As to Johnson's Poets,° I have seen them and have read all his prefaces; Mr. Unwin has them; consequently I have them whenever I please.—I have read Extracts from Hayley's works in the Review,° and have admired some of them, but I know that he has published now and then a performance which I have no curiosity to be better acquainted with than I am already by

means of the aforesaid Review. Especially some Dramatic
pieces in verse. Why therefore should I put you to the expence
of his works at large, in which perhaps are more things than
his plays that I should at most but slightly run over and
merely to satisfy curiosity? The Quarto volume that you
mention,° in which He and Goldsmith who is a favorite of
mine, figure together, will suit me well. I want it, send it, I am
impatient 'till it arrives. Wine, my dearest Cousin, is an article
on which I have something to say that will not please you, and
something that will. You must know that some years since,
not many, when we began to feel ourselves a little pinched in
our finances, I made an heroic resolution that I would drink
no more. Accordingly I substituted half a pint of a certain
Malt liquor called Ale instead of it, much against Mrs. Unwin's
will, who opposed the innovation with all her might. But I was
obstinate and had my own way as I generally have. The
consequences were such a concert of Music within, such
squeaking, croaking and scolding of stomach and bowels
denied their wonted comfort, and such perpetual indigestions
withal, that I was constrained to return again to the bottle. I
have a stomach that is good for little at the best, and that bids
fair to be the first part of me that shall fail altogether in the
performance of its functions; I find it necessary therefore to
drink wine in order to keep it in tolerable humour, to the
amount of three or four glasses after dinner and Supper. A
bottle accordingly serves me two days and sometmes two and
a half, which I mention principally with a view to commend
my own sobriety. I drink nothing but Port. The Port therefore
my Dear which you offer me, I accept. It is to me a medicine
which I cannot do without, and yet a medicine as times go,
rather too costly for me. Shrub° I never drink, for my
quarrelsome Stomach will bear neither the juice of Orange or
Lemon, nor do I touch Brandy more than twice in a
twelvemonth. Brandy and Shrub therefore my Cousin, you
shall send me none. Now I do assure you that I have been as
faithfull and as explicit as if upon oath, and in all I have said
upon these subjects have not sacrificed a tittle of Truth to false
delicacy or to any such squeamish impertinence. Now for the
Conveyance.—We have two. The Wellingborough Coach
passes through Olney, on Tuesdays, Thursdays and Saturdays

in its way from London. It sets out from Town at 5 in the Morning on those days, and starts from the Cross Keys in St. John Street—Smithfield. Rogers' Waggon sets out every Wednesday and Saturday from the Wind mill in St. John Street. Rogers the Proprietor lives at a Village called Sherrington three Miles short of Olney, but Olney is the goal he drives at. You are now in possession of the whole matter in detail.

Although I do not suspect that a secret to you my Cousin is any burthen, yet having maturely consider'd that point since I wrote my last, I feel myself altogether disposed to release you from the injunction to that effect under which I laid you. I have now made such a progress in my Translation, that I need neither fear that I shall stop short of the end, nor that any other Rider of Pegasus should overtake me. Therefore if at any time it should fall fairly in your way or you should feel yourself invited to say that I am so occupied, you have my Poetship's free permission. My heart bounds at the thought of being introduced to Mrs. Montague,° I have heard of her, and have heard of her all that you relate. You are certainly to be my Introducer into notice. I have found by experience that without exactly such help as you will afford me, it is no easy matter to engage attention. Dr. Johnson read and recommended my first Volume, and the favorable account of it that appeared in the Monthly Review, was written by a friend of his° to whom he consigned that office. But your interest my beloved Cousin, will I doubt not promote that of my present publication far more.

Adieu! Bless you—So say we both—Yours
Wm Cowper.

P.S. | They are just going to publish a new Edition of Johnson's Dictionary° revised by himself and much improved. It is to come out at first in Weekly Numbers, and will be completed in a year and half or little more, 2 Vols. 4to.—At that time therefore I will beg you to send it to me—It is a work that ev'ry Writer should be possessed of.

My Dear, if I can produce a Translation of the Old Bard that the Literati shall prefer to Pope's, which I have the assurance to hope that I may, it will do me more honour than any thing that I have performed hitherto. At present they are all agreed that Pope's is a very inadequate representation of him.

To Harriot Hesketh

Olney Decr. 6. 1785

My dearest Cousin,

I write not *upon* my Desk, but *about* it. Having in vain expected it by the waggon that followed your letter, I again expected it by the next; and thinking it likely that it might arrive last night at Sherrington, I sent a man over thither this morning, hoping to see him return with it. But again I am disappointed. I have felt an impatience to receive it that you yourself have taught me, and now think it necessary to let you know that it is not come, lest it should perhaps be detained in London by the negligence of some body to whom you might entrust the packing of it or its carriage to the Inn.

I shall be obliged to be more concise than I chuse to be when I write to you, for want of time to indulge myself in writing more. How, will you say, can a man want time, who lives in the country, without business, and without neighbours, who visits nobody, and who is visited himself so seldom? My Dear, I have been at the races this morning, and have another letter to write this evening; the Post sets out at 7, and it is now drawing near to six. A fine day you will say for the races, and the better no doubt because it has rained continually ever since the morning. At what races do you suppose then that I have been? I might leave you to guess; but loving you too well to leave you under the burthen of an employment that must prove for ever vain, I will e'en tell you, and keep you no longer in suspense. I have been at Troy, where the principal heroes of the Iliad have been running for such a prize as our Jockeys would disdain to saddle a horse for; and yet I assure you they acquitted themselves most nobly, though a kettle and a frying-pan were to reward their labours.°

I never answer'd your question concerning my strong

partiality to a Common. I well remember making the speech of which you remind me, and the very place where I made it. It was upon a Common in the neighborhood of Southampton, the name of which however I have forgot. But I perfectly recollect that I boasted of the sagacity that you mention, just after having carried you over a dirty part of the road that led to it. My nostrils have hardly been regaled with those wild odours from the day to the present. We have no such here. If there ever were any such in this country, the inclosures have long since destroyed them. But we have a scent in the fields about Olney, that to me is equally agreeable, and which even after attentive examination I have never been able to account for. It proceeds, so far as I can find, neither from herb nor tree nor shrub. I should suppose therefore that it is in the soil. It is exactly the scent of amber when it has been rubbed hard, only more potent. I have never observed it except in hot weather, or in places where the sun shines powerfully and from which the air is excluded. I had a strong poetical desire to describe it when I was writing the Common scene in the Task,° but feared lest the unfrequency of such a singular property in the earth, should have tempted the reader to ascribe it to a fancifull nose, at least to have suspected it for a deliberate fiction.

I have been as good as my word, and have sent for the Doctor.° But having left him the whole week to chuse out of, am uncertain on what day I shall fall under his consideration. I have been in his company. He is quite a gentleman, and a very sensible one, and as to skill in his profession I suppose that he has few superiors.

Mrs. Unwin (who begs to be mentioned to you with affectionate respect) sits knitting my stockings at my elbow with a degree of industry worthy of Penelope herself. You will not think this an exaggeration, when I tell you that I have not bought a pair these 20 years, either of thread, silk, or worsted.

Adieu my most beloved Cousin. If you get this before I have your answer to my last, let me soon have an answer to them both.

Truely yours.
Wm Cowper.

To Harriot Hesketh

Olney | Feb. 9:86. Thursday.

My dearest Cousin,

I have been impatient to tell you that I am impatient to see you again. Mrs. Unwin partakes with me in all my feelings upon this subject, and longs also to see you. I should have told you so by the last Post, but have been so completely occupied with this tormenting Specimen,° that it was impossible to do it. I sent the General a letter on Monday that will distress and alarm him; I sent him another yesterday that will, I hope, quiet him again. Johnson has apologized very civilly for the multitude of his friend's strictures,° and his friend has promised to confine himself in future to a comparison of me with the Original, so that I doubt not we shall now jog on merrily together. And now my Dear let me tell you once more that your kindness in promising us a visit has charmed us both. I shall see you again, I shall hear your voice, we shall take walks together, I will show you my prospects, the hovel, the Alcove, the Ouse, and its banks, every thing that I have described. I anticipate the pleasure of those days not very distant, and feel a part of it at this moment. Talk not of an Inn, mention it not for your life. We have never had so many visitors but we could easily accommodate them all, though we have received Unwin and his wife and his Sister and his Son all at once. I shall carry you back now, having particular occasion to do it, to a period mentioned in one of my former letters. When I plunged into the gulph of 1773, my disorder was such, that it was not possible to leave me day or night. Mrs. Unwin sat up with me herself as long as it was possible for one person to bear the fatigue of it. Then Servants, then people hired for the purpose. But servants and hirelings were an abomination to me alike, and I would endure nobody but Mrs. Unwin. She therefore ordered a bed to be spread for her in a corner of the chamber, and slept upon it in her cloaths. For a long time my nights were disturbed to a great degree, and bad as my days were, were still worse than they. Even to this moment I have occasion for some person in the chamber with me in the night. Accordingly she has now, for more than

12 years, been that person, for the remembrance of St. Albans makes me abhor a stranger or a servant in that office. For 12 years she has never been within curtains but once, when having occasion to watch me several nights together and being worn out, she took the Maid's bed and sent her into the sick man's chamber. But the sick man would not, could not bear it, so she immediately occupied her post again. It is a long time for a Lady to have slept in her cloaths, and the patient at first sight seems chargeable with much inhumanity who suffers it. But God knows how great has been the occasion. To this disposition of things it is owing that our house not large, is yet more capacious than it otherwise would be. We can without much difficulty, with very little indeed, make two spare beds, and if requisite, can with equal ease accommodate a servant into the bargain.—My Dear, I will not let you come 'till the end of May or beginning of June, because before that time my greenhouse will not be ready to receive us, for it is the only pleasant room belonging to us. When the plants go out, we go in. I line it with mats, and spread the floor with mats, and there you shall sit with a bed of Mignonette at your side, and a hedge of Honeysuckles, Roses and Jassamine; and I will make you a bouquet of Myrtle every day. Sooner than the time I mention the Country will not be in complete beauty. And now I will tell you what you shall find on your first entrance. Imprimis, as soon as you have enter'd the Vestibule, if you cast a look to either side of you, you shall see on your right hand a box of my making. It is the Box in which have been lodged all my hares, and in which lodges Puss at present. But he, poor fellow, is worn out with age, and promises to die before you can see him. On the right hand, stands a cupboard the work of the same Author. It was once a dove-cage, but I transformed it. Opposite to you stands a table which I also made. But a merciless servant having scrubbed it 'till it is become paralytic, it serves no purpose now but of ornament, and all my clean shoes stand under it. On the left hand at the farther end of this superb vestibule you will find the door of the parlour into which I will conduct you and where I will introduce you to Mrs. Unwin (unless we should meet her before) and where we will be as happy as the day is long. Order yourself dear Cousin, to the Swan at Newport and there

you shall find me prepared to escort you to Olney.—Our house when we first found it was inhabited by Basket-makers, but they vanished at our appearance. It cost Mrs. U. as much money as it is worth, to make but an indifferent house of it at last. But it was at that time the only abode to be procured at Olney, and you will find it, incommodious and aukward as it is, good enough for people to be very happy in who love one another.

I will promise you that your Squire shall not be dressed in a Bag.° By some Instinct in me it has come to pass, that immediately after telling you that I wore a bag, I of my own mere motion exchanged it for a queeüe.° That ever I wore a bag constantly was owing to Lady Austen, who in France had been used to see nothing else. Nevertheless I shall not be altogether a Beau, for leather breeches I have none, and boots I have none, having ever had an antipathy to a saddle. But in so unfashionable a place as Newport, I shall be taken for a Gentleman even though I should happen to be dressed like one.

I forgot to observe to you in the description that I gave of the Landscape that embellishes the Snuff box° sent me by Anonymous, that the drawer of it has attended particularly to the characters of the three hares given in the Gentleman's Magazine. One is sprightly, one is fierce, and one is gentle. The box has done me no small honour in the eyes of 2 or 3 to whom I have shown it.

My dear I have told Homer what you say about Casks and Urns, and have asked him whether he is sure that it is a Cask in which Jupiter keeps his wine. He swears that it is a Cask, and that it will never be any thing better than a Cask to eternity. So if the God is content with it, we must even wonder at his Taste and be so too—Adieu my Dearest, Dearest Cousin—Your

Wm C.

To William Unwin

Olney July 3. 1786

My dear William,—

After long silence, I begin again. A day given to my friends is a day taken from Homer, but to such an interruption now and then occurring, I have no objection. Lady Hesketh is as you observe arrived, and has been with us near a fortnight. She pleases every body, and is pleased in her turn with every thing she finds at Olney; is always cheerful and sweet temper'd, and knows no pleasure equal to that of communicating pleasure to us and to all around her. This disposition in her, is the more comfortable, because it is not the humour of the day, a sudden flush of benevolence and good spirits occasion'd merely by a change of scene, but it is her natural turn and has govern'd all her conduct ever since I knew her first. We are consequently happy in her society, and shall be happier still to have you to partake with us in our joy. I can now assure you that her complexion is not at all indebted to art, having seen a hundred times the most convincing proof of its authenticity; her colour fading and glowing again alternately, as the weather or her own temperature have happen'd to affect it, while she has been sitting before me.—I am fond of the sound of Bells, but was never more pleased with those of Olney, than when they rang her into her new habitation. It is a Compliment that our performers upon those instruments have never paid to any other personage (Lord Dartmouth excepted) since we knew the town. In short she is, as she ever was, my pride and my joy, and I am delighted with every thing that means to do her honour.—Her first appearance was too much for me. My Spirits, instead of being greatly raised as I had inadvertently supposed they would be, broke down with me under the pressure of too much joy, and left me flat, or rather melancholy throughout the day to a degree that was mortifying to myself and alarming to her. But I have made amends for this failure since, and in point of cheerfulness have far exceeded her expectations; for she knew that sable had been my suit for many years.

And now I shall communicate Intelligence that will give

you pleasure. When you first contemplated the front of our abode you were shock'd. In your eyes it had the appearance of a prison, and you sighed at the thought that your Mother dwelt in it. Your view of it was not only just, but even prophetic. It not only had the aspect of a place built for purposes of Incarceration, but has actually served that purpose through a long, long period, and we have been the prisoners. But a Gaol-delivery is at hand. The bolts and bars are to be loosed, and we shall escape. A very different mansion both in point of appearance and accommodation expects us, and the expence of living in it not greater than we are subjected to in this. It is situated at Weston, one of the prettiest villages in England, and belongs to Mr. Throckmorton. We all three dine with him to day, by invitation, and shall survey it in the afternoon, point out the necessary repairs, and finally adjust the treaty. I have my Cousin's promise that she will never let another year pass without a Visit to us, and the house is large enough to contain us and our suite, and her also with as many of hers as she shall chuse to bring. The change will I hope prove advantageous both to your Mother and me in all respects. Here we have no neighborhood, there we shall have most agreeable neighbors in the Throck——ns. Here we have a bad air in the Winter impregnated with the fishy-smelling fumes of the Marsh Miasma, there, we shall breathe in an atmosphere untainted. Here, we are confined from September to March, and sometimes longer, there we shall be upon the very verge of pleasure-grounds in which we can always ramble, and shall not wade through almost impassable dirt to get at them. Both your Mother's constitution and mine have suffer'd materially by such close and long confinement, and it is high time, unless we intended to retreat into the grave, that we should seek out a more wholesome residence. A pretty deal of new furniture will be wanted, especially chairs and beds, all which my kind Cousin will provide, and fit up a parlour and a Chamber for herself into the bargain.——So far is well, the rest is left to heav'n.°

I have hardly left myself room for an answer to your Queries concerning my friend John & his studies. What the supplement of Hirtius° is made of, I know not. We did not read it at Westminster. I should imagine it might be dispensed with. I should recommend the *Civil War* of Cæsar, because he wrote it, who ranks I believe as the best Writer as well as soldier of his day. There are books, (I know not what they are but you do and can easily find them) that will inform him clearly of both the Civil and Military management of the Romans, the several officers, I mean, in both departments, and what was the peculiar province of each. The study of some such book would, I should think, prove a good Introduction to that of Livy, unless you have a Livy with notes to that effect. A want of Intelligence in those points has heretofore made the Roman History very dark and difficult to me. Therefore I thus advise.

Our Love is with all your Lovelys both great and small.

Yours
W.C.

To Harriot Hesketh

Weston Lodge Nove. 26. 1786

It is my birth day my Cousin, and I determine to employ a part of it, in order that it may not be altogether destitute of festivity, in writing to you. The dark thick fog that has obscured it would have been a burthen to me at Olney, but here I have hardly attended to it. The neatness and snugness of our abode compensates all the dreariness of the season, and whether the ways are wet or dry, our house at least is always warm and commodious. Oh for you my Cousin, to partake these comforts with us! I will not begin already to teaze you upon that subject, but Mrs. U. remembers to have heard from your own lips that you hate London in the Spring. Perhaps therefore by that time you may be glad to escape from a scene which will be every day growing more disagreeable, that you may enjoy the comforts of the Lodge. You well know that the best house has a desolate appearance, unfurnish'd. This house accordingly, since it has been occupied by us and our meubles is as much superior to what it was when you saw it, as you can imagine. The parlour is even elegant, and pray tell Mrs. Cowper that her Bell-ropes are our admiration, as they will be of others in due time, but they have been so lately put up, that only ourselves and the Carpenter have yet seen them. He who has seen all the fashionable Bell-ropes in the country, declares that he has never seen their equals. When I said that the Parlour is elegant, I did not mean to insinuate that the study is not so. When it shall be furnished with our new chairs, which as you observe are not yet arrived, it will not at all yield in that respect to the parlour. In the mean time it is neat, warm, & silent, and a much better study than I deserve if I do not at last produce in it a most incomparable Translation of Homer. I think every day of those lines of Milton, and congratulate myself on having attained before I am quite superannuated, what He seems not to have hoped for sooner.—

> And may at length my weary age
> Find out the peaceful hermitage!°

For if it be not a hermitage at least it is a much better thing, and you must always understand my Dear, that when poets talk of Cottages, hermitages, and such like matters, they mean a house with 6 sashes in front, two comfortable parlours, a smart Stair-case, and three bed-chambers of convenient dimensions; in short, exactly such a house as this.

The Thro—ns are, as ever, the most obliging neighbors in the world. One morning in the last week, She called and took Mrs. Unwin out to walk with her in the Garden. The next, he invited me to a walk at my own hour. I accordingly called on him between 1 and 2, and they both went with me to the Cliffs. A scene my Dear in which you would delight beyond measure, but which you cannot visit except in the Spring or Autumn. The heat of Summer and the clinging dirt of Winter would destroy you, for it is almost as far hence as from hence to Olney. What is called the Cliff is no Cliff nor at all like one, but a beautiful terras sloping gently down to the Ouse, and from the brow of which, though not lofty, you have a view of such a valley as makes that which you see from the hills near Olney, and which I have had the honour to celebrate,° an affair of no consideration. It forms a part, but a very small part of the prospect. Cattle indeed there are in abundance, for they who have fruitful meads will be sure to have beasts to graze them. We even enter'd a field from which we were forced to retreat immediately, for the oxen being well-fed and wanton, caper'd so immoderately at our approach that Mrs. T—n was afraid to proceed. But it is easy, especially in a dry season, to avoid them by turning into fields that are only conversant with the plough.—Yesterday they sent us a present of fish—Not the oxen my Dear, but the Throck—ns. And I have lent Mr. T—n the first Volume of my favourite the Don,° which he reads to his wife in an Evening.

I burn a lamp in my chamber. The wicks were all consumed save two, and they are only to be had at Newport. I sent Mr. Bull a note upon that subject which he received yesterday morning, and between 1 and 2 he brought hither a box himself, but unfortunately we were gone to Olney, called thither by several occasions. It was the first time that Mrs. U has visited the place since we left it. Thus it happen'd that we saw not Domine Bull, but he is to dine with us some day this week.

Wintry as the weather is do not suspect that it confines me. I ramble daily and every day change my ramble. Wherever I go, I find short grass under my feet, and when I have travell'd perhaps 5 miles come home with shoes not at all too dirty for a drawing-room. I was pacing yesterday under the elms that surround the field in which stands the great alcove, when lifting my eyes I saw two black genteel figures bolt through a hedge into the path where I was walking. You guess already who they were and that they could be nobody but our neighbors. They had seen me from a hill at a distance, and had traversed a great turnip-field to get at me. You see therefore my Dear, that I am in some request.

Alas! in too much request with some people. The verses of Cadwallader have found me at last; those terrible poems with which the Welshman threat'ned me° while you were here, and which I had good hope were lost for ever. They reach'd me yesterday and came accompanied by a letter so simple, honest and civil, that sometime or other I must read them. He tells me that he has added some lines to those which he subjoined to the letter that you saw, and has sent them to the Press. Oh happy I, with a Taffy to bind on my laurels—He adds too by way of Postscript those lines of Pope—

Say, shall my litle bark attendant sail,
Pursue the triumph, and partake the gale?°

Neither does he forget to tell me that he has 3 sons and 3 daughters and a tame magpie. Riches enough I think in all conscience for a poet, especially a Welsh one. But he has another string to his bow, for he is an attorney into the bargain.—Higher honours than this attended me by the same conveyance. The Coach that brought me yesterday all this good news from Wales, brought me also a pacquet from the Howardian Committee. It contained however only the poem called the Triumph of Benevolence.°

Mrs. Unwin had a letter this day from her daughter-in-law, informing her that her son is greatly recover'd and that they hope in a few days to leave Winchester. I am charm'd with your account of our little Cousin at Kensington,° if the world does not spoil him hereafter, he will be a valuable man. We have received 2 hampers, viz 8 dozen of Port, from my good and kind friend the General, sans one broken bottle.

Adieu Dear Dear Cousin. My back and my knuckles both ache, and if I am not at the end of my prate at least I am of my paper, so good night and may God bless thee.

With Mrs. Unwin's love, farewell.
Wm Cowper.

Mrs. Forrester° is gone, and the Dowager Throck—n. Mr. G.° is seldom visible unless one dines there, being much engaged with his gun.

You never send trifles my Dear, neither can you send any thing that we should account such. A thousand thanks from us both for the things that you announce, and from me in particular for the Smelling bottle that you sent me by Hannah the day you went. I often put it to my nose and think of you.

To John Newton

[William Unwin died suddenly at Winchester on 29 Nov. 1786, while visiting Henry Thornton.]

Weston Underwood. | Jan. 13. 1787.

My dear friend—

It gave me pleasure, such as it was, to learn by a letter from Mr. H. Thornton,° that the Inscription° for the tomb of poor Unwin has been approved of. The Dead have nothing to do with human praises, but if they died in the Lord they have abundant praises to render to Him, which is far better. The Dead, whatever they leave behind them, have nothing to regret. Good Christians are the only creatures in the world that are truely good, and them they will see again and see them improved, therefore them they regret not. Regret is for the Living. What we get we soon lose, and what we lose we regret. The most obvious consolation in this case seems to be, that we who regret others, shall quickly become objects of regret ourselves, for Mankind are continually passing off in a rapid succession.

I have many kind friends who, like yourself, wish that instead of turning my endeavours to a Translation of Homer, I had proceeded in the way of Original poetry. But I can truely say that it was order'd otherwise; not by me, but by the Providence that governs all my thoughts and directs my intentions as he pleases. It may seem strange but it is true, that after having written a volume, in general, with great ease to myself, I found it impossible to write another page. The mind of man is not a fountain, but a cistern, and mine, God knows, a broken one. It is my Creed, that the Intellect depends as much both for the energy and the multitude of its exertions, upon the operations of God's agency upon it, as the Heart for the exercise of its Graces, upon the influences of the Holy Spirit. According to this persuasion I may very reasonably affirm that it was not God's pleasure that I should proceed in the same track, because he did not enable me to do it. A whole year I waited, and waited in circumstances of mind that made a state of non-employment peculiarly irksome. I long'd for the pen as the only remedy, but I could find no subject. Extreme distress of spirit at last drove me, as if I mistake not, I told you some time since, to lay Homer before me and to translate for amusement. Why it pleased God that I should be hunted into such a business, of such enormous length and labour, by miseries for which he did not see good to afford me any other remedy, I know not. But so it was. And jejune as the consolation may be, and unsuited to the exigencies of a mind and heart that once were spiritual, yet a thousand times have I been glad of it, for a thousand times it has served at least to divert my attention in some degree from such terrible tempests as I believe have seldom been permitted to beat upon a human mind. Let my friends therefore who wish me some little measure of tranquillity in the performance of the most turbulent voyage that ever Christian mariner made, be contented that having Homer's mountains and forests to windward, I escape under their shelter from the force of many a gust that would almost overset me; especially when they consider that not by choice but by necessity I make *them* my refuge. As to fame and honour and glory that may be acquired by poetical feats of any sort, God knows that if I could lay me down in the grave with Hope at my side, or sit with Hope at my side in a dungeon all the residue of my days, I would cheerfully waive them all. For the little fame that I have already earned, has never saved me from one terrible night or from one despairing day since I first acquired it. *For* what I am reserved, or *to* what, is a mystery. I would fain hope not merely that I may amuse others, or only to be a Translator of Homer.

Sally Perry's case° has given us much concern ever since we heard it. I have no doubt that it is distemper, and heartily wish her cured. But distresses of mind that are occasion'd by distemper are the most difficult of all to deal with. They refuse all consolation, they will hear no reason. God only, by his own immediate impressions can remove them, as after an experience of 13 years' misery I can abundantly testify.

The Oysters after whose arrival you enquired reach'd us safe, and were excellent. The Cocoa nut was equally good in its way. Our thanks are due for both and we pay them heartily. Mrs. Unwin is pretty well, and I as well as I

generally am at this season of the year, when an obstructed
perspiration is apt to affect me feverishly. Accept our united
love to yourself and Mrs. Newton, and believe me, as ever,

Your affectionate
Wm Cowper.

To Harriot Hesketh

The Lodge Sunday Jan. 14. 1787°

My dearest Cousin—

I have been so much indisposed in the course of the last
week with the fever that I told you had seized me, as not to be
able to follow my last letter with another, sooner, which I
should otherwise certainly have done, because I know that
you will feel some anxiety about me. My nights during the
whole week may be said to have been almost sleepless, for
waking generally about One in the morning, I slept no more
till toward the time when I commonly used to rise. The
consequence has been that except the translation of about 30
lines at the conclusion of the 13th book, I have been forced to
abandon Homer entirely. This was a sensible mortification to
me, as you may suppose, and felt the more, because my spirits
of course failing with my strength, I seemed to have peculiar
need of my old amusement. It seemed hard therefore to be
forced to resign it just when I wanted it most. But Homer's
battles cannot be fought by a man who does not sleep well,
and who has not some little degree of animation in the day
time. Last night however, quite contrary to my expectation,
the fever left me entirely, and I slept quietly, soundly, and
long. If it please God that it returns not, I shall soon find
myself in a condition to proceed. I would now take the Bark,°
but my stomach will not bear it, either the gross bark or the
Tincture. Hoffman,° and Daffy,° and now and then a very
small quantity of Magnesia, are the only medicines that do
not seem to poison me, and they in their turn have each of
them done me service. I walk constantly, that is to say Mrs.
Unwin and I together, for at these times I keep her

continually employ'd and never suffer her to be absent from me many minutes. She gives me all her time and all her attention and forgets that there is another object in the world.

I believe my Dear I sent you very slovenly thanks for the Contents of the Box and basket. If I did, it was owing partly to want of room at the top of my letter, and partly to a cause that always prevents my being very diffuse on that topic, which is that to a heart generous and kind as yours a great deal of acknowledgement is only another word for a great deal of trouble. I now however repeat my thanks for all in general, and for the green cloth I give my Uncle thanks in particular. Present my Love to him into the bargain, and tell him that I hope he will live to give me such another piece when this shall be worn out. The leaves for fruit and the baskets are beautiful, and we shall rejoice to see them filled with raspberries, strawberries and cherries for you. Thanks also for the neat smart Almanac. And now I am on the subject of Thanksgiving, I beg that when you shall next see or write to my name-sake of Epsom,° you will mention me to him with much gratitude and affection, for him alone of all my benefactors I seem to forget, though in fact I do not forget him but have the warmest sense of his kindness. I shall be happy if it please God to spare my life 'till an opportunity may offer, to take him by the hand at Weston.

Mrs. Carter° thinks on the subject of dreams as every body else does, that is to say according to her own experience. She has had no extraordinary ones, and therefore accounts them only the ordinary operations of the Fancy. Mine are of a texture that will not suffer me to ascribe them to so inadequate a cause, or to any cause but the operation of an exterior agency. I have a mind my Dear (and to you I will venture to boast of it) as free from superstition as any man living, neither do I give heed to dreams in general as predictive, though particular dreams I believe to be so. Some very sensible persons, and I suppose Mrs. Carter among them, will acknowledge that in old times God spoke by dreams, but affirm with much boldness that he has since ceased to do so. If you ask them, Why? They answer because he has now reveal'd his Will in the Scripture, and there is no longer any need that he should instruct or admonish us in dreams—. I grant that with respect to doctrines and precepts, he has left us in want of nothing; but has he thereby precluded himself in any of the operations of his Providence? Surely not. It is perfectly a different consideration; and the same need that there ever was of his interference in this way, there is still and ever must be, while man continues blind and fallible and a creature beset with dangers which he can neither foresee, nor obviate. His operations however of this kind are I allow very rare, and as to the generality of dreams, they are made of such stuff and are in themselves so insignificant, that though I believe them all to be the manufacture of others, not our own, I account it not a farthing matter who makes them. As to my own peculiar experience in the dreaming way I have only this to observe. I have not believed that I shall perish because in dreams I have been told it, but because I have had hardly any but terrible dreams for 13 years, I therefore have spent the greatest part of that time most unhappily. They have either tinged my mind with melancholy or filled it with terrour, and the effect has been unavoidable. If we swallow arsenic we must be poison'd, and he who dreams as I have done, must be troubled. So much for dreams.

　　Tuesday.
I have always worn the three-corner'd kerchiefs, and Mrs. U. will easily find an use for the odd bit, therefore will not trouble you with the muslin again.

　　Thanks my Dear for the very handsome Turchas° dish which arrived safe last night.—My fever is not yet gone, but sometimes seems to leave me. It is altogether of the nervous kind and attended now and then with much dejection.

　　A young Gentleman called here yesterday who came 6 miles out of his way to see me. He was on a journey to London from Glasgow, having just left the University there. He came I suppose partly to satisfy his own curiosity, but chiefly as it seemed to bring me the thanks of some of the Scotch professors for my 2 volumes. His name is Rose,° an Englishman and very genteel. Your spirits being good you will derive more pleasure from this incident than I can at present, therefore I send it.

Adieu Dearest, Dearest Cousin. Yours
Wm C.

To Harriot Hesketh

The Lodge Novbr. 10. 1787.

The Parliament my dearest Cousin, prorogued continually, is a meteor dancing before my eyes, promising me my wish only to disappoint me, and none but the King and his Minister can tell when you and I shall come together.° I hope however that the period, though so often postponed, is not far distant, and that once more I shall behold you and experience your power to make Winter gay and sprightly.

I have always forgotten (never say forgot) to tell you the reason why Mr. Bull did not fulfill his engagement to call on you in his return from the West. It was owing to an accident that happen'd to one of those legs of his. At Exmouth he chose to wallow in the sea and made use of a Bathing machine for that purpose. It has a Ladder, as you know, attach'd to its tail. On the lowermost step of that Ladder he stood, when it broke under him. He fell of course, and with his knee on the point of a large nail which pierced it almost to the depth of two inches. The consequence was that when he reach'd London, he could think of nothing but getting home as fast as possible. The wound has been healed some time, but is occasionally still painful, so that he is not without apprehensions that it may open again, which considering that he is somewhat gross in his habit, is not impossible. But I have just sent to invite him to dine with us on Monday.

I have a kitten my Dear, the drollest of all creatures that ever wore a Cat-skin. Her gambols are not to be described, and would be incredible if they could. She tumbles head over heels several times together, she lays her cheek to the ground and presents her rump at you with an air of most supreme disdain, from this posture she rises to dance upon her hind feet, an exercise that she performs with all the grace imaginable, and she closes these various exhibitions with a loud smack of her lips, which for want of greater propriety of expression, we call Spitting. But though all cats spit, no cat ever produced such a sound as she does. In point of size she is likely to be a kitten always, being extremely small of her age, but time I suppose, that spoils every thing will make her also a

Cat. You will see her I hope before that melancholy period shall arrive, for no wisdom that she may gain by experience and reflection hereafter, will ever compensate the loss of her present hilarity. She is dress'd in a tortoise-shell suit, and I know that you will delight in her.

Mrs. Throck. carries us to-morrow in her chaise to Chicheley.° Mr. Chester has been often here, and Mrs. Chester as I told you, once; and we are glad and obliged to our neighbor for an opportunity to return their visits, at once so convenient and inviting. The event however must be supposed to depend in some degree on the elements, at least on the state of the atmosphere which is at present turbulent beyond measure. Yesterday it thunder'd. Last night it lighten'd, and at 3 this morning I saw the sky as red as a city in flames could have made it. I have a Leech in a bottle my Dear, that foretells all these prodigies and convulsions of nature. No. Not as *you* will naturally conjecture, by articulate utterance of oracular notices, but by a variety of gesticulations which here I have not room to give an account of. Suffice it to say that no change of weather surprizes him, and that in point of the earliest and most accurate intelligence he is worth all the Barometers in the world. None of them all indeed even make the least pretence to foretell thunder, a species of sagacity of which he has frequently given the most unequivocal evidence. I gave but sixpence for him, which is a groat more than the market price, though he is in fact, or rather would be if Leeches were not found in every ditch, an invaluable acquisition.

Mrs. Throck. sola dined with us last Tuesday. She invited herself. The particular reason of her so doing was that her husband and brother dined at Horton.° The next day we Dined at the Hall.

Mrs. Wrighte's is still consider'd as a melancholy case,° though we learn this evening that she has twice or thrice taken airings in the chaise, and must therefore I suppose be better. Pray my Dear add to what I have already desired you to bring with you, a roll or two of green wax candle° to go upon a spindle, spindle, spindle. I repeat it 3 times having more than once experienced how apt that circumstance is to escape the memory. I have no room for any other addition than that of our best Love, and to assure you how truely I am ever yours

Wm Cowper.

To Harriot Hesketh

The Lodge | Feb. 16. 1788

I have now three Letters of yours, my dearest Cousin, before me, all written in the space of a Week, and must be indeed insensible of kindness did I not feel yours upon this occasion. I cannot describe to you, neither could you comprehend it if I should, the manner in which my mind is sometimes impressed with melancholy on particular subjects. Your late silence was such a subject. I heard, saw and felt a thousand terrible things which had no real existence, and was haunted by them night and day 'till they at last extorted from me the doleful Epistle which I have since wish'd had been burn'd before I sent it. But the cloud has pass'd, and as far as you are concern'd, my heart is once more at rest.

Before you gave me the hint, I had once or twice as I lay on my bed watching for the break of day, ruminated on the subject which in your last but one, you recommend to me. Slavery, or a release from slavery such as the poor Negroes have endured, or perhaps both those topics together, appeared to me a theme so important at the present juncture, and at the same time so susceptible of poetical management, that I more than once perceived myself ready to start in that career, could I have allowed myself to desert Homer for so long a time as it would have cost me to do them justice. While I was pondering these things, the public prints informed me that Miss Moore was on the point of publication,° having actually finished what I had not yet begun. The sight of her advertisement convinced me that my best course would be that to which I felt myself most inclined, to persevere without turning aside to attend to any other call however alluring, in the business that I have in hand. It occurred to me likewise that I have already borne my testimony° in favour of our Black Brethren, and that I was one of the earliest, if not the first of those who have in the present day, expressed their detestation of the diabolical traffic in question. On all these accounts I judged it best to be silent, and especially because I cannot doubt that some effectual measures will now be taken to alleviate the miseries of their condition, the whole nation being in possession of the case, and it being impossible also to alledge an argument in behalf of Man-merchandize that can deserve a hearing. I shall be glad to see Hannah Moore's poem; she is a favorite writer with me, and has more nerve and energy both in her thoughts and language than half the He rhimers in the kingdom. The Thoughts on the manners of the great will likewise be most acceptable. I want to learn as much of the world as I can, but to acquire that learning at a distance, and a book with such a title promises fair to serve that purpose effectually. For poor Hannah's sake I thank you, as does Mrs. Unwin, heartily, for your kind intentions to send her Mrs. Trimmer's publication.° She is at present a very good girl, affectionate and studious to please, and will I verily believe turn that Lady's instructions to as good account as any of her little disciples.

I recommend it to you, my Dear, by all means to embrace the fair occasion, and to put yourself in the way of being squeezed and incommoded a few hours, for the sake of hearing and seeing what you will never have opportunity to see and hear hereafter, the trial of a man° who has been greater and more feared than the Mogul himself, and of his Myrmidon Sir Elijah.° Whatever we are at home, we have certainly been Tyrants in the East; and if these men have, as they are charged, riotted in the miseries of the innocent, and dealt death to the guiltless with an unsparing hand, may they receive a retribution that shall make all future Governors and Judges of ours in those distant regions tremble. While I speak thus, I equally wish them acquitted. They were both my Schoolfellows and for Hastings I had a particular value. As to our friends at the Hall, whether on this subject or any other, I never find them violent. If they dispute, as they do sometimes, it is with each other, never with me. To me and to mine they are always equally obliging, kind and friendly. Poor Mrs. Throg is doing Lent pennance at this time, a discipline which I assure you does not at all agree with her. A Diet differing so much from that which she allows herself in common, affects both her looks and her spirits. The Gentlemen, the Padre excepted, are less scrupulous than she, and consequently fare better. Mr. Throg goes to town to morrow, but designing to stay there only till Thursday next, he will hardly have time to call upon you.

I have lately had a Letter from a Lady unknown to me, tho'
she tells me she was intimate with my brother. Her name is
Margaret King,° and she lives at Perton Hall near Kimbolton.
I answer'd it 2 or 3 days ago, and shall probably hear from her
again. The consequence will be that I shall have a new
Correspondent; an acquisition that I can hardly afford to
make.

The terrible Curate° of whom I told you, is become to me
less terrible, having left Weston and taken up his abode at
Ravenstone. I have had the good hap to see him but once, and
may now hope that I shall see him no more.

Farewell, my dearest Cousin, with Mrs. Unwin's affectionate
respects, I conclude myself I Ever Yours

Wm Cowper.

All Advertisements that you may see in the name of Andrew
Fridze° are my compositions.

The Letter that you mention of which Padre Postlethwaite°
was so much the subject, came safe to hand.

To Harriot Hesketh

The Lodge I Mar. 3. 1788—Monday.

My dearest Coz—

He who can sit up all night at a Gaming table,° knowing
that he is to spend the next day in the accusation of another at
the Bar of the first Court of Judicature in the world, is not a jot
more innocent than he whom he accuses. If he has not
committed the same offences it is only because he never had
the same opportunity, for profligate he must be to a degree
that no Governor of Fort St. George° past, present, or to come
can possibly surpass. This may look like an assertion built
upon grounds too slight to bear it, but if I were not writing to
my Cousin whom I would not entertain merely with logical
deductions, I think I could make it appear probably at least, if
not absolutely certain.

One day last Week, Mrs. Unwin and I having taken our
morning walk, and returning homeward through the wilderness,

met the three Throckmortons. A minute after we had met
them, we heard the cry of hounds at no great distance, and
mounting the broad stump of an Elm which had been felled,
& by the aid of which we were enabled to look over the
Wall, we saw them. They were at that time in our Orchard.
Presently we heard a Terrier belonging to Mrs. Throg, which
you may remember by the name of Fury, yelping with much
vehemence, and saw her running through the thickets within
few yards of us at her utmost speed as if in pursuit of
something which we doubted not was the Fox. Before we
could reach the other end of the wilderness, the hounds
enter'd also; and when we arrived at the Gate which opens
into the grove, there we found the whole dirty and weary
cavalcade assembled. The Huntsman dismounting begg'd
leave to follow his hounds on foot, for he was sure, he said,
that they had killed him. A conclusion which I suppose he
drew from their profound silence. He was accordingly
admitted, and with a sagacity that would not have dishonour'd
the best hound in the world, pursuing precisely the track
which the Fox and the dogs had taken, though he had never
had a glimpse of either after their first entrance through the
rails, soon arrived where he found the slaughter'd prey,
videlicet in the Pit of a certain place called Jessamy Hall,° into
which both the Fox and the dogs had enter'd by a large
aperture in the Brick-work at the bottom of it. Being himself
by far too staunch to boggle at a little filth contracted in so
honourable a cause, he soon produced dead Reynard, and
rejoined us in the grove with all his dogs about him. Having
an opportunity to see a ceremony which I was pretty sure
would never fall in my way again, I determined to stay and to
notice all that passed with the most minute attention. The
Fox's tail, or brush as I ought to call it, was given to one of the
Hall Foot-boys, who bearing it in his hat-band, ran with it to
his mistress, and in the height of his transport offer'd it to her
fair hand, neither so clean nor so sweet as it had been while
the Fox possess'd it. Happily however for Mrs. Throg, not
being quite so enraptured, she had the presence of mind to
decline the offer. The boy therefore for aught I know, remains
to this hour in possession both of the tail and the stink that
belongs to it. The Huntsman having by the aid of a Pitchfork

lodged Reynard on the arm of an Elm at the height of about 9 feet from the ground, there left him for a considerable time. The Gentlemen sat on their horses contemplating the Fox for which they had toiled so hard, and the hounds assembled at the foot of the tree with faces not at all less expressive of the most rational delight, contemplated the same object. The Huntsman remounted. He cut off a foot and threw it to the hounds. One of them swallow'd it whole like a Bolus. He then once more alighted, and drawing down the fox by his hinder legs, desired the people who were by this time rather numerous to open a lane for him to the right and left. He was instantly obey'd, when throwing the fox to the distance of some yards, and screaming like a fiend as he is—Tear him in pieces—at least six times repeatedly, he consign'd him over absolutely to the pack, who in a few minutes devour'd him completely. Thus, my Dear, as Virgil says,° What none of the Gods could have ventured to promise me, time itself pursuing its accustom'd course has of its own accord presented me with.—I have been In at the death of a Fox—and you now know as much of that matter as I, who am as well inform'd as any Sportsman in England.

A thousand thanks my Dear for your kind intention to furnish me not only with Books but with Shelves also to set them on. I am in reality equally in want of both, having no shelf in the world but an Encoignure° which holds a Lexicon and a Dictionary.

My Dog turns out a most beautiful creature but is at present apt to lift up his leg in the house, on which subject he and I had a terrible quarrel this morning. My Cat is the most affectionate of all her kind, and in my eyes a beauty also.— The Throgs with whom we walked this morning enquired after you as they often do, when I made your remembrances as you desired.

Adieu my dearest Coz, with Mrs. Unwin's very best and warmest respects, I remain ever Yours—

Wm Cowper.

I often think of my Uncle though I do not always mention him. Few days pass in which he is not in my thoughts—Give my Love to him.

To Margaret King

My dear Madam,

You must think me a tardy correspondent, unless you have had charity enough for me to suppose that I have met with other hindrances than those of indolence and inattention. With these I cannot charge myself, for I am never idle by choice, and inattentive to you I certainly have not been, but on the contrary can safely affirm that every day I have thought on you. My silence has been occasion'd by a malady to which I have all my life been subject, an inflammation of the eyes. The last sudden change of weather from excessive heat to a wintry degree of cold, occasion'd it, and at the same time gave me a pinch of the rheumatic kind, from both which disorders I have just recover'd. I do not suppose that our climate has been much alter'd since the days of our forefathers the Picts, but certainly the Human Constitution in this country has been alter'd much. Inured as we are from our cradles to every vicissitude in a climate more various than any other, and in possession of all that modern refinement has been able to contrive for our security, we are yet as subject to blights as the tenderest blossoms of Spring, and are so well admonished of every change in the atmosphere by our bodily feelings as hardly to have any need of a weather-glass to mark them. For this we are no doubt indebted to the multitude of our accommodations, for it was not possible to retain the hardiness that originally belong'd to our race under the delicate management to which for many ages we have now been accustom'd. I can hardly doubt that a Bull dog or a Game cock might be made just as susceptible of injuries from weather as myself, were he dietted and in all respects accommodated as I am. Or if the project did not succeed in the first instance (for we ourselves did not become what we are at once) in process of time however and in a course of many generations, it would certainly take effect. Let such a dog be fed in his infancy with pap, Naples biscuit,° and boiled Chicken, let him be wrapt in flannel at night, sleep on a good feather-bed, and ride out in a Coach for an Airing, and if his

posterity do not become slight limb'd, puney and valetudinarian
it will be a wonder. Thus our parents, and their parents, and
the parents of both were managed; and thus ourselves; and the
consequence is that instead of being weather-proof even
without cloathing, furs and flannels are not warm enough to
defend us. It is observable however that though we have by
these means lost much of our pristine vigour, our days are not
the fewer. We live as long as those whom on account of the
sturdiness of their frame the poets supposed to have been the
progeny of Oaks. Perhaps too they had little feeling, and for
that reason also might be imagined to be so descended. For a
very robust athletic habit seems inconsistent with much
sensibility. But sensibility is the *sine quâ non* of real happiness.
If therefore our lives have not been shorten'd and if our
feelings have been render'd more exquisite as our habit of
body has become more delicate, on the whole perhaps we have
no cause to complain but are rather gainers by our degeneracy.

Do you consider what you do when you ask one poet his
opinion of another? Yet I think I can give you an honest
answer to your question and without the least wish to nibble.
Thomson was admirable in description, but it always seemed
to me that there was somewhat of affectation in his stile, and
that his numbers are sometimes not well harmonized. I could
wish too with Dr. Johnson° that he had confined himself to
this country, for when he describes what he never saw, one is
forced to read him with some allowance for possible misrepresentation. He was however a true poet and his lasting fame
has proved it. Believe me, my Dear Madam, with my best
respects to Mr. King—most truly Yours

                                        Wm Cowper.

P.S. I am extremely sorry that you have been so much
indisposed, and hope that your next will bring me a more
favorable account of your health. I know not why, but I rather
suspect that you do not allow yourself sufficient air and
exercise; the physicians call them Non-naturals.° I suppose to
deter their patients from the use of them.

To Harriot Hesketh

The Lodge | June 27. 1788

For the sake of a longer visit, my dearest Coz, I can be well content to wait. The Country, this country at least, is pleasant at all times, and when Winter is come, or near at hand, we shall have the better chance for being snug. I know your passion for *Retirement indeed*, or for what we call here *Deedy*° Retirement, and the Frogs intending to return to Bath with their mother when her visit to the Hall is over, you will then find here exactly the retirement in question. I have made in the Orchard the best Winter walk in all the parish, shelter'd from the East and from the North East, and open to the Sun, except at his rising, all the day. Then we will have Homer and Don Quixote, and then we will have saunter and Chat, and one Laugh more before we die. Our Orchard is alive with creatures of all kinds, poultry of ev'ry denomination swarms in it, and pigs the drollest in the world. By that time indeed they will have ceased to be pigs and will probably be converted into pork or bacon, but we have also a most fruitful sow from whom we expect a continual and endless succession of pigs similar to these. At her first litter she produced Nine to the wonder of the whole village, and on that occasion all the Connoisseurs in such matters came to visit her, with a man called John Watson° at the head of them who attends as man midwife at the production of all such births in the neighborhood. It is not common you must know, my Dear, for swine to produce so many at their first accouchement, and we were accordingly the envy of all around us.

I rejoice that we have a Cousin Charles° also, as well as a Cousin Henry,° who has had the address to win the goodlikings of the chancellor. May he fare the better for it! As to myself, I have long since ceased to have any expectations from that quarter. Yet if he were indeed mortified as you say (and no doubt you have particular reasons for thinking so) and repented to that degree of his hasty exertions in favour of the present Occupant, who can tell? He wants neither means nor management, but can easily at some future time redress the evil, if he chuses to do it. But in the mean time life steals away, and shortly neither he will be in circumstances to do me a kindness nor I to receive one at his hands. Let him make haste therefore or he will die a promise in my debt which he will never be able to perform. Your communications on this subject are as safe as you can wish them. We divulge nothing but what might appear in the Magazine, nor that neither without great consideration.

I have a stomach that is the plague of my life, and tomorrow morning, just when other people will be rising with a good appetite to their Breakfasts, I shall swallow Tartar Emetic,° alias one abomination in order to get rid of half a dozen. Till One o'clock this morning I was employed, sitting upright in bed, in the sort of exercise that such a stomach always makes necessary, and have for three or four days past been occupied in the same agreeable manner, after dinner. It is not possible tamely to submit to it any longer.

I must tell you a feat of my Dog Beau. Walking by the River-side I observed some Water-Lilies floating at a little distance from the Bank. They are a large white flower with an Orange colour'd Eye, and extremely beautiful. I had a desire to gather one, and having your long Cane in my hand, by the help of it endeavor'd to bring one of them within my reach. But the attempt proved vain and I walked forward. Beau had all the while observed me very attentively. Returning soon after toward the same place, I observed him plunge into the river while I was about 40 yards distant from him, and when I had nearly reached the spot, he swam to land with a Lily in his mouth, which he came and lay'd at my foot.

Mr. Rose, whom I have mentioned to you heretofore as a visitor of mine for the first time soon after you left us, writes me word that he has seen my Ballads against the Slavemongers,° but not in Print. Where he met with them I know not. Mr. Bull begged hard for leave to Print them at Newport pagnel, and I refused, thinking that it would be wrong to anticipate the Nobility, Gentry and others at whose pressing instance I composed them, in *their* designs to print them. But perhaps I need not have been so squeamish, for the opportunity to publish them in London seems now not only ripe but rotten. I am well content. There is but one of the three with which I am myself satisfied, though I have heard them all well spoken of.

But there are very few things of my own composing that I can
endure to read when they have been written a month, though
at first they seem to me to be all perfection.

Mrs. Unwin who has been much the happier since the time
of your return hither has been in some sort settled, begs me to
make her kindest remembrances—Yours my Dear most truly
                                                    Wm Cowper.

P.S. The Fish was not from Sephus.°

To Margaret King

Weston Underwood | October 11. 1788

My dear Madam,
     You are perfectly secure from all danger of being over-
whelm'd with presents from me. It is not much that a poet can
possibly have it in his power to give; when he has presented
his own works, he may be supposed to have exhausted all
means of donation. They are his only superfluity. There was a
time, but that time was before I commenced Writer for the
Press, when I amused myself in a way somewhat similar to
yours; allowing I mean for the difference between masculine
and female operations. The scissors and the needle are your
chief implements; mine were the chissel and the saw. In those
days you might have been in some danger of too plentiful a
return for your favours. Tables, such as they were, and Joint-
stools, such as never were, might have travell'd to Pirtenhall
in most inconvenient abundance. But I have long since
discontinued this practise and many others which I found it
necessary to adopt, that I might escape the worst of all evils
both in itself and in its consequences, an idle life. Many arts I
have exercised with this view, for which Nature never design'd
me, though among them were some in which I arrived at
considerable proficiency by mere dint of the most heroic
perseverance. There is not a Squire in all this country who can
boast of having made better Squirrel houses, hutches for
rabbits, or bird-cages than myself; and in the article of
Cabbage-nets I had no Superior. I even had the hardiness to

take in hand the pencil, and studied a whole year the art of drawing. Many figures were the fruit of my labours which had at least the merit of being unparallel'd by any production either of Art or Nature; but before the year was ended, I had occasion to wonder at the progress that may be made in despight of natural deficiency, but dint alone of practise; for I actually produced three Landscapes which a Lady thought worthy to be framed & glazed. I then judged it high time to exchange this occupation for another, lest by any subsequent productions of inferior merit, I should forfeit the honour I had so fortunately acquired. But Gardening was of all employments that in which I succeeded best, though even in this, I did not suddenly attain perfection. I began with Lettuces and Cauliflowers; from them I proceeded to cucumbers; next to Melons. I then purchased on Orange tree, to which in due time I added two or three Myrtles. These served me day and night with employment during a whole severe winter. To defend them from the frost in a situation that exposed them to its severity, cost me much ingenuity and much attendance. I contrived to give them a fire heat, and have waded night after night through the snow with the bellows under my arm, just before going to bed, to give the latest possible puff to the embers, lest the frost should seize them before Morning. Very minute beginnings have sometimes important consequences. From nursing 2 or 3 little evergreens I became ambitious of a Greenhouse, and accordingly built one, which, Verse excepted, afforded me amusement for a longer time than any expedient of all the many to which I have fled for refuge from the misery of having nothing to do. When I left Olney for Weston I could no longer have a Greenhouse of my own, but in a neighbour's garden I find a better, of which the sole management is consign'd to me.

I had need take care when I begin a letter, that the subject with which I set off be of some importance, for before I can exhaust it, be it what it may, I have generally filled my paper. But self is a subject inexhaustible, which is the reason that though I have said little, and nothing, I am afraid, worth your hearing, I have only room to add that I am | My dear
Madam, | Most truly Yours
Wm Cowper.

Mrs. Unwin bids me present her best Compliments and say how much she shall be obliged to you for the Receipt to make that most excellent Cake which came hither in its native pan. There is no production of yours that will not be always most welcome at Weston.

To Samuel Rose

The Lodge July 23. 1789

You do well, my dear Sir, to improve your opportunity. To speak in the rural phrase, this is your sowing time, and the sheaves you look for can never be yours unless you make that use of it. The colour of our whole life is generally such as the three or four first years, in which we are our own masters, make it. Then it is that we may be said to shape our own destiny, and to treasure up for ourselves a series of future successes or disappointments. Had I employed my time as wisely as you in a situation very similar to yours, I had never been a poet perhaps, but I might by this time have acquired a character of more importance in society, and a situation in which my friends would have been better pleased to see me. But three years mis-spent in an attorney's office were almost of course followed by several more equally mis-spent in the Temple, and the consequence has been, as the Italian Epitaph says—Sto qui°—The only use I can make of myself now, at least the best, is to serve in terrorem to others when occasion may happen to offer, that they may escape, so far as my admonitions can have any weight with them, my folly and my fate. When you feel yourself tempted to relax a little the strictness of your present discipline and to indulge in amusements incompatible with your future interests, think on your friend at Weston.

Having said this, I shall next with my whole heart invite you hither, and assure you that I look forward to approaching August with great pleasure because it promises me your company. After a little time (which we shall wish a longer) spent with us, you will return invigorated to your studies and pursue them with the more advantage. In the mean time, in point of season, you have lost little by being confined to London. Incessant rains and meadows under water have given to the summer the air of winter, and the country has been deprived of half its beauties. We begin to be seriously alarmed for the harvest. The hay has most of it already perished, and the corn having spired into a stalk of uncommon length, will consequently be productive of little. A very intelligent neighbour assured me two days ago, that the present wet weather continuing another fortnight will certainly cause a great dearth, if not a famine. The millers and Bakers even now find it difficult to procure wheat, and a lean crop succeeding will reduce us to a penury in the article of bread such as is seldom felt in England.

It is time to tell you that we are all well and often make you our subject. Lady Hesketh desires to be kindly remember'd to you, as does Mrs. Unwin. We comfort ourselves as well as we can under all these threatening appearances with cheerful chat and the thought that we are once more together. This is the third meeting that my Cousin and we have had in this country, and a great instance of good fortune I account it in such a world as this, to have expected such a pleasure thrice without being once disappointed. Add to this wonder as soon as you can, by making yourself of the party—I am truly Yours

Wm Cowper

To John Newton

[1 December 1789]

My dear Friend

On this fine first of December, under an unclouded sky and in a room full of sunshine, I address myself to the payment of a debt long in arrear but never forgotten by me, however I may have seemed to forget it. I will not waste time in apologies. I have but one, and that one will suggest itself unmention'd. I will only add that you are the first to whom I write of several to whom I have not written many months, who all have claims upon me and who I flatter myself are all grumbling at my silence. In your case perhaps I have been less anxious than in the case of some others, because if you have not heard from myself, you have heard from my better self, Mrs. Unwin. From her you have learn'd that I live, that I am as well as usual, and that I translate Homer. Three short Items, but in which is comprized the whole detail of my present history. Thus I fared when you were here, thus I have fared ever since you were here, and thus, if it please God, I shall continue to fare some time longer, for though the work is done it is not finished; a riddle which you who are a brother of the Press, will solve easily. I have also been the less anxious, because I have had frequent opportunities to hear of you, and have always heard that you are in good health and happy. Of Mrs. Newton too I have heard more favorable accounts of late, which have given us both the sincerest pleasure. Mrs. Unwin's case is at present my only subject of uneasiness that is not immediately personal and properly my own. She has almost consant headaches, almost a constant pain in her side which nobody understands, and her lameness, within the last half year, is very little amended. But her spirits are good, because supported by comforts which depend not on the state of the body, and I do not know that with all these pains her looks are at all alter'd since we had the happiness to see you here, unless perhaps they are alter'd a little for the better. I have thus given you as circumstantial an account of ourselves as I could; the most interesting matter, I verily believe, with which I could have filled my paper, unless I could have made spiritual mercies to myself the subject. In my next, perhaps, I shall find leisure to bestow a few lines on what is doing in France and in the Austrian Netherlands;° though to say the truth I am much better qualified to write an essay on the siege of Troy, than to descant on any of these modern revolutions. I question if in either of the countries just mention'd, full of bustle and tumult as they are, there be a single character whom Homer were he living, would deign to make his hero. The populace are the heroes now, and the stuff of which gentlemen heroes are made, seems to be all expended.

I will endeavour that my next letter shall not follow this so tardily as this has followed the last, and with our joint affectionate remembrances to yourself and Mrs. Newton, remain as ever—Sincerely Yours

Wm Cowper

To Lady Hesketh

[In Jan. 1790 John Johnson paid a surprise visit to Cowper, who had not been in touch with his mother's family for twenty-seven years.]

The Lodge | Jan. 23. 1789°

A thousand thanks my dear for a basket full of excellent things on which I shall fare deliciously day and night.

In lieu of deserts, unwholesome and dear,
Pickled olives and Lodi° shall bring up the rear.

I had a letter yesterday from the wild boy Johnson, for whom I have conceived a great affection. It was just such a letter as I like, of the true helter-skelter kind, and though he writes a remarkable good hand, scribbled with such rapidity that it was barely legible. He gave in it a droll account of the adventures of Lord Howard's note,° and of his own in pursuit of it, all which I presume were occasioned by me who forgot, as I suppose, when I told you that he was come to visit me, to tell you his name also. He feels very sensibly the kindness of your reception of him, is very much pleased with Mr. Rose whom he had the good fortune to find with you, and adds that he is to meet him this day also—Saturday—at your dinner. He addressed his letter to Mrs. Unwin like an *inconsiderate* youth; on a presumption, as he says, that I should not be able to find time to read it; like an *inconsiderate* youth never recollecting that it would cost me as much time to hear it. The truth, I suppose was, that he thought he should have a better chance of an answer. In this he judged right, for Mrs. Unwin replied to him on the instant, which I could not have done, nor probably 'till he had returned to Cambridge.

The poem he brought me came as from Lord Howard with his Lordship's request that I would revise it. It is in the form of a Pastoral, and is entitled the *Tale of the Lute or the beauties of Audley-End*. I read it attentively; Was much pleased with part of it, and part of it I equally disliked. I told him so, and in such terms as one naturally uses when there seems to be no occasion to qualify or to alleviate censure. I observed him afterward somewhat more thoughtful and silent, but occasionally as pleasant as usual, and in Kilwick wood° where we walked the next day, the truth came out; that he was himself the Author; that Lord H. not approving it altogether, and several friends of his own age to whom he had shown it, differing from his Lordship in opinion and being highly pleased with it, he had come at last to a resolution to be set down by my judgment, a measure to which Lord H by all means advised him. He accordingly brought it, and will bring it again in the summer, when we shall lay our heads together and try to mend it.

I have lately had a letter also from Mrs. King, to whom indeed I had written to enquire whether she were living or dead. It was followed by a basket containing also good things but of a different kind from yours, chiefly Preserves and pastry. She tells me that the Critics expect from my Homer every thing in some parts, and that in others I shall fall short. These are the Cambridge Critics, and she has her intelligence from the Botanical Professor Martyn.° That Gentleman in reply assures them that I shall fall short of nothing, but shall disappoint them all.—It shall be my endeavour to do so, and I am not without hope of succeeding.

Beau's Love and Mrs. Unwin's must finish, only let me not forget to thank you on my own part for your kindness shown to Johnson on my recommendation. For though he be my Cousin, to thee is he not at all related.

Ever yours, my Dear,
Wm Cowper.

To Harriot Hesketh

Friday, I believe Feb. 26. 1790 | but am not sure.

You have set my heart at ease my Cousin, so far as you were yourself the subject of its anxieties. What other troubles it feels can be cured by God alone. But you are never silent a week longer than usual without giving an opportunity to my imagination ever fruitful in flowers of a sable hue, to teaze me with them day and night. London is indeed a pestilent place as you call it, and I would with all my heart that thou had'st less to do with it. Were you under the same roof with me, I should know you to be safe and should never distress you with melancholy letters.

Many thanks are due to you for adding Mrs. Howe° to the number of your acquaintance for my sake, and I shall be glad if the measure answer to you, though I should never be much the better for it myself; to say the truth I have learn'd not to be very sanguine in expectations of advantage in this way. The rich and the great are so little apt to interest themselves in favour of such folks as I, that I believe I might scratch in the soil of this world a whole century, and never turn up a single jewel. I feel myself however well enough inclined to the measure that you propose, and will show her, with all my heart, a sample of my translation. But it shall not be, if you please, taken from the Odyssey. It is a poem of a gentler character than the Iliad, and as I purpose to carry her by a coup de main, shall employ Achilles, Agamemnon and the two armies of Greece and Troy in my service. I will accordingly send you in the box that I received from you last night, the two first books of the Iliad for that Lady's perusal. To those I have given a third revisal; for them therefore I will be answerable, and am not afraid to stake the credit of my work upon *them*, with her or with any living wight, especially who understands the Original. I do not mean that even they are finished, for I shall examine and cross-examine them yet again, and so you may tell her, but I know that they will not disgrace me, whereas it is so long since I have look'd at my Odyssey that I know nothing about it. They shall set sail from Olney on Monday morning in the Diligence, and will reach you, I hope, in the Evening. As soon as she has done with them I shall be glad to have them again, for the time draws near when I shall want to give them the last touch.

I am delighted with Mrs. Bodham's kindness in giving me the only picture of my own mother° that is to be found, I suppose, in all the world. I had rather possess it than the richest jewel in the British crown, for I loved her with an affection that her death 52 years since has not in the least abated. I remember her too, young as I was when she died, well enough to know that it is a very exact resemblance of her, and as such, it is to me invaluable. Every body loved her, and with an amiable character so impress'd on all her features, every body was sure to do so. Should I mount when I die, I shall see her again, else, never.

I have a very affectionate and a very clever letter from Johnson who promises me the transcript of the books entrusted to him in a few days. I have a great love for that young man. He has some drops of the same stream in his veins that once animated the original of that dear picture.

Should the wretch be detected° who has aspersed Lord Cowper in this second instance, and should I learn his name, *Birth, parentage* and *education,* I may perhaps find an opportunity to pay him in *my* way. Should that happen, he shall not complain that he is overlook'd.

I am truly concerned for poor Rose and have little doubt that we shall lose him. Johnson the Bookseller told me lately that he was very so so, and intended writing to me in a few days. When he does, I will answer him soon, and say as you desire me.

The Oysters were not bad, but not so good as we have seen from your monger. The haddocks and lobsters are excellent.

As to Cambridge's conclusion° I shall only say that when you sent me a prose account of it, you express'd the thought yourself much better.

She has all she can wish, and she asks *for* no more. If you do not allow this to be a shabby line both on account of tautology and language, I shall say that you are partial, and admire That in Him which you would not endure in me. Adieu my Dearest Coz—with Mrs. U.'s best affections | Ever thine—

Wm Cowper.

The Box contained also a letter from Mrs. Bodham which if I should have answered it before I screw up the box I will send you. Nothing can be kinder or better expressed.

You will also receive per box two new pieces of mine, should Mrs. U. be well enough to copy them. They are both gone to Enfield's Speaker.°

To Anne Bodham

Weston Underwood near Olney, Bucks. | Feb. 27. 1790

My dearest Rose,

Whom I thought wither'd and fallen from the stalk but who I find are still alive, nothing could give me greater pleasure than to know it and to learn it from yourself. I loved you dearly when you were a child and love you not a jot the less for having ceased to be so. Every creature that bears any affinity to my own mother is dear to me, and you, the daughter of her brother,° are but one remove distant from her; I love you therefore and love you much, both for her sake and for your own. The world could not have furnish'd you with a present so acceptable to me as the picture which you have so kindly sent me. I received it the night before last, and view'd it with a trepidation of nerves and spirits somewhat akin to what I should have felt had the dear Original presented herself to my embraces. I kissed it and hung it where it is the last object that I see at night, and, of course, the first on which I open my eyes in the morning. She died when I had completed my sixth year, yet I remember her well and am an ocular witness of the great fidelity of the Copy. I remember too a multitude of the maternal tendernesses which I received from her and which have endeared her memory to me beyond expression. There is in me, I believe, more of the Donne than of the Cowper, and though I love all of both names and have a thousand reasons to love those of my own name, yet I feel the bond of nature draw me vehemently to your side. I was thought in the days of my childhood much to resemble my mother, and in my natural temper, of which at the age of 58 I must be supposed a competent judge, can trace both Her and my late uncle your father. Somewhat of his irritability, and a little, I would hope, both of his and of her—I know not what to call it without seeming to praise myself which is not my intention, but speaking to *you* I will e'en speak out and say—Good nature. Add to all this, that I deal much in poetry as did our venerable ancestor the Dean of St. Paul's, and I think I shall have proved myself a Donne at all points.° The truth is that whatever I am, I love you all.

I account it a happy event that brought the dear boy your nephew to my knowledge, and that, breaking through all the restraints which his natural bashfulness imposed on him, he determined to find me out. He is amiable to a degree that I have seldom seen, and I often long with impatience to see him again.

My dearest Cousin, what shall I say in answer to your affectionate invitation? I *must* say this. I cannot come now, nor soon, and I wish with all my heart I could. But I will tell you what may be done perhaps, and it will answer to us just as well. You and Mr. Bodham can come to Weston, can you not? The summer is at hand, there are roads and wheels to bring you, and you are neither of you translating Homer. I am crazed that I cannot ask you all together for want of House room, but for Mr. Bodham and yourself we have good room, and equally good for any third in the shape of a Donne, whether named Hewitt,° Bodham, Balls° or Johnson or by whatever name distinguished. Mrs. Hewitt has particular claims upon me, she was my playfellow at Berkhamstead and has a share in my warmest affections. Pray tell her so. Neither do I at all forget my Cousin Harriot. She and I have been many a time merry at Catfield° and have made the parsonage ring with laughter. Give my love to her. Assure yourself my dearest Cousin that I shall receive you as you were my sister, and Mrs. Unwin is for my sake prepared to do the same. When she has seen you she will love you for your own.

I am much obliged to Mr. B. for his kindness to my Homer, and with my love to you all and with Mrs. Unwin's kind respects, am | my dear dear Rose—Ever yours

Wm Cowper.

P.S. | I mourn the death of your poor brother Castres° whom I should have seen had he lived, and should have seen with the greatest pleasure. He was an amiable boy and I was very fond of him.

P.S. | Your nephew tells me that his Sister in the qualities of the mind resembles you; that is enough to make her dear to me, and I beg you will assure her that she is so. Let it not be long before I hear from you.

Still another P.S.—I find on consulting Mrs. Unwin that I

have under-rated our capabilities and that we have not only room for you and Mr. Bodham, but for two of your sex and even for your nephew into the bargain. We shall be happy to have it all so occupied.

To Harriot Hesketh

The Lodge—March 22. 1790

I rejoice my dearest Coz that my MSS have roam'd the earth so successfully and have met with no disaster. The single book excepted that went to the bottom of the Thames and rose again, they have been fortunate without exception.° I am not superstitious, but have nevertheless as good a right to believe that adventure an omen and a favorable one, as Swift had to interpret, as he did, the loss of a fine fish which he had no sooner laid on the bank than it flounced into the water again. This, he tells us himself, he always consider'd as a type of his future disappointments,° and why may not I, as well, consider the marvellous recovery of my lost book from the bottom of the Thames as typical of its future prosperity? To say the truth, I have no fears now about the success of my translation, though in time past I have had many. I knew that there was a stile somewhere, could I but find it, in which Homer ought to be render'd and which alone would suit him. Long time I blunder'd about it e'er I could attain to any decided judgment on the matter. At first I was betrayed, by a desire of accommodating my language to the simplicity of his, into much of the quaintness that belong'd to our writers of the fifteenth century. In the course of many revisals I have deliver'd myself from this evil, I believe, entirely; but I have done it slowly, and as a man separates himself from his mistress when he is going to marry. I had so strong a predilection in favour of this stile at first that I was crazed to find that others were not as much enamoured with it as myself. At every passage of that sort which I obliterated, I groan'd bitterly, and said to myself I am spoiling my work to please those who have no taste for the simple Graces of antiquity. But in measure as I adopted a more modern phraseology, I became a convert to their opinion, and in the last revisal which I am now making am not sensible of having spared a single expression of the obsolete kind. I see my work so much improved by this alteration that I am filled with wonder at my own backwardness to assent to the necessity of it, and the more when I consider that Milton, with whose manner I account myself intimately acquainted, is never quaint, never twangs through the nose, but is every where grand and elegant without resorting to musty antiquity for his beauties. On the contrary he took a long stride forward, left the language of his own day behind him, far behind him, and anticipated the expression of a century yet to come.

I have now, as I said, no longer any doubt of the event; but I will give thee a shilling if thou wilt tell me what I shall say in my preface. It is an affair of much delicacy and I have as many opinions about it as there are whims in a weather cock.

Send my MSS and thine when thou wilt. In a day or two I shall enter on the last Iliad. When I have finished it I shall give the Odyssey one more reading, and shall therefore shortly have occasion for the copy in thy possession, but you see that there is no need to hurry.

Thanks for all your labours and for all the new names which you have added. I leave the little remnant of paper for Mrs. Unwin's use,° who means I believe to occupy it, and am evermore thine most truly

Wm Cowper.

I want a new coat, but must first, it seems have a fashionable pattern. Wilt thou send me one when thou sendest or dost send the MSS.?

A pattern button is wanted also.

To John Johnson

Weston Underwood | March 23. 1790

My dear Cousin,

Your cold has perhaps by this time left you, and if it has, I rejoice. But forget not the advice given you here, to furnish yourself with a bed that may stand decently in your Keeping-room° (as I think you call it) for you will else incur consequences painful to yourself and to me, because I feel that I am interested in your well-being.

Your MSS have arrived safe in New Norfolk Street,° and I am much obliged to you for your labours. Were you now at Weston I could furnish you with employment for some weeks, and shall perhaps be equally able to do it in the summer, for I have lost my best amanuensis in this place—Mr. George Throckmorton, who is gone to Bath.

You are a man to be envied who have never read the Odyssey, which is one of the most amusing story-books in the world. There is also much of the finest poetry in the world to be found in it, notwithstanding all that Longinus has insinuated° to the contrary. His comparison of the Iliad and Odyssey to the Meridian and to the declining sun, is pretty, but, I am persuaded, not just. The prettiness of it seduced him; he was otherwise too judicious a reader of Homer to have made it. I can find in the latter, no symptoms of impair'd ability, none of the effects of age. On the contrary it seems to me a certainty that Homer, had he written the Odyssey in his youth, could not have written it better, and if the Iliad in his old age, that he would have written it just as well. A Critic would tell me that instead of *written* I should have said *composed*. Very likely—but I am not writing to one of that snarling generation.

My Boy, I long to see thee again. It has happen'd some way or other that Mrs. Unwin and I have conceived a great affection for thee. That I should, is the less to be wonder'd at because thou art a shred of my own mother; neither is the wonder great that she should fall into the same predicament, for she loves every thing that I love. You will observe that your own personal right to be beloved makes no part of the consideration. There is nothing that I touch with so much tenderness as the vanity of a young man, because I know how extremely susceptible he is of impressions that might hurt him, in that particular part of his composition. If you should ever prove a coxcomb, from which character you stand just now at a greater distance than any young man I know, it shall never be said that I have made you one. No—you will gain nothing by me but the honour of being much valued by a poor poet who can do you no good while he lives and has nothing to leave you when he dies. If you can be contented to be dear to me on those conditions, so you shall be, but other terms more advantageous than these or more inviting, none have I to propose. Farewell. Puzzle not yourself about a subject when you write to either of us. Every thing is subject good enough from those we love. With Mrs. Unwin's best remembrances I am much Yours

Wm Cowper.

To Joseph Hill

Weston Underwood | May 2. 1790

My dear friend—

My letters all begin with thanks, which is a proof that you are kind whether it prove my gratitude or not, *That* I should be glad to prove by longer and more frequent letters, did my situation afford me subjects or my occupation leisure.° At present however I thank you for two parcels of excellent maccarel; the first at least was such teste me ipso,° and a few hours hence I shall be equally qualified, I doubt not, to attest the goodness of the latter.

I am still at the old sport; Homer all the morning and Homer all the Evening. Thus have I been held in constant employment, I know not exactly how many, but I believe these six years, an interval of eight months excepted. It is now become so familiar to me to take Homer from my shelf at a certain hour, that I shall no doubt continue to take him from my shelf at the same time, even after I have ceased to want him. That period is not far distant. I am now giving the last touches to a work, which had I foreseen the difficulty of it, I should never have meddled with, but which, having at length nearly finished it to my mind, I shall discontinue with regret.

My very best Compliments attend Mrs. Hill whom I love unsight unseen as they say, but yet truly.

Yours ever
Wm Cowper.

To John Newton

Weston. Mar. 29. 1791

My dear friend—

It affords me sincere pleasure that you enjoy serenity of mind after your great loss° It is well in all circumstances, even in the most afflictive, with those who have God for their comforter. You do me justice in giving entire credit to my expressions of friendship for you; no day passes in which I do not look back to the days that are fled, and consequently none in which I do not feel myself affectionately reminded of you and of Her whom you have lost for a season. I cannot even see Olney spire from any of the fields in the neighbourhood, much less can I enter the town, and still less the vicarage, without experiencing the force of those mementos, and recollecting a multitude of passages to which you and yours were parties.

The Past would appear in a dream, were the remembrance of it less affecting. It was, in the most important respects, so unlike my present moment, that I am sometimes almost tempted to suppose it a dream. But the difference between dreams and realities long since elapsed, seems to consist chiefly in this, that a dream however painful or pleasant at the time, and perhaps for a few ensuing hours, passes like an arrow through the air, leaving no trace of its flight behind it; but our actual experiences make a lasting impression; we review those which interested us much when they occurred, with hardly less interest than in the first instance, and whether few years or many have intervened, our sensibility makes them still present; such a mere nullity is time to a creature to whom God gives a feeling heart and the faculty of recollection.

That you have not the first sight, and sometimes perhaps have a late one, of what I write, is owing merely to your distant situation. Some things I have written not worth your perusal, and a few, a very few, of such length, that engaged as I have been to Homer, it has not been possible that I should find opportunity to transcribe them. At the same time Mrs. Unwin's constant pain in her side has almost forbidden her the use of the pen; she cannot use it long without encreasing that pain, for which reason I am more unwilling than herself that she should ever meddle with it. But whether what I write be a trifle, or whether it be serious, you would certainly, were you present, see them all. Others get a sight of them by being so, who would never otherwise see them, and I should hardly withold them from you whose claim upon me is of so much older a date than theirs. It is not indeed with readiness and good will that I give them to any body, for, if I live, I shall probably print them, and my friends who are previously well acquainted with them, will have the less reason to value the book in which they shall appear. A trifle can have nothing to recommend it but its novelty. I have spoken of giving copies, but in fact I have given none; they who have them, made them; for till my whole work shall have fairly pass'd the press, it will not leave me a moment more than is necessarily due to my correspondents. Their number has of late encreased upon me, by the addition of many of my maternal relations, who having found me out about a year since, have behaved to me in the most affectionate manner, and have been singularly serviceable to me in the article of my Subscription. Several of them are coming from Norfolk to visit me in the course of the Summer.

I enclose a copy of my last mortuary verses. The Clerk° for whom they were written is since dead, and whether his successor the late Sexton,° will chuse to be his own dirge-maker, or will employ me, is a piece of important news that has not yet reached me.

Our best remembrances attend yourself and Miss Catlett, and we rejoice in the kind providence that has given you, in her, so amiable and comfortable a companion.

Adieu—my dear friend—I am sincerely yours.
Wm C

To Samuel Rose

Weston. Decr. 21. 1791

My dear Friend—

It grieves me, after having indulged a little hope that I might perhaps have the pleasure to see you in the holidays, to be obliged to disappoint myself. The occasion too is such as will insure to me your sympathy.

On Saturday last, while I was at my desk near the window, and Mrs. Unwin at the fire-side opposite to it, I heard her suddenly exclaim—Oh Mr. Cowper, don't let me fall—I turn'd and saw her actually falling together with her chair, and started to her side just in time to prevent her. She was seized with a violent giddiness which lasted, though with some abatement, the whole day, and was attended too with some other most alarming symptoms. At present however she is relieved from the vertigo, and seems in all respects better, except that she is so enfeebled as to be unable to quit her bed for more than an hour in a day.

She has been my faithful and affectionate nurse for many years, and consequently has a claim on all my attentions. She has them, and will have them as long as she wants them, which will probably be, at the best, for a considerable time to come.

I feel the shock as you may suppose in every nerve. God grant that there may be no repetition of it. Another such stroke upon her would, I think, overset me completely. But at present I hold up bravely.

Lady Hesketh is also far from well. She has ventur'd these two last days to dine in the study, else she has kept her chamber above this fortnight. She has suffer'd however by this first sally and has taken cold as I fear'd she would.

Thus are we a house of Invalids, and must wait for the pleasure of receiving you here 'till it shall please God to restore us to health again.

With my best Compliments to Mrs. Rose, and with those of the two Ladies, I remain, my dear friend | most Sincerely yours

Wm Cowper.

To William Hayley

[Hayley had written to Cowper at Joseph Johnson's on 7 Feb. 1792, but the letter remained in London for almost six weeks before someone thought to send it on to Weston. Cowper was dismayed that Johnson had been so careless about transmitting the letter, and he answered Hayley the same day he received it.]

Weston-Underwood | near Olney—Bucks. | March 17. 1792.

My Dear Sir—

Your Letter gives me the sincerest pleasure, and at the same time, the late arrival of it, the greatest uneasiness. What must you think of a man who could leave so valuable a favour almost six weeks unacknowledged? A Liberality like that of the amiable writer was certainly such as entitled him to other treatment, and even you, candid and generous as you are, must at least have begun by this time to suspect me of the most stupid insensibility. But let the blame be imputed to the blameworthy, and let the innocent go free. Your pacquet dated the 7th. of last month, reached me not till six o'clock this evening. Thanks to my Bookseller who neglected to send it sooner, and by his unreasonable delay has put my nerves and spirits to a trial, not the first of the kind that they have sustained from Him, but certainly the severest.

When I saw the Newspaper° to which you allude, and in which we seem'd to be match'd like two racehorses against each other, my first sensations were not unpleasant, for I felt myself not a little flatter'd by the supposed competition between us. But sensations of a very different kind succeeded, and such as were nearly akin to the most dispiriting despondence. I never thought myself very well qualified for my present enterprize, for though I have all my life been at times occupied in reading and admiring Milton, I had not once look'd into him with the eyes of a Commentator; nor did I, nor had I any reason to judge myself in any measure equal to yourself either in point of Learning or other ability for such an employment. Guess then how I must feel myself relieved by the information you give me that we are to act each in a distinct province, and that I shall have no disgrace to fear on this occasion save from myself only.—He who knows the hearts of all, knows that in thus speaking and in thus describing my feelings in this instance, I have spoken nothing but truth.

I rejoice that you are employed to do justice to the character of a man, perhaps the chief of all who have ever done honour to our country, and whose very name I reverence. Here we shall not clash or interfere with each other, for a Life of Milton is no part of my bargain. In short we will cope with each other in nothing but that affection which you avow for me, unworthy of it as I am, and which your character and writings and especially your kind letter have begotten in my heart for you.

A thousand thanks to you for your Subscription, though the honour of your name is all the benefit that I shall derive from it, who am, on this occasion, Bookseller's Labourer, and nothing more. As many also for your Sonnet,° of which you speak more modestly than justly, and which I will not call a Compliment because I will not wrong your sincerity, or even seem to do it. May I always so write and so act as to continue in your good opinion, and send me now and then a line to tell me that I still possess it. Believe me, my Dear Sir, duly sensible of your kindness, as in truth I am, and your much obliged and | affectionate humble Servant

Wm Cowper.

Every remark of yours on Milton will be highly valued by me.

To William Hayley

Weston-Underwood | Mar. 24. 1792

My dear friend—

For though I am seldom very precipitate in using that stile of address, and have never 'till now address'd with it any of my correspondents in the beginning of our intercourse, with you I am sure that I may use it safely. Your letters will not suffer me to doubt your friendship for me, and I need only consult my own heart for a moment to be convinced that on my side there is no deficiency. None, I mean, of present feelings such as constitute friendship, and so far as frail man may dare to answer for himself, I may venture to affirm, I believe, that there shall be none hereafter.

So long as my letter to you was on the road, I had uneasy sensations that I cannot better describe than by saying in Lady's language that I was in the fidgets. At last I said to a friend of mine, by this time Mr. Hayley has received my letter. Yes, he replied, unless he happens to be in London. This cruel scruple threw me back again, and left the matter in such a state of uncertainty that I found all quiet of mind impossible and hopeless till I should receive your answer. I am bound to thank you therefore for sending me one so speedily, and such a one too as in every line of it, the line excepted in which you speak of yourself as an Invalide, gives me pleasure. I have been used, I know not why, to consider you as a much younger man than myself who have seen my sixtieth birthday, and cannot therefore be reconciled to the thought of your being habitually indisposed, while, with a greater load of years on my back, I am myself in tolerable health. I would with all my heart that we had known each other while approximation was possible. But how should I who have not journey'd 20 miles from home these 20 years, how should I possibly reach your country? You will wonder perhaps, after hearing me boast of my freedom from disease, wherein the impossibility can consist. But consider what habit is, and consider how every year that is spent entirely at home, adds terrours to the thought of quitting it. To this consideration add another, of which at present you are not apprized, that though I labour under no bodily disability properly so call'd, I have sad spirits, a mind continually subject to melancholy, and sometimes cover'd with the darkest shade of it. Your state of body therefore, not more than my state of mind, seems to lour on the hope of our meeting till we shall meet in a long hereafter. But in the mean time we may be affectionately disposed to each other, and I trust shall be so, for though not very superstitious nor apt much to be govern'd by prognostics, I have every day and all day long a pleasure in the thought of the acquisition I have made in you, that seems to assure me we shall not soon become indifferent to each other.

It gives a lift to my spirits to hear you say that you think me qualified for my undertaking, but let me set you right in one particular. You think, and naturally enough, having seen me blazon'd as the Translator of Milton's Italian poems, that I am a Master of that language. But the fact is otherwise. I never studied it but during one winter, a winter that pass'd thirty years ago, and since that time, except the Sonnets in question, have never even seen any thing written in it. Those however I have translated, by the assistance of a kind interpreter, my neighbor Mr. Courteney. I love you therefore and am very sensibly obliged to you for your kind offer to procure me such Italian authors as I may wish to see, but instead of wishing to see them, must confine myself to a modester wish, that I could understand them. Mr. Steevens the editor of Shakespear, though a stranger to me, has communicated to me a scarce and curious book, the Adamo of Andreini,° which however is likely, for the reason mention'd, to avail me little. It is the shield of Achilles° given to Ajax, which Ulysses in Ovid tells him, was too mysterious for the comprehension of such a block head.

I believe you perfectly right in tracing that passage in Comus to the text you quote from Job.° The Lines of Milton are as you say most beautiful, and in many a green lane in Hartfordshire I have repeated them to myself, when a boy, with rapture. But I have filled my paper e'er half is said. Adieu, my dear friend, let it not be long before you write again, and believe me | most sincerely yours

Wm Cowper.

On recurring to your letter which I have read many times, I have, I perceive, inferr'd too hastily from what you say of your valitudinary state, that you *never* leave your home. Were it possible that you could leave it for mine, here you may be as much a hermit° as you can be any where, and here shall you be nursed as I am, and with what pleasure should I receive you!

To William Hayley

Weston-Underwood | April 6. 1792.

My dear Friend—

God grant that this friendship of ours may be a comfort to us all the rest of our days in a world where true friendships are rarities, and especially where, suddenly form'd, they are apt soon to terminate. But, as I said before, I feel a disposition of heart toward you, that I never felt for one whom I had never seen, and that shall prove itself, I trust, in the event a propitious omen.

You tell me a tale of woes that move my compassion much, and my sorrow both for your past and present sufferings. I remember indeed to have seen it pathetically related in a poem of yours,° many years ago. From that poem I took my first impressions of you, and more favorable impressions of you I could not have taken from any thing. Horace says somewhere, though I may quote it amiss perhaps, for I have a terrible memory

> Utrumque nostrum incredibili modo
> Consentit astrum—°

I have been all my life subject to inflammations of the eye, and in my boyish days had specks on both that threaten'd to cover them. My father alarm'd for the consequences, sent me to a female oculist° of great renown at that time, in whose house I abode two years, but to no good purpose. From her I went to Westminster school where at the age of 14 the small-pox seized me and proved the better oculist of the two, for it deliver'd me from them all. Not however from great liableness to inflammation, to which I am in a degree still subject, though much less than formerly, since I have been constant in the use of a hot foot-bath every night, the last thing before going to rest. If you have never tried it I will earnestly recommend it to you.—But *our stars consent*, at least have had an influence somewhat similar, in another and more important article. I cannot indeed say that I have ever been actually deprived of understanding, but near thirty years ago I had a disorder of mind that unfitted me for all society, and was in fact during many months sequester'd from it. In sufferings therefore we are brethren, brethren too in occupation, and brethren I hope we shall be hereafter in heart and affection.— So much for our respective infirmities; and now as you see I have made myself a proper object of my own satyr, and if I have not inspired you with the wish of a *peevish hearer*, it is owing more to your good nature than to my prudence.

It gives me the sincerest pleasure that I may hope to see you at Weston, for as to any migrations of mine, they must I fear, notwithstanding the joy I should feel in being a guest of yours, be still consider'd in the light of Impossibles. Come then, my friend, you and your good handmaid of 40,° and be as welcome, as the country people say here, as *the flowers in May*. I am happy as I say in the expectation, but the fear or rather the consciousness that I shall not answer on a nearer view, makes it a trembling kind of happiness, and a doubtful.

After my escape into the world again out of that privacy which I have mention'd above, I went to Huntingdon. Soon after my arrival there I took up my quarters at the house of the Revd. Mr. Unwin. I lived with him while he lived, and ever since his death have lived with his widow. Her therefore you will find mistress of the house, and I judge of you amiss, or you will find her just such as you would wish. To me she has been often a nurse, and invariably the kindest friend, through a thousand advertisities that I have had to grapple with in the course of almost 30 years.—I thought it better to introduce her to you thus, than to present her to you at your coming, quite a stranger.—Bring with you any books that you think may be useful to my commentatorship, for, with you for an interpreter, I shall be afraid of none of them. And in truth if you think that you shall want them, you must bring books for your own use also, for they are an article with which I am *heinously unprovided*, being much in the condition of the man whose library Pope describes as

> no mighty store,
> His own works neatly bound, and little more.°

You shall know how this has come to pass hereafter.

Tell me my friend, are your letters in your own handwriting?° If so, I am in pain for your eyes, lest by such frequent demands upon them I should hurt them. I had rather write you three letters for one, much as I prize your letters, than *that* should happen.

And now for the present adieu! I am going to accompany Milton into the lake of fire and brimstone,° having just begun my annotations, which I suppose will turn out but a poor business, for all the bushes had been well beaten before I took the field.

Yours very affectionately
Wm Cowper.

To Harriot Hesketh

[On 22 May, while Hayley was a guest at Weston Lodge, Mrs Unwin suffered her second paralytic stroke. Hayley immediately offered practical and spiritual comfort.]

I would with all my heart, my Dearest Coz, that I had not ill news for the subject of the present letter, but when, so far as myself am concerned, shall I be able to send thee any better? My friend, my Mary, in whom thou knowest that I live and have my Being far more than in Him from whom I received that Being,° has again been attack'd by the same disorder that threaten'd me last year with the loss of her, and of which you were yourself a witness. Gregson would not allow that first stroke to be paralytic, but this he acknowledges to be so, and with respect to the former I never had myself any doubt that it was, but this has been much the severest. Her speech has been almost unintelligible from the moment when she was struck. It is with difficulty that she opens her eyes and she cannot keep them open, the muscles necessary to the purpose being contracted, and as to self moving powers from place to place, and the use of her right hand and arm, she has entirely lost them.

It has happen'd well, that of all men living the man most qualified to assist and comfort me, is here, though 'till within these few days I never saw him, and a few weeks since had no expectation that I ever should. You have already guessed that I mean Hayley. Hayley the most benevolent and amiable of his kind, and who loves me as if he had known me from my cradle. When he returns to Town, as he must alas! too soon, he will pay his respects to you; and you will then find him to deserve all that could be said to his advantage in many words, and I have used but few.

I will not conclude without adding that our poor patient is beginning I hope to recover from this stroke also. But her amendment is slow, as must be expected at her time of life, and in such a disorder. I am as well myself as you have ever known me in a time of much trouble, and even better.

It was not possible to prevail on Mrs. Unwin to let me send for Dr. Kerr,° but Hayley has written to his friend Dr. Austen° a representation of her case, and we expect his opinion and advice to-morrow In the mean time we have borrowed an Electrical Machine° from our neighbour Socket,° the effect of which she tried yesterday and the day before, and we think it has been of material service.

She was seized while Hayley and I were walking, and while Mr. Greatheed, who called while we were abroad, was with her.

I forgot in my last to thank thee for the proposed amendments of thy friend.° Whoever he is, make my Compliments to him and thank him. The passages to which he objects have been all alter'd, and when he shall see them new-dress'd I hope he will like them better.

As to the lines I sent you of which Hastings° was the subject, trouble not thyself about them.

Mrs. U.'s Love and Mr. H.'s best Compliments attend thee.

Thine ever
Wm Cowper.

The Lodge | May 24. 1792.

She was taken ill last Tuesday.

I have no need to trouble thee for viands of any sort on H.'s account. He drinks only water, and eats little beside mustard.

To William Hayley

All's well.

Which words I place as conspicuously as possible and prefix them to my letter, to save you the pain, my friend and Brother, of a moment's anxious speculation. Poor Mary proceeds in her amendment still, and improves I think even at a swifter rate than when you left her. The stronger she grows the faster she gathers strength, which is perhaps the natural course of recovery. She waked so well this morning that she told me at my first visit she had entirely forgot her illness, and she spoke so distinctly and had so much her usual countenance that, had it been possible, she would have made me forget it too. Yesterday she moved into the electrifying room with very little help from her supporters, and carried herself more erect than at any time before. She seems however to have a better opinion of your spark-eliciting faculties than of mine, and once or twice was so riotous that I had much ado to manage her. She even had the hardiness to tell me of your superior skill, and when the snaps were smart and frequent to say, Hayley would not do thus if *he* was here. The truth is, I believe, that her Feelings are quicker than they were, and that the inconvenience of which she complains is rather owing to the Patient's amendment than to any want of dexterity in the Agent. She bids me tell you that she loves you dearly, and that were you her brother she could not love you more. She is desirous too that you should know her own opinion of her disorder. She judges it to be a nervous rheumatism accompanied by those spasms to which she has so many years been subject. Formerly they affected her bosom, and now she judges them to be the same that have seized her limbs. It is certain that they go and come, and that in the course of the same day her face is sometimes drawn aside and sometimes not, and that her speech varies in the same manner. Last night she enquired of Gregson if Steers's Opodeldoc° might not be useful to her. He thought it might. Therefore having a little left at the bottom of a bottle that Lady Hesketh brought with her, she had it rubb'd into her back at bed-time, and it seems to have been of prodigious use to her. We can easily, I believe, get more of it at Northampton. She wishes much for an aperient electuary,° and if Dr. Austen can prescribe one that will be effectual, will hold it a great additional obligation. Whether in prose or verse I shall always love and honour *him*, and so will Mary.

And now my dear fellow let me tell you how much we love you, and how much we have regretted you. We talk of you all the day long, and always say of you more than I will now tell you. Neither are we quite singular in this, for you have left a regret of you in the hearts of all our family and of all our visitors. Every creature is sorry that you are gone, only in this sorrow *we* claim the preeminence, having far most reason.

Here I shall leave a gap to be fill'd after the Post comes in, and proceed to sing you a song which you will find in the next page, and which would have been better had you been here to mend it.

—Return'd from my walk, blown to tatters and all in a dissolution. Found two things in the Study, your Letter and my Mary. She is bravely well, and your beloved epistle does us both good. How kind is Carwarden.° Bless him, and tell him that I say so. As to your own kindness you shall hear no more about that from me, for the more I say of it, the more attentive you become to me, and the less to yourself. For instance, you would leave Murphy's book° at last, though I said all I could to dissuade you from it, and now you will poison yourself with the steams of old Babylon in hopes of doing me service. But beware, for shouldst thou kill thyself in my cause, I shall never love thee after. I found your kind pencil-note in my song-book as soon as I came down on the morning of your departure, and Mary was vex'd to the heart that the simpletons who watch'd her supposed her asleep when she was not, for she learn'd soon after you were gone that you would have peep'd at her had you known her to be awake. I perhaps might have had a peep too, and therefore was as vext as she. But if it please God we shall make ourselves large amends for all lost peeps by and by at Eartham.—I have no doubt that all is well there, tho' you found no letter, but I wish you had found for your own peace's sake. Adieu. God be with you. Amen.

Sonnet.

Hayley—thy tenderness fraternal shown
    In our first interview, delightful guest!
    To Mary and me for her dear sake distress'd,
Such as it is has made my heart thy own
Though heedless now of new engagements grown;
    For threescore winters make a wintry breast,
    And I had purpos'd ne'er to go in quest
Of Friendship more, except with God alone.
    But Thou has won me. Nor is God my Foe,
Who e're this last afflictive scene began
    Sent Thee to mitigate the dreadful blow
    My Brother, by whose sympathy I know
Infallibly thy true deserts to scan,
Not more t'admire the Bard, than love the Man.

                                        W Cowper.

———

Mrs. Socket whom I told that I was writing to you, desires me to give her duty to yourself and her love to Mrs. Mary and to her son.° She has nothing to add, except that she is very well.

I shall long to hear from you, but would not worry you to write unless when you can find a tranquil moment, if such can be found in London.

To Samuel Teedon

June 5. 1792.

Dear Sir—

Mrs. Unwin has had a very indifferent night, and is far from being so well this morning as I hoped she would be, having seen her yesterday much better than on any former day since she was taken ill. I can attain in short to no settled hope of her recovery. Every paralytic stroke exposes a person more to the danger of another, and I am in constant fear of a repetition, from which it is evident that enfeebled as she is, and at her time of life, she could not be restored without an absolute miracle. I cannot but observe too that none of your notices° go the length we wish, none of them speak plainly concerning a recovery, they are all open to a spiritual interpretation and seem almost to demand it. When she had the atrophy 27 years ago,° I had clear notice of her restoration in these words, *she shall recover.* And in these—*she is yours for many years.* And when she was taken ill last December I had one equally clear to the same purport in these—*Your watch must be wound up again.* But on the present occasion I have none such. On the contrary I am continually threaten'd with the loss of her. My nocturnal experiences are all of the most terrible kind. Death, Church yards and carcases, or else thunder storms and lightnings, God angry, and myself wishing that I had never been born. Such are my dreams, and when I wake it is only to hear something terrible, of which she is generally the subject.

Who can hope for peace amid such trouble? I cannot. I live a life of terrour. My prospects respecting this life as well as another seem all intercepted; I am incapable of proceeding in the work I have begun, and unless it pleases God to give me a quieter mind shall be obliged to free myself from my engagement, while Johnson has yet time enough before him to employ another.

I write thus that you may accommodate your prayers to my condition and circumstances, and not that I may make you more a partaker with me in my distresses than you are already. I should not wish that evil even to an enemy, much less to you.

Yours
Wm Cowper.

To William Hayley

Weston. June 7. 1792

Love you? Yes to be sure I do. Do you take me for a stock or a stone that you make a question of it? Have you not taken a more ardent interest in me and my poor Mary than ever man did? Of what materials can you suppose me made, if after all the rapid proofs that you have given me of your friendship, I do not love you with all my heart and regret your absence continually? But you must permit me nevertheless to be melancholy now and then, or if you will not, I must be so without your permission; for that sable thread is so intertwined with the very thread of my existence as to be inseparable from it; at least while I exist in the body. I tell you my man, I was occasionally sad even in the days when I believed that God himself lov'd me, and who are you, that I should not be so now? The most humane, the kindest, the tenderest of all our sex indeed, for such I am persuaded you are, but still a poor mortal like myself, whom neither the winds nor the stars will obey, nor the humours that influence my spirit. Be content therefore, let me sigh and groan, but always be sure that I love you.

You will be well assured that I should not have indulged myself in this rhapsody about myself and my melancholy, had my present mood been of that complexion, or had not our poor Mary seem'd still to advance in her recovery. So in fact she does, and has perform'd several little feats to day such as either she could not perform at all, or very feebly while you were with us.—We received your basket of medicine, and your Mary's kind remembrancer this afternoon in perfect safety. For the former we thank both you and our dear Physician with all our hearts, and are particularly sensible of his kindness in getting the medicines made by his own Chemist. You have been a fortunate man indeed to meet with both a physician and a parson° so similar to yourself. May you long enjoy *them*, and may they long enjoy *you*! I can wish neither of you much greater felicity. Hannah is charm'd with the Hat, remembers the kind Donor° of it with much affection, and returns her many thanks.

But it is time that I should advert to your letter. Your note to the Chancellor, which I thank your Mary for copying, is so proper that nothing could be better. I observe a circumstance in it that gives me hope of the success of your attempt to enter his castle at least, if you prevail no farther. I mean the commission to which you allude, and which you have been entrusted to execute for his Lordship and his Daughter. This cannot fail I think to interest him,° whatever it may be, and he will wish of course to see you for that, if for no other reason.

Friday Morning

Thus far I proceeded last night, for Mary having risen early went early to bed, and left me to amuse myself with you 'till suppertime. She has had a good night and is cheerful this morning, but I shall be able to give a better account of her when I have seen her in the study.—At this last word I received a summons to her chamber. I found that she had just been rubb'd with the embrocation and she told me that she felt herself in a glow after it. Her speech is in its best order at present, distinct and clear, but will probably thicken a little as the day goes on. She will rise presently and I will tell you more of her when she does.

Mrs. Socket call'd on me yesterday and sat with me about a quarter of an hour. She sends her love to her son and expresses herself completely happy in his situation. I assur'd her she had all the reason in the world to be so and she believed me.

If you call'd at my Cousin's on Thursday evening you saw perhaps my moody letter to her written on Wednesday. Two very sleepless nights had weaken'd our patient a little and dishearten'd me. But all that mischief is now repair'd again. I shall be glad if you have seen Johnny as I call him, my Norfolk Cousin; he is a sweet lad but as shy as a bird. It costs him always 2 or 3 days to open his mouth before a stranger, but when he does, he is sure to please by the innocent cheerfulness of his conversation. His sister too is one of my idols for the resemblance she bears to my mother.

I wish'd you to fall in love with my Cousin of Norfolk Street as much as she has fallen in love with you. She only regrets that she must lose you and that you are going to hide yourself in Sussex. But my wish it seems is accomplish'd, and as Pistol says, I rejoice therefore.°

I began your fine poem on History° this morning and already perceive that I am reading for my humiliation. To tell you the truth I am become very little in my own eyes, much less than ever I was, since I have known you. This I doubt will do me no good as a poet, but as a man it will do me much, and an humble man is a better thing than a lofty-minded poet.—I shall keep the other side for Mary.

Being bright this morning, I guess the commission°

mention'd in your note to the Chancellor, though last night I had not the wit to discover it.

Shall have no room for Mary at last. I have forgot to tell you till now that at my friend Rose's request I sent him an Introduction to you, and since you do not leave town to day, it is possible that he may find you. I have made I believe a very stiff formal letter on the occasion, but the occasion itself is stiff & formal, and I could not help it.

I have this moment received yours by the Post. Am grieved for your eyes; get into the country as fast as you can or London will blind you. A thousand times obliged to you for thinking of so proper a compliment° to the kind Doctor, and for the excellent 2 stanzas with which you will adorn the present. I am a beast for not preventing you, but Mary and you have all my thoughts, and how should it be otherwise?— —How is it that you contrive to write beautiful verses and to think of ev'ry proper thing in the midst of such a bustle?—You are at this moment with the Chancellor, and Mary is with me. She looks well, is better, and loves you dearly. Adieu my brother.

WC.

To Harriot Hesketh

Weston Underwood | July 21. 1792

My Dearest Coz—

I am crazed with having much to do and doing nothing. Every thing with me has fallen into arrear to such a degree that I almost despair of being able by the utmost industry to redeem the time that I have lost. With difficulty it is that I can steal even now a moment to address a few lines to thee. They must be as few as I can make them. Briefly therefore I say thus—

My Pourtrait° is nearly finish'd. An excellent one in my mind and in the opinion of all who see it, both for drawing and likeness. It will be completed I believe on Monday. I shall keep it a short time after Abbot is gone that my 2 or 3 friends in this neighbourhood may be gratified with a sight of it, and shall then send it to his house in Caroline Street Bloomsbury, where it will remain some time. Should it be your wish to view it, you will then have an opportunity, and trust me I think it will afford you as much pleasure, nay perhaps even more, than a sight of the Original myself; for you will see it with this thought in your mind, that whether I live or die, while this picture subsists my charming lineaments and proportions can never be forgotten.

We have not even yet determined absolutely on our journey to Eartham, but shall I believe in 2 or 3 days decide in favour of it. Hayley interests himself so much in it, and I am persuaded that it bids fair to do us both so much good, that I am sincerely desirous of going. A thousand Lions, monsters and giants are in the way, but perhaps they will all vanish if I have but the courage to face them. Mrs. Unwin, whose weakness might justify her fears, has none. Her trust in the Providence of God makes her calm on all occasions.

Should Anonymous have consign'd his half year's remittance to your hands and my namesake William his annual one,° thou canst not do better than send them, for I hear a flying rumour that travelling is costly, and that consequently money will be wanted.—This moment I receive yours. Many thanks for it and for the Draft contain'd in it.

I learn'd lately from Sephus that you are not very well, and know you too well not to know that you hide from me the worst half of your malady let it be what it may. God preserve thee, restore thy health and give us a comfortable meeting once more in the winter.

Sam's wife° shall be paid. Mrs. Unwin sends her best Love. Johnny goes to Eartham, but not with us, because Sam will be more useful by the way. Johnny therefore and Nanny Roberts will jog thither in the stage. You shall hear from me as soon as I can after my arrival.

Adieu—must go to be painted—can't add another syllable except that I am ever Thine

Wm Cowper.

My dear Johnny sends his affectionate Compliments. He goes with us. All in a coach together which Abbot will send us from town. To morrow will be my last sitting, and I verily think the Pourtrait, exclusive of the likeness which is the closest imaginable, one of the best I ever saw. You will see by this P.S. that the journey is already determined on—Would to heaven that you could join us!

To William Hayley

Weston-Underwood | July 22. 1792

This important affair, my dear Brother, is at last decided, and we are coming. Wednesday se'nnight, if nothing occur to make a later day necessary, is the day fixt for our journey. Two days it will certainly cost us, and it is not possible to say 'till we make the trial, that it will not cost us a third. This is unpleasant, because it leaves you at an uncertainty when to look for us and will therefore worry your spirits; but there is no remedy. Our rate of travelling must depend on Mary's ability to bear it.—How foolish I am to represent a thing as uncertain which in fact ascertains itself! I forgot that our mode of travelling will occupy three days unavoidably, for we shall come in a coach. Abbot finishes my picture tomorrow, on Wednesday he returns to town, and is commission'd to order one down for us with your steeds to draw it.

Hollow pamper'd jades of Asia°
That cannot go but forty miles a day.

Send us our route,° for I am as ignorant of it almost as if I were in a strange country. We shall reach St. Albans I suppose the first day. Say where we must finish our second day's journey and at what Inn we may best repose? As to the end of the third day, we know where that will find us—viz in the arms and under the roof of our beloved Hayley. General Cowper having heard a rumour of this intended migration desires to meet me on the road, that we may once more see each other. He lives at Ham near Kingston. Shall we go through Kingston, or near it? for I should wish to give him as little trouble as possible, though he offers very kindly to come as far as Barnet for that purpose. Nor must I forget Carwardine, who so kindly desired to be inform'd what way

we should go. On what point of the road will it be easiest to
him to find us? On all these subjects you must be my oracle.—
My friend and brother we shall overwhelm you with our
numbers; this is all the trouble that I have left. My Johnny of
Norfolk, happy in the thought of accompanying us, would be
broken-hearted to be left behind. Sam and Sam's wife also will
be part of your burthen, but they, being one flesh, will occupy
one bed only. Four beds therefore will serve us all, and fewer
will not. Tell me if you can supply them without miserable
inconvenience, for to distress you would make me miserable,
and I would leave Sam behind though I foresee that he will be
every thing to us upon the road. These are questions that you
must answer by the return of the post, otherwise I shall hardly
have time to give General Cowper and Carwardine sufficient
notice. In the midst of all these solicitudes I laugh to think
what they are made of, and what an important thing it is for
me to travel. Other men steal away from their homes silently
and make no disturbance, but when I move, houses are turn'd
upside down, maids are turn'd out of their beds, and all the
counties through which I pass appear to be in an uproar.
Surrey greets me by the mouth of the General, and Essex by
that of Carwardine. How strange does all this seem to a man
who has seen no bustle and made none for 20 years together!

You already perceive that, escorted as we shall be, there is
no need to trouble your Mary to assist mine. She gives her
love to you and thanks you for the offer. God bless you my
dear brother and afford us the blessing of a happy meeting! I
have had this week past a rheumatism in my back, commonly
call'd the lumbago, which has sometimes almost crippled me.
I am now better, but feel that this writing posture encreases
my pain again. Adieu therefore. With Johnny's best bow and
Mary's best love to you and yours, I remain | Your
affectionate

                                        Wm Cowper.

Hannah is mending fast, sends her duty and goes to her school
on Wednesday.

To Harriot Hesketh

[During his first visit to Weston in May 1792, Hayley invited Cowper and Mrs Unwin to Eartham. After much debate, Cowper determined on 20 July to accept the offer. He, Mrs Unwin, John Johnson, Sam and Nanny Roberts, and Beau left Weston on 1 Aug. and reached Hayley on the 3rd. They began their return on 17 Sept., arriving back at Weston on the 19th.]

Eartham Augt. 11. 1792

My dearest Coz,

I would gladly have devoted to you my first hour after breakfast, while my mind was fresh and unfatigued with study, but Hayley who is never so happy as when he can render me some service, insisted on my passing the time with him till eleven o'clock, in the revisal of my Miltonic labours. Now therefore I can give you nothing but the vapid lees of an imagination already jaded, and in no condition to describe what I felt in this memorable journey. Much anxiety I felt before it, and much in the course of it, fearful of its effects on Mrs. Unwin, and that she would want strength to endure the fatigue of it. We reach'd Barnet on the Evening of the first day, where, though she boasted herself unwearied, I suffer'd inconceivable dejection on her account, finding her power of articulation and even her voice almost entirely lost through weariness, and the Inn so noisy that she seem'd to have no chance to sleep. The next morning however I found her sufficiently refresh'd, and with Mr. Rose added to our party who had kindly walk'd from London the Evening before to meet us, we began our second day's journey. I pass'd through London, as he I suppose has told you, less affected by the scene than I had hoped I should be. Him we dropp'd at the Surrey end of Westminster bridge, and proceeded to Kingston. There, as you have learn'd, we met the good General, whom we found already at the Sun expecting us. So alter'd indeed was he, that neither his face, his person, nor the sound of his voice announced him to me, who had not seen him almost 30 years. But I guess'd him, or rather found him out by inference, and hasting to embrace him, soon learn'd that I was not mistaken. We pass'd somewhat more than an hour together when he went home to dinner, having first made me promise, if possible, to dine with him on my return. From Kingston we proceeded to Ripley, where if we did not find the most splendid of all receptacles for travellers, we found at least, what was more valuable to us, tolerable chambers and a silent house. Mrs. Unwin slept better than the preceding night, and when she rose appear'd so well and in such good spirits that I had no fears left respecting her ability to perform the remainder of the journey. Accordingly she perform'd it well, and between nine and ten, having pass'd some of the Sussex hills by moon-light with more terrour to myself than her, we arrived safe at the gate of our beloved Hayley. Here we inhabit a paradise. His pleasure ground is a hill about 3 quarters of a mile in circuit, beautiful beyond my power or opportunity to describe at present, and commanding a noble view of both sea and land from the summit. Mrs. Unwin, I thank God, seems already somewhat the better for the journey, the fine air and the exercise that this delightful place affords her. She has slept almost twice as much ev'ry night since we came, as she did at Weston, and has had twice the appetite, for at Weston she has for some time hardly eaten enough to sustain her. Her amendment in short has been such that I could not expect a single week to do more for her even at Eartham, and as to myself, I was never better.—So much for our journey, and such consequences of it as we have at present experienced.

I have fill'd my paper and said nothing in answer to yours.—Yet not so, for I have told you on recollection what you chiefly desired to know. I can at present only add that you are every day affectionately remember'd by us all, and ev'ry day wish'd for, and that Hayley who always speaks of you with delight, challenged me yesterday to drink your health in a bumper, which was done accordingly. Johnny, once Sir John Croydon,° but now better known by the title of the Reverend Doctor Pelbarto,° desires to live always in your remembrance and good opinion, as does our host the benevolent Hayley, and Mrs. Unwin who has just join'd me in the Library, sends her best love. How long we shall stay I know not, but I already see that to depart will be an affair of some difficulty.—

Adieu, my Dear, I am | Ever thine
Wm Cowper.

To Harriot Hesketh

Eartham. Sund. Augt. 26. 1792

I know not how it is my dearest Coz, but in a new scene, and surrounded by strange objects I find my powers of thinking dissipated to a degree that makes it difficult to me even to write a letter, and even a letter to you. But such a letter as I can, I will, and have the fairer chance to succeed this morning, Hayley and Romney and Hayley's son and Beau being all gone to the sea together for bathing. The sea, you must know is nine miles off, so that unless stupidity prevent, I shall have opportunity to write not only to you but to poor Hurdis also, who is broken-hearted for the loss of his favorite sister lately dead,° and whose letter giving an account of it, and which I received yesterday, drew tears from the eyes of all our party. My only comfort respecting even yourself is that you write in good spirits and assure me that you are in a state of recovery, otherwise I should mourn not only for Hurdis but for myself, lest a certain event should reduce me, and in a short time too, to a situation as distressing as his; for though Nature design'd you only for my Cousin, you have had a sister's place in my affections ever since I knew you. The reason is I suppose, that having no sister the daughter of my own mother, I thought it proper to have one the daughter of *yours*. Certain it is that I can by no means afford to lose you, and that unless you will be upon honour with me to give me always a true account of yourself, at least when we are not together, I shall always be unhappy, because always suspicious that you deceive me.

Now for ourselves. I am, without the least dissimulation, in perfect health. My spirits are about as good as you have ever seen them, and if encrease of appetite and a double portion of sleep be advantages, such are the advantages that I have received from this migration. As to that gloominess of mind which I have had these 20 years, it cleaves to me even here, and could I be translated to paradise, unless I left my body behind me, would cleave to me there also. It is my companion for life and nothing will ever divorce us. So much for myself— Mrs. Unwin is evidently the better for her jaunt, though by no means as well as she was before this last attack, still wanting help when she would rise from her seat and a support in walking, neither can she use her knitting-needles, nor read with ease, or long together. But she is able to use more exercise than she could at home, and moves with rather a less tottering step. God knows what he designs for me, but when I see those who are dearer to me than myself, distemper'd and enfeebled, and myself as strong in the days of my youth, I am shock'd to my very heart and tremble for the solitude in which a few years may place me. I wish her and you to die before me indeed, but not till I am more likely to follow you immediately. Enough of this.

Charlotte Smith's last novel° I have not read, therefore can say nothing of its merits, but it seems to have the fate of all writings tinged with Politics, to be censured or commended according to the political opinions of her readers. I advise you however to read it, and the rather because I know that she has bestow'd in it high encomiums on the British constitution. She will soon publish another which I believe you will find excellently written, and not exceptionable on the same account.

Romney has drawn me in crayons,° and in the opinion of all here, with his best hand and with the most exact resemblance possible.—But I must remember that I am near the end of my paper.

The 17th. of September is the day on which I intend to leave Eartham. We shall then have been six weeks resident here, a holiday-time long enough for a man who has much to do, and who can do nothing except at home.

I have made both Hayley and Romney acquainted with the flattering things you say of them, and they are at least as much flatter'd by them as wise men ought to be.—Each presents his best thanks and Compliments. Hayley, who knows you, never mentions you but with admiration—.And now farewell my Dearest Coz, let me soon hear from you, and if it please God have a favorable account of you. Tell me too, that soon after our return to Weston, we shall have the happiness to see you there. Farewell—with Mrs. U.'s sincere and affectionate best wishes I remain ever thine

Wm Cowper.

P.S. Hayley, whose love for me seems to be truly that of a brother, has given me his picture drawn by Romney about 15 years ago. An admirable likeness,° and which you will rejoice the more to see, because it will effectually displace a certain Hob-owchin° that you wot of.

To William Hayley

Weston Thursday | Sepr. 21. 1792.°

My Dear Hayley—
   Chaos himself, even the Chaos of Milton, is not surrounded with more confusion nor has a mind more completely in a hubbub than I experience at the present moment. At our first arrival after long absence, we find a hundred orders to servants necessary, a thousand things to be restored to their proper places, and an endless variety of minutiæ to be adjusted, which though individually of little importance, are most momentous in the aggregate. In these circumstances I find myself so indisposed to writing, that, save to yourself only, I would on no account attempt it. But to you I will give such a recital as I can of all that has pass'd since I sent you that short note from Kingston, knowing that if it be a perplext recital, you will consider the cause and pardon it.°
   I will begin with a remark in which I am inclined to think you will agree with me; that there is sometimes more true Heroism passing in a corner and on occasions that make no noise in the world, than has often been exercised by those whom that world esteems her greatest Heroes and on occasions the most illustrious. I hope so at least—for all the Heroism I have to boast, and all the opportunities I have of displaying any, are of a private nature. After writing that note, I immediately began to prepare myself for my appointed visit to Ham; but the struggles that I had with my own spirit, labouring as I did under the most dreadful dejection, are never to be told. I would have given the world to have been excused, sensible that I was unfit for company, and fearing lest I should unavoidably discover that unfitness by a countenance too faithful to my feelings. I went however, and

carried my point against myself, assuming a cheerful aspect and behaving cheerfully, with a heart riven asunder. I had reasons for all this anxiety which I cannot relate now, and you would hardly deem me in my senses if you knew them. The visit however pass'd off well, and we return'd in the dark to Kingston; I with a lighter heart than I had known since my departure from Eartham, and Mary too; for she had suffer'd hardly less than myself, and chiefly on my account. That night we rested well in our Inn, and at 20 minutes after eight next morning set off for London. Exactly at 10 we reach'd Mr. Rose's door, and as *we* drove up to it one way, the chaises he had order'd to meet us, drove up to it the other. We drank a dish of chocolate with him which cost us about 20 minutes, and proceeded, Mr. Rose riding bodkin with us as far as St. Albans where his mother is, and Johnny riding ditto with the servants. From this time forth we met with no impediment; at every Inn we found horses and chaises as ready as if they had been provided, and saving another downfall of one of our servants' horses, which however was attended with no mischief, met with nothing worth recording. In the dark, and in a storm, and at eight at night we found ourselves at our own back door. Mrs. Unwin was very near slipping out of the chair in which she was taken from the chaise, but at last was landed safe.

We have all had a good night and are all well this morning, Johnny having recover'd from a violent cholic which tormented him all the way from Wooburn to Weston. God bless you my Dearest brother! Mrs. Unwin joins me in most affectionate remembrances to yourself and our dearest Tom, and Johnny sends a thousand thanks for all your kindness. It grieved me much to learn from him, that when we parted from you at the end of the wood, you had great uneasiness in your Hip and talk'd of going to bed at your return. Let me hear from you and tell me that you are better.

Ever yours
Wm Cowper.

Socket's Letter is deliver'd and his parents are well.°

To Samuel Teedon

Friday Mor. [26 October 1792]

Dear Sir—

I am not well, but far from being so. I wake almost constantly under the influence of a nervous fever, by which my spirits are affected to such a degree that the oppression is almost insupportable. Since I wrote last I have been plunged in Deeps unvisited, I am convinced, by any human soul but mine, and though the day in its progress bears away with it some part of this melancholy, I am never cheerful because I can never hope, and am so bounded in my prospects, that to look forward to another year to me seems madness.

In this state of mind how can I write? It is in vain to attempt it. I have neither spirits for it, as I have often said, nor leisure.—Yet vain as I know the attempt must prove, I purpose in a few days to renew it.

Mrs. Unwin is as well as when I wrote last, but, like myself, dejected. Dejected both on my account and on her own. Unable to amuse herself either with work or reading, she looks forward to a new day with despondence, weary of it before it begins, and longing for the return of night.

Thus it is with us both. If I endeavour to pray, I get my answer in a double portion of misery. My petitions therefore are reduced to three words, and those not very often repeated—God have Mercy!

Adieu—Yours
Wm Cowper

To Samuel Teedon

[16–17 November 1792]

Dear Sir—

To avoid constant repetition of the same complaints which is tiresome even to myself, I shall give you my intelligence, I believe, for the future in the form of a journal. On the night of Tuesday the 13th. I enter'd on the practise recommended by you, and used the Evening Collect,° paraphrasing it a little and instead of *perils* and *dangers* which are the same thing, praying to be deliver'd from all perils and *terrours*. That night my sleep was frequently broken, but not much disturb'd. In the morning I used the proper Collect, omitting to the best of my remembrance the word *safely*, because it seems to me that whosoever has lost all his evidences and all his hopes, cannot justly be said to have been brought *safely* on. Wednesday was a day of no particular mark, I was only stupid and melancholy as I always am. Wednesday night was much like the night preceding, and Thursday much such another day as Wednesday.

Friday Novr. 16.—I have had a terrible night—such a one as I believe I may say God knows no man ever had. Dream'd that in a state of the most insupportable misery I look'd through the window of a strange room being all alone, and saw preparations making for my execution. That it was but about 4 days distant, and that then I was destined to suffer everlasting martyrdom in the fire, my body being prepared for the purpose and my dissolution made a thing impossible. Rose overwhelm'd with infinite despair, and came down into the study execrating the day when I was born with inexpressible bitterness. And while I write this, I repeat those execrations, in my very soul persuaded that I shall perish miserably and as no man ever did. Every thing is, and for 20 years has been, lawful to the Enemy against *me*.

Such was Friday morning, and the rest of the day, especially the Evening, unfit for description.

Saturday 17.—Had much less sleep than usual, but the sleep I had was quiet.—Terrour turns to wrath, wrath promotes unadvised speech, unadvised speech brings guilt, and guilt terrour again. In this circle I have moved, and all my waking hours in the night and my rising in the morning have been miserable accordingly. It is now past Ten in the forenoon and I seem settling into a calm habitual melancholy, which is the happiest frame of mind I ever know.

To Samuel Teedon

Jan. 2. 1793°

Dear Sir—

It is with great unwillingness that I write, knowing that I *can* say nothing but what will distress you. I despair of every thing, and my despair is perfect, because it is founded on a persuasion that there is no effectual help for me, even in God.

From 4 this morning till after 7 I lay meditating terrour, such terrours as no language can express, and as no heart I am sure but mine ever knew. My very fingers' ends tingled with it, as indeed they often do. I then slept, and dream'd a long dream, in which I told Mrs. U. with many tears that my salvation is impossible for the reasons given above. I recapitulated in the most impassion'd accent and manner, the unexampled severity of God's dealings with me in the course of the last 20 years, especially in the year 73 and again in 86, and concluded all with observing that I *must* infallibly perish, and that the Scriptures which speak of the insufficiency of Man to save himself, can never be understood *unless* I perish.

I then made a sudden transition in my dream to one of the public streets in London, where I was met by a dray; the fore horse of the team came full against me, and in violent anger, I Damn'd the Drayman for it.

Such are my nocturnal experiences, and my daily ones are little better.—I know that I have much fever, but it is a fever for which there is no cure, and is as much the afflictive hand of God upon me, as any other circumstance of my distress.

I thank you for your two last. Delay is no Denial indeed, but in extremities such as mine it is very severe and hard to bear.

I am, Dear Sir—Yours sincerely

Wm C.

To William Hayley

Weston Feb. 24. 1793

My dear Hayley,

Your letter, so full of kindness and so exactly in unison with my own feelings for you, should have had, as it deserved to have, an earlier answer, had I not been perpetually tormented with inflamed eyes, which are a sad hindrance to me in every thing. But to make amends, if I do not send you an early answer, I send you at least a speedy one, being obliged to write as fast as my pen can trot, that I may shorten the time of poring upon paper as much as possible. Homer too has been another hindrance, for always when I can see, which is only during about 2 hours in a morning and not at all by candle-light, I devote myself to Him, being in haste to send him a second time to the Press, that nothing may stand in the way of Milton. By the way, where are my Dear Tom's remarks° which I long to have, and must have soon or they will come too late?

Oh you rogue! what would you give to have such a dream about Milton as I had about a week since? I dream'd that being in a house in the city and with much company, looking toward the lower end of the room from the upper end of it, I descried a figure which I immediately knew to be Milton's. He was very gravely but very neatly attired in the fashion of his day, and had a countenance which fill'd me with those feelings that an affectionate child has for a beloved father. Such for instance as Tom has for you. My first thought was wonder where he could have been conceal'd so many years, my second a transport of joy to find him still alive, my third, another transport to find myself in his company, and my fourth a resolution to accost him. I did so, and he received me with a complacence in which I saw equal sweetness and dignity. I spoke of his Paradise Lost as every man must who is worthy to speak of it at all, and told him a long story of the manner in which it affected me when I first discover'd it, being at that time a school-boy. He answer'd me by a smile and a gentle inclination of his head. I told him we had poets in *our* days, and no mean ones, and that I was myself intimate with the best of them. He replied—I know Mr. Hayley very well by his writings. He then grasp'd my hand affectionately and with a smile that charm'd me said—Well—you, for your part, will do well also. At last recollecting his great age, for I understood him to be about 200 years old, I fear'd that I might fatigue him by much talking and took my leave, and he took his with an air of the most perfect good-breeding. His person, his features, his dress, his manner, were all so perfectly character- istic, that I am persuaded an apparition of him could not represent him more completely.—This may truly be said to have been one of the dreams of Pindus,° may it not?

How truly I rejoice that you have recover'd Guy!° That man won my heart the moment I saw him, give my love to him and tell him I am truly glad he is alive again.

There is much sweetness in those lines° from the Sonneteer of Avon, and not a little in Dear Tom's. An earnest, I trust, of good things to come.

My friend Hurdis is encouraged to stand for the Poetry- professorship at Oxford,° a vacancy being expected to happen soon. Can you do him any service? I know if you can you will.—With Mary's kind love, I must now conclude myself, my dear brother, ever Yours

Lippus.°

To Samuel Teedon

April 26. 1793

Dear Sir—

Your experiences have a difference in them. If you are cast down, you are comforted and raised again. But as for mine, they proceed in one dull train, unvaried, unless sometimes by darker shades than usual. Thus it has happen'd to me since I saw you. During two days I rejected entirely all your notices, and if I have since exercised some little degree of belief in them, it has not been on account of the smallest encourage- ment, for I have received none; but, perhaps, because the temptation to cast them away is abated.

I have nothing farther to add respecting my state of mind which hardly ever affords me a new subject of any thing worth communicating. It seems strange however that the prayers and promises of some years should remain still so entirely unanswered and unaccomplished.

We are much as usual in our health, and with our united thanks for your spiritual services | I remain, Dear Sir—Yours sincerely

Wm Cowper.

To John Johnson

Weston Undd. | Novr. 30. 1793.

My Dearest Johnny,

That I may begin my Sabbath pleasantly at least, though not so piously as yourself, I begin it with a letter to you. To pay a debt that has been long owing cannot be a bad deed on any day. Time was when on Sabbath mornings in winter I rose before day, and by the light of a lanthorn trudged with Mrs. Unwin, often through snow and rain, to a prayer-meeting at the Great House,° as they call it, near the Church at Olney. There I always found assembled 40 or 50 poor folks who preferred a glimpse of the light of God's countenance and favour to the comforts of a warm bed, or to any comforts that the world could afford them; and there I have often, myself, partaken that blessing with them. If I live a different life now, it is not because I have found, or think that I have found a better way of living, but because for reasons too long and too unpleasant to be enumerated here, I have been constrained to do so. God knows with how much sorrow and misery to myself, on account of the loss of his presence which is better than life. I will not tell you how I lost it, and probably I never shall, and that merely because it would do you no good to know it, the story being absolutely incredible; but I know the truth of it, and have for 20 years suffered things not to be expressed, in consequence. The instruction however to be collected from it I will give you, and it is this: never shut your eyes against a known duty, nor close your ears to an express providential call, however uncommon and even unprecedented it may be, and however difficult the service that it enjoins.

Thus, my dear Johnny, without intending it when I began, I have preach'd to you, who are now preparing to preach to others. God help you to profit by the lesson, which I am sure is a good one, and heal the wounds that I have incurr'd and long time languish'd under, because I neglected it! Amen—.

It is of no consequence that you had not time to see Johnson, for Hayley has seen him, and conferred with him much to my satisfaction. Diverse matters, all very agreeable to me, were the subjects of it, but the most agreeable of all, in the result of it, was this new edition of Milton; on which subject I learn that the publication is postponed on account of the war,° which leaves the world no leisure for literary amusements; Johnson accordingly thinks it would be too hazardous to send forth so expensive a work at present. I have therefore leisure, when Homer is finished, which will soon be the case, instead of acting the dull part of a commentator, to perform the poet's part, far pleasanter and more adapted to my natural propensity. You will not be displeased to learn that Lawrance's sketch of me is to be engraved by Bartolozzi,° though for private use only; and that a new edition of my poems with embellishments by Lawrance is in contemplation.°

You do kindly and like yourself to gratify your sister's preference of landed honours° to vile cash, though your compliance is certainly an expensive one. Her pride in this instance is of a kind that I have no quarrel with.

Adieu—We are as well as usual. Lady Hesketh is here. Hers and Mrs. Unwin's best love attend you.

Yours ever
Wm Cowper.

Give my love to your sister, whose likeness to my mother insures to her always my tenderest attachment—and my love to all friends.

I hope you have by this time heard from Mr. Newton.

I have nothing more to do with Homer now but to go over the last book of the Iliad with Clarke's notes,° to write a new preface, and to transcribe the alterations.

To Samuel Teedon

Jan: 10. 1794.

Dear Sir—

I have suffer'd much since I wrote last. More than tongue can tell. My despair and terrour have been equal to, if not greater than any I felt in the dreadful time of my first convictions, and the reasons I had for them, seem to have been not less important.

While I thought on my last note to you, in which I express'd my apprehensions that I had little to expect from any promises given you in my favour, because no terms are to be kept with me whom God I fear considers as a traytor—these words were distinctly spoken to me—

You understand me right, William.

Again, I dream'd that in our parlour at Olney my thoughts were suddenly carried to the offence of which I have in time past inform'd you, and from which originated all my misery twenty years since, when my soul seem'd to be taken as it were out of me and carried up to heaven, though I saw nothing nor heard any voice, where it was for a few seconds fill'd with infinite despair and horror, after which I awoke and heard these words.

The dreadful visit is paid.

I tremble, while I write, at the recollection of these things, and lest they should make you despair of me as much as I of myself. Whatever be the effect, write nothing that may distress poor Mrs. Unwin who has already suffer'd too much for my sake, and more than her health could bear.

Yours sincerely
Wm Cowper.

To Harriot Hesketh

[There are fifteen letters extant from the Norfolk years, eleven of which are printed here. Their unrelenting grimness stands in marked contrast to the buoyant optimism of the earliest surviving letter of Cowper's, that to Walter Bagot of 12 Mar. 1749/50.]

Mundesley,° near North Walsham,° Aug. 27, 1795.

Hopeless as ever, and chiefly to gratify myself by once more setting pen to paper, I address a very few lines to one whom it would be a comfort to me to gratify as much by sending them. The most forlorn of beings I tread a shore under the burthen of infinite despair, that I once trod all cheerfulness and joy. I view every vessel that approaches the coast with an eye of jealousy and fear, lest it arrive with a commission to seize me. But my insensibility, which you say is a mystery to you, because it seems incompatible with such fear, has the effect of courage, and enables me to go forth, as if on purpose to place myself in the way of danger. The cliff is here of a height that it is terrible to look down from; and yesterday evening, by moonlight, I passed sometimes within a foot of the edge of it, from which to have fallen would probably have been to be dashed in pieces. But though to have been dashed in pieces would perhaps have been best for me, I shrunk from the precipice, and am waiting to be dashed in pieces by other means. At two miles' distance on the coast is a solitary pillar of rock, that the crumbling cliff has left at the high water-mark. I have visited it twice, and have found it an emblem of myself. Torn from my natural connexions, I stand alone and expect the storm that shall displace me.

I have no expectation that I shall ever see you more, though Samuel assures me that I shall visit Weston again, and that you will meet me there. My terrors, when I left it, would not permit me to say—Farewell for ever—which now I do; wishing, but vainly wishing to see you yet once more, and equally wishing that I could now as confidently, and as warmly as once I could, subscribe myself affectionately yours; but every feeling that would warrant the doing it, has, as you too well know, long since forsaken the bosom of

W.C.

Mr. Johnson is gone to North Walsham, and knows not that I write.

Mrs. Unwin sends her affectionate respects and compliments.

To Harriot Hesketh

[5 September 1795]

Mr. Johnson is again absent; gone to Mattishall,° a circumstance to which I am indebted for an opportunity to answer your letter as soon almost as I have received it. Were he present, I feel that I could not do it.—You say it gives you pleasure to hear from me, and I resolve to forget for a moment my conviction that it is impossible for me to give pleasure to any body. You have heard much from my lips that I am sure has given you none; if what comes from my pen be less unpalatable, none has therefore so strong a claim to it as yourself.

My walks on the sea-shore have been paid for by swelled and inflamed eyelids, and I now recollect that such was always the condition of mine in the same situation. A natural effect I suppose, at least upon eyelids so subject to disorder as mine, of the salt spray and cold winds, which on the coast are hardly ever less than violent. I now therefore abandon my favourite walk, and wander in lanes and under hedges. As heavy a price I have paid for a long journey, performed on foot to a place called Hazeborough.° That day was indeed a day spent in walking. I was much averse to the journey, both on account of the distance and the uncertainty of what I should find there; but Mr. Johnson insisted. We set out accordingly, and I was almost ready to sink with fatigue long before we reached the place of our destination. The only inn was full of company; but my companion having an opportunity to borrow a lodging for an hour or two, he did so, and thither we retired. We learned on enquiry, that the place is eight miles distant from this, and though, by the help of a guide, we shortened it about a mile in our return, the length of the way occasioned me a fever, which I have had now these four days, and perhaps shall not be rid of in four more; perhaps never.

Mr. J. and Samuel, after dinner, visited the light-house.° A gratification which would have been none to me for several reasons, but especially because I found no need to add to the number of steps I had to take before I should find myself at home again. I learned however from them that it is a curious structure. The building is circular, but the stairs are not so, flight above flight, with a commodious landing at every twentieth stair, they ascend to the height of four stories; and there is a spacious and handsome apartment at every landing. The light is given by the patent lamp, of which there are two ranges: six lamps in the upper range, and five in the lower; both ranges, as you may suppose, at the top of the house. Each lamp has a broad silver reflector behind it. The present occupant° was once commander of a large merchant-man, but, having chastised a boy of his crew with too much severity, was displaced and consequently ruined. He had, however, a friend in the Trinity-House,° who, soon after this was built, asked him if he would accept the charge of it; and the cashiered captain, judging it better to be such a lamp-lighter than to starve, very readily and very wisely closed with the offer. He has only the trouble of scouring the silver plates every day, and of rising every night at twelve to trim the lamps, for which he has a competent salary, (Samuel forgets the amount of it,) and he and his family a pleasant and comfortable abode.

I have said as little of myself as I could, that my letter might be more worth the postage. My next will perhaps be less worth it, should any next ensue; for I meet with little variety, and shall not be very willing to travel fifteen miles on foot again, to find it. I have seen no fish since I came here, except a dead sprat upon the sands, and one piece of cod, from Norwich, too stale to be eaten. Adieu.

W.C.

To Harriot Hesketh

Jan. 22, 1796.

I little thought ever to have addressed you by letter more. I have become daily and hourly worse, ever since I left Mundsley: there I had something like a gleam of hope allowed me, that possibly my life might be granted me for a longer time than I had been used to suppose, though only on the dreadful terms of accumulating future misery on myself, and for no other reason; but even that hope has long since forsaken me, and I now consider this letter as the warrant of my own dreadful end; as the fulfilment of a word heard in better days, at least six and twenty years ago. A word which to have understood at the time when it reached me, would have been, at least might have been, a happiness indeed to me; but my cruel destiny denied me the privilege of understanding any thing that, in the horrible moment that came winged with my immediate destruction, might have served to aid me. You know my story far better than I am able to relate it. Infinite despair is a sad prompter. I expect that in six days' time, at the latest, I shall no longer foresee, but feel the accomplishment of all my fears. Oh, lot of unexampled misery incurred in a moment! Oh wretch! to whom death and life are alike impossible! Most miserable at present in this, that being thus miserable I have my senses continued to me, only that I may look forward to the worst. It is certain, at least, that I have them for no other purpose, and but very imperfectly even for this. My thoughts are like loose and dry sand, which the closer it is grasped slips the sooner away. Mr. Johnson reads to me, but I lose every other sentence through the inevitable wanderings of my mind, and experience, as I have these two years, the same shattered mode of thinking on every subject, and on all occasions. If I seem to write with more connexion, it is only because the gaps do not appear.

Adieu.—I shall not be here to receive your answer, neither shall I ever see you more. Such is the expectation of the most desperate and the most miserable of all beings.

W. C.

To Harriot Hesketh

February 19, 1796.

Could I address you as I used to do, with what delight should I begin this letter! But that delight, and every other sensation of the kind, has long since forsaken me for ever. The consequence is, that I neither know for what cause I write, nor of what materials to compose what shall be written; my groans, could they be expressed here, would presently fill the paper. I write, however, at the instance of Mr. Johnson, and, as I always think, so always on the last occasion more assuredly than on any of the former, for the very last time. He, I know, enquired in a letter he lately sent you, when we might expect you here. Whatever day you name in your reply, will be a day that I shall never see; nor have I even the hope, unless it come to-morrow, that your reply itself will reach this place before I am taken from it. The uncertainty is dreadful, and all remedy for it impracticable. But why tell you what I think of myself, of my present condition, and of the means employed to reduce me to it? My thoughts on all these subjects are too well known to you to need any recital here. All my themes of misery may be summed in one word. He who made me, regrets that ever he did. Many years have passed since I learned this terrible truth from Himself, and the interval has been spent accordingly. Adieu—I shall write to you no more. I am promised months of continuance here, and should be somewhat less a wretch in my present feelings, could I credit the promise, but effectual care is taken that I shall not. The night contradicts the day, and I go down the torrent of time into the gulf that I have expected to plunge into so long. A few hours remain, but among those few not one is found, a part of which I shall ever employ in writing to you again. Once more therefore adieu—and adieu to the pen for ever. I suppress a thousand agonies to add only

W. C.

Mr Johnson says he shall expect me to resume the pen and my former employments on Tuesday se'nnight. But what I have written here, on my reperusal of it, convinces me, as it may him, that it will be in vain. Some other dreadful thing will happen to me, and not the desirable one announced.

To Harriot Hesketh

[30 May 1796]

Obliged to write, but more disqualified for it than ever, I once again address you in the stile of misery and the deepest despair. One thing and only one is left me, the wish that I had never existed. Hunted into this terrible state of mind so long since, what now can I look for? What can remain for me to say, but what all my former letters said, and what now I repeat in this? To exist in this place if I might, and not to suffer immediately what I am threaten'd with, oh that I could hope for it! and Oh that there could be pity, or if not that, at least forebearance for the most forlorn of Beings! Farewell.

W.C.

To Harriot Hesketh

[c.15 May 1797]

To you once more, and too well I know why, I am under cruel necessity of writing. Every line that I have ever sent you, I have believed, under the influence of infinite despair, the last that I should ever send. This I know to be so. Whatever be your condition, either now or hereafter, it is heavenly compared with mine even at this moment. It is unnecessary to add that this comes from the most miserable of beings, whom a terrible minute made such.

To William Hayley

[c.19 June 1797]

Ignorant of every thing but my own instant and impending Misery, I know neither what I do when I write nor can do otherwise than write because I am bidden to do so. Perfect Despair the most perfect that ever possess'd any Mind has had Possession of mine you know how long, and knowing that, will not need to be told who writes.

Harriot Hesketh

June 1, 1798.

Under the necessity of addressing you, as I have done in other days, though these are such as seem to myself absolutely to forbid it,—I say as usual, my dear cousin; and having said it, am utterly at a loss to proceed. Mr. Johnson says that we are going on Monday to Mundsley, and bids me to tell you so; but at present he acknowledges himself that it is uncertain whether we go or not, since we cannot know till to-morrow whether there is a place for us there, or the lodgings be already full.

Whether the journey be practicable or otherwise, and wherever I am, my distress is infinite; for I see no possible way of escape, in my circumstances, from miseries such, as I doubt not, will far exceed my most terrible expectations. To wish, therefore, that I had never existed, which has been my only reasonable wish for many years, seems all that remains to one who once dreamed of happiness, but awoke never to dream of it again, and who under the necessity of concluding as he began, subscribes himself your affectionate

Wm. Cowper.

To John Newton

Dear Sir—

Few letters have pass'd between us, and I was never so incapable of writing as now, nor ever so destitute of a subject. It is long since I received your last, to which I have as yet return'd no answer, nor is it possible that, though I write, I should even now reply to it. It contain'd I remember, many kind expressions, which would have encouraged, perhaps, and consoled any other than myself, but I was, even then, out of the reach of all such favourable impressions, and am, at present; less susceptible of them; than at any time since I saw you last. I once little thought to see such days as these, for almost in the moment when they found me, there was not a man in the world who seem'd to himself to have less reason to expect them. This you know, and what can I say of myself that you do not know?

I will only add, therefore, that we are going to the sea-side to morrow, where we are to stay a fortnight, at the end of which time I expect to find a letter from you directed to me at Dereham.

I remain in the mean time | yours as usual,
Wm Cowper.

July 29. 1798.
Mr. Johnson is well and desires to be kindly remember'd to you.

To Harriot Hesketh

Dear Cousin—

You describe delightful scenes, but you describe them to One, who if he even saw them, could receive no delight from them; who has a faint recollection, and so faint as to be like an almost forgotten dream, that once he was susceptible of pleasure from such causes. The country that you have had in prospect,° has been always famed for its beauties, but the wretch who can derive no gratification from a view of nature even under the disadvantage of her most ordinary dress, will have no eyes to admire her in any. In one day, in one moment I should rather have said, she became an universal blank to me, and, though from a different cause, yet with an effect as difficult to remove, as blindness itself. In this country, if there are not mountains, there are hills, if not broad and deep rivers, yet such as are sufficient to embellish a prospect, and, an object still more magnificent than any river, the ocean itself is almost immediately under the window. Why is scenery like this, I had almost said, why is the very scene, which many years since I could not contemplate without rapture, now become, at the best, an insipid wilderness to me? It neighbours nearly and as nearly resembles the scenery of Catfield, but with what different perceptions does it present me! The reason is obvious. My state of mind is a medium through which the beauties of paradise itself could not be communicated with any effect but a painful one.

There is a wide interval between us, which it would be far easier for you, than for me to pass. Yet I should in vain invite you. We shall meet no more. I know not what Mr. Johnson said of me in the long letter he addressed to you yesterday,° but nothing, I am sure, that could make such an event seem probable.

I remain, as usual, | Dear Cousin, | yours

Wm Cowper.

Mundsley, Oct. 13. 1798.

To John Newton

Dereham— | Apr: 11. 1799.

Dear Sir—

Your last letter so long unanswer'd may, and indeed must, have proved sufficiently, that my state of mind is not now more favourable to the purpose of writing than it was when I received it; for had any alteration in that respect taken place, I should certainly have acknowledged it long since, or at whatsoever time the change had happen'd, and should not have waited for the present call upon me to return you my thanks at the same time for the letter and for the book° which you have been so kind as to send me. Mr. Johnson has read it to me. If it afforded me any amusement, or suggested to me any reflections, they were only such as served to imbitter, if possible, still more the present moment, by a sad retrospect to those days when I thought myself secure of an eternity to be spent with the Spirits of such men as He whose life afforded the subject of it. But I was little aware of what I had to expect, and that a storm was at hand which in one terrible moment would darken, and in another still more terrible, blot out that prospect for ever.—Adieu Dear Sir, whom in those days I call'd Dear friend, with feelings that justified the appellation—

I remain yours
Wm Cowper.

[Cowper died quietly at 4. 55 p.m. on Friday 25 Apr. 1800. The physician who attended him said he died of a worn-out constitution. Cowper spoke his final words during Thursday night when refusing a cordial: 'What can it signify?']

NOTES

1 *1749.* Cowper has used Julian or Old Style for this letter; Gregorian or New Style dating was not accepted in England until 2 Sept. 1752.

Morgan's. Almost surely Charles Morgan (b. *c.* 1733) from Llandovery, Carmarthenshire; he was a classmate of Cowper's at Westminster.

Prison. Walter was still a student at Westminster.

Father Antick the Law. 1 Henry IV, i. ii. 59.

Argus. Possibly Pierson Lloyd, the Second or Under Master.

Toby. Chase Price. See Biographical Register.

2 *Chapman's.* The lawyer with whom Cowper resided in Greville Street.

3 *Flummery.* Mere flattery or empty compliment.

Noblest work of God. An Essay on Man, iv. 248.

Chambers. Cowper does not seem to have taken up his chambers until 15 Nov. 1753.

4 *Elfrida.* This play by William Mason (1724–97), the friend and literary executor of Thomas Gray, had been published in Mar.

Brown's Coffee House. Located in Mitre Court, this place was popular with lawyers.

A certain Person. Probably Theadora.

Simile agit in Simile. Like leads on like.

5 *Honest Impudence.* Although his citation does not appear in the play, Cowper is probably referring to Ranger in Benjamin Hoadly's *The Suspicious Husband* (1747), who claims to be an honest, if impudent, person.

6 *the Enclosed.* Probably Cowper's poem, 'Written in a Quarrel'.

8 *prepare.* Cowper is commissioning Hill to have his chambers at the Middle Temple ready upon his return from a visit to his father at Berkhamsted.

Stalking Horse. Someone who covers for someone else.

more comfortable place. Than Berkhamsted.

a Friend or two. Cowper is referring to friends such as Jones Redman (1695?–1763), the physician, Richard Bard Harcourt (1724?–1815), a boyhood friend, and Mary Essington, a landowner in Berkhamsted.

9 *will everlastingly be mine.* Cowper is referring to sentiments expressed in Plutarch's *Life of Cicero.*

mother. Rebecca (d. 1762), Cowper's step-mother, whom John Cowper married on 8 Jan. 1740/1.

10 *Mrs. Essington.* See note p. 8.

11 *Nonsense Club*. A group of seven Old Westminsters who dined together every Thursday. Among the members were James Bensley, Robert Lloyd, George Colman the Elder, Bonnell Thornton, and Cowper.

12 *pip*. Probably diarrhoea.

chincough. Whooping cough.

Madge. A barn owl. The members of the Nonsense Club may have taken the names of animals or birds in a quasi-serious attempt at secrecy.

first minister. At this time, Cowper may have been the Prime Minister or leader of the Club.

Brighthelmston. Brighton.

Iö Triumphe. A Latin and Greek expression of exaltation.

13 *Carr*. Arthur Carr (b. 1727) had attended Trinity College, Dublin, before being admitted to the Middle Temple on 3 Feb. 1746/7; Cowper and Carr had been close friends, had drifted apart when Cowper went to the Inner Temple, but, at the time of the writing of this letter, Carr had become extremely solicitous of his troubled friend.

14 *Servant*. Sam Roberts.

Turkish Spy says. Cowper is referring to Book i, Letter i of the first volume of *Letters Writ by a Turkish Spy* (1684; English trans. 1687), which is attributed to Giovanni Paolo Marana (1642–93).

Fluellin. Henry V, iv. vii. 30.

18 *the Month of October has proved rather unfavourable*. Heavy rains had caused extensive flooding on the south coast.

Parson Adams. Fielding's comical parson in *Joseph Andrews*.

19 *Rousseau's Description of an English Morning. La Nouvelle Héloïse*, v, Letter iii: '. . . nous avons passé aujourd'hui une matinée à l'angloise, réunis et dans le silence, goûtant à la fois le plaisir d'être ensemble et la douceur du recueillement. Que les délices de cet état son connues de peu de gens!'

Wapping and Redriff. A facetious reference to the high proportion of robberies for which these two districts of London were notorious.

Mr. Grey's Stanza. Cowper has slightly misquoted ll. 53–6 of *Elegy Written in a Country Churchyard*.

Eamonson. Probably an oilman, of a firm in Cannon Street, to whom Cowper owed money.

Child's. The merchant bank, which was the first such establishment in London.

poor George's Illness. There is an asterisk in the text of the holograph accompanied by the statement: 'he meant Charles's'. Cowper had thought that George Cowper (1754–87) was the son of Maria Cowper suffering from 'Epidemical Fever'; the son in question was Charles (b. 1765), still an infant.

20 *Martin's Collection*. As early as 1760 Martin Madan had brought out a

little volume of 171 selected *Psalms and Hymns*, chiefly from Charles Wesley and Isaac Watts.

21 *Mrs. Maitland*. Penelope Maitland (1730–1805), Mrs Madan's daughter and sister of Martin Madan and Maria Cowper.

The Newspaper. Among others, the *Public Advertiser* of 6 July and the *Saint James's Chronicle* of 4–7 July had carried the notice.

when our Lord cometh. Matthew 24: 42.

22 *Haweis*. Revd Thomas Haweis (1734–1820), rector of Aldwinkle, Northants.

Conyers. Revd. Richard Conyers (1724–86), vicar of Helmsley (1756–76) and Kirby Misperton, Yorks. (1763–8).

23 *It will be empty at Michaelmass*. This house at Emberton was not rented, probably because the tenant who had offered the house to Newton could not come to an agreement with the owner.

Cowper and Mrs Unwin moved to Olney on 14 Sept.; they first lived in a house occupied by the Newtons temporarily, and then at the Vicarage. Cowper's house (Orchard Side) was not ready until 15 Feb. 1768.

near her Son. At this time, curate of Comberton, Cambridgeshire.

24 *Stanzas*. Untraced.

made perfect. Hebrews 12: 23.

25 *Gift proceeds*. James 1: 17.

Oh for a closer Walk with God. No. 3 in Book i of the *Olney Hymns*.

28 *Physician*. Probably Robert Glynn, afterwards Clobery (1719–1800).

When I can hear my Saviour say. These lines, probably not by Cowper, are untraced.

29 *hartshorn or lavender*. Burnt hartshorn and oil of lavender were widely used in the treatment of 'nervous disorders'.

The sheet anchor of the soul was wanting. See Hebrews 6: 19.

30 *unloose the seals*. Revelation 5: 9.

32 *to his God and my God*. John 20: 18.

his Living. John had in 1765 been appointed rector of Foxton (south-west of Cambridge).

The Master. The Revd John Barnardiston (d. 17 June 1778) had been elected Master of Bene't (Corpus Christi College) on 7 July 1764.

Mrs Cowper at York. She was staying with her brother Spencer Madan.

33 *Mr. Morley . . . Mr. Rawlinson's Address*. Francis Morley, once a friend of the Unwin family, had premises at 155 Cheapside; his replacement, William Rawlinson, was at 94 Cornhill.

34 *the Fair*. Cherry Fair, celebrated on 29 June.

34 *the Tower*. The royal menagerie, housed in the Tower until 1835, included lions in the eighteenth century.

the Paper tells us. In an effort to shorten the tedious delays in Chancery transactions, Thurlow had been examining various documents at Chancery Lane.

Miss Shuttleworth. William's sister-in-law.

little John. William's son was 3 at this time.

Mr. James Martin, Glazier. Unidentified.

35 *The Hoy*. A small boat, usually rigged as a sloop, which carried passengers and goods for short distances along the coast.

Tumbled down for Nothing. Cowper is describing the strange residence at Kingsgate, near Margate, which the dissolute politician Henry Fox (1705–74; created Baron Holland of Foxley in 1763) had constructed. The place is immortalized in Gray's 'On Lord Holland's Seat near Margate, Kent'.

Sam: Cox the Council. Cox (1720–76), one of the builders of the residences in Dean's Yard for students at Westminster, was also a protector of many of the boys from that school who went on to the Inner Temple. He used to take vacations at such places as Ramsgate and Margate with Cowper and his friends.

36 *Pine Plants*. Pineapples.

another Tax upon that Commodity. The tax on window glass had been increased in 1778.

Emilius. In *Émile* (1762), Rousseau's imaginary pupil was sent to learn a trade.

37 *Cox or Langford the Auctioneers*. Christopher Cock (d. 1748) and Abraham Langford (1711–74). In 1749 Langford succeeded Cock at the latter's establishment. At the time of his death, Langford was the best-known auctioneer in England.

Arnold's. The firm of Arnold & Pearkes, Tobacconists.

Johnson's Biography. Unwin had sent Cowper the first four volumes of *Prefaces, Biographical and Critical, to the Works of the English Poets*.

Pensioner. Johnson was granted a royal pension of £300 a year in 1762.

38 *Sentence of Condemnation upon Lycidas*. In part, Johnson claimed (in *Prefaces*, ii. 153–4): 'One of the poems on which much praise has been bestowed is *Lycidas*; of which the diction is harsh, the rhymes uncertain, and the numbers unpleasing. . . . In this poem there is no nature, for there is no truth; there is no art, for there is nothing new.'

the unfitness of the English Language for Blank Verse. *Prefaces*, ii. 220–1: 'Blank verse makes some approach to that which is called the *lapidary stile*; has neither the easiness of prose, nor the melody of numbers, and therefore tires by long continuance.'

39 *most Zealous Mob . . . Cause of Religion.* The Gordon Riots. They were fuelled by Protestant resistance, led by Lord George Gordon (1751–93), to the removal of civil restrictions from Catholics.

Great Queen Street. Where the Hills lived.

they are undone. The removal of tarrifs on Irish goods and thus the destruction of a market for English lace must have been the concern of the residents of Olney, many of whom were lace-makers. David Murray, Viscount Stormont (1727–96), was Secretary of State for the Southern Department from Oct. 1779 until July 1782.

Lord Dartmouth. William Legge (1731–1801), 2nd Earl of Dartmouth, knew Cowper from their days at Westminster School. Dartmouth was an ardent evangelical, particularly devoted to the plight of the poor.

40 *Mr. Newton having desired me to be of the Party.* Newton wrote to Cowper on 14 July telling him that he would be dining at Maria Cowper's on Friday the 21st and suggesting that on the 20th Cowper write to her so that his letter would arrive when Newton was her guest at Grosvenor Square. This letter was in fulfilment of this request, but Newton did not dine there until the 28th.

Shod with Felt. King Lear, IV. vi. 186–7.

41 *late Scene.* The Gordon Riots.

42 *knotting or Netting.* Forms of knitting which involve making knots (for fringes) and net (for purses etc.) respectively.

45 *Conversation.* One of the moral satires in *Poems* (1782).

Raban. Thomas Raban, the Olney carpenter.

Mr. Symonds's. The Revd Joshua Symonds was minister of Bunyan Meeting, Bedford. Cowper and Mrs Unwin eventually found the missing letters.

46 *bene vixit qui bene latuit.* Ovid. *Tristia,* III, iv. 25: 'He who hides well, lives well.'

it should have been the motto to my Book. The mottoes actually used were from Caraccioli and Virgil.

an excellent one for Retirement. Cowper finally used a motto from Virgil's *Georgics* for 'Retirement', the final moral satire in *Poems* (1782).

47 *Quarme.* Probably the Robert Quarme who was a subscriber to Cowper's translation of Homer in 1791. In the 1740s, Cowper had known George Quarme (1716?–75), a friend of his uncle Ashley and later a Commissioner of Taxes and Excise. Robert was probably related to George.

the Boy & his Trunk. Unidentified.

48 *present awfull Crisis.* The American war of independence.

49 *King Critic.* 'Johnson' was inserted in the holograph in another hand.

50 *Priar.* Matthew Prior (1664–1721), the poet and diplomat.

50 *have stood in a different order. Prefaces*, vi. 58–9: 'His expression has every mark of laborious study; the line seldom seems to have been formed at once; the words did not come till they were called, and were then put by constraint into their places, where they do their duty, but do it sullenly.'

Curl or Dennis. Edmund Curll (1675–1747), the publisher of pirated material and antagonist of Alexander Pope; John Dennis (1657–1734), the boisterous literary critic who advocated the Longinian sublime.

51 *some of Dryden's Fables. Fables, Ancient and Modern* was published in 1700.

Ithuriel and Zephon. The confrontation between these cherubs and Satan takes place in *Paradise Lost*, iv. 788–856.

Thomson's Seasons. Published as a unit in 1730.

Ships I have none. Since Cowper had 'renounced' drawing because it hurt his eyes, he was unable to supply little John with a 'ship'.

53 *his Chancellorship.* Edward Thurlow. See Biographical Register.

a certain Eastern Monarch. Ahazuerus. See Esther 6: 1 ff. and the story of Mordecai and Haman.

your Letter to their Worships. A letter in support of prisoners, one of Unwin's favourite causes.

Mrs. Powley. Unwin and his family planned to visit Susanna in Yorkshire before arriving at Olney.

54 *Dr. Johnson's opinion.* See p. 116 for evidence concerning Johnson's reading of Cowper's *Poems*.

Night Thoughts. Edward Young's *The Complaint: or Night Thoughts on Life, Death, and Immortality* (1742–6).

Renny. Unidentified further.

55 *in the end.* These events inspired Cowper's poem, 'The Colubriad'.

Mr. Small's. Alexander Small (1747–1816), who had inherited his father's house at Clifton Reynes, close to Olney.

another child. William, son of Thomas and Jane Scott. The Revd Thomas Scott (1747–1821) was curate at Olney from 1781 to 1785.

56 *Mrs. Bouverie's.* Elizabeth Bouverie of Barham Court, Teston, Kent, was a friend of Hannah Moore.

57 *Lady Austen's behaviour.* Cowper's reconcilement with her had occurred c.June–July 1782.

Hares. Cowper's pets. See his letter to the *Gentleman's Magazine* of 28 May 1784.

Mr. Scott. See note p. 55.

58 *a Physician.* Probably William Kerr (1737–1824), the doctor from Northampton who regularly attended Cowper and Mrs Unwin after 1784.

59 *Minister of three parishes.* In addition to Stock, Ramsden Bellhouse and Ramsden Crayes in Essex.

60 *Miss Green.* Martha Richardson, Lady Austen's sister, married Richard Greene on 1 Nov. 1763, and Ann was their daughter. After his death, Martha married Thomas Jones on 15 May 1778.

Mrs. Scott's delivery. See note p. 55.

visiting the prisoners. Unwin had visited the prisoners at Chelmsford Gaol, a place infamous for its inhuman conditions.

62 *Soals.* Sole.

as Horace observed. Epistles, I. xvii. 35.

One Man. Cowper is referring to the dissolute early life of Henry Fox (see note p. 35) before his entering Parliament in 1735.

63 *the apple of his eye.* See Deuteronomy 32: 10 and Psalm 17: 8.

64 *box.* A compartment partitioned off in the public room of a coffee house.

busy periwigs. The sworn clerks of the Chancery Office.

papers tell me that peace is at hand. The peace preliminaries, by which Spain agreed to leave Gibraltar in English hands, were signed on 20 Jan. 1783.

65 *Elliott's medicines.* An eye ointment prepared by John Elliot, MD (1747–87).

Æsculapius. Legendary Greek physician and god of medicine.

66 *The papers inform me that Lord Bute is at the bottom of all this mischief.* John Stuart, 3rd Earl of Bute (1713–92), retired from active political life in 1766 and subsequently travelled abroad incognito. At this time, it was widely suspected that he was negotiating with the French on behalf of England.

the Etching you recommended. A stipple engraving of Thurlow dated 21 Apr. 1781 and published by E. Hodges at 92 Cornhill.

68 *She wanted words to a tune.* This poem was set to the air 'The Lass of Pattie's Mill'.

70 *nihil est ab omni parte beatum.* Horace, *Odes*, II. xvi. 27–8: 'No perfect good exists.'

Mr. Fytche. Lewis Disney (1738–1822), who had assumed the surname and arms of ffytche on 27 Sept. 1775. In 1781 ffytche, who owned the living of Woodham Walter in Essex, attempted to present John Eyre to that parish. However, when the bishop of London learned that Eyre had given ffytche a bond of £3,000, he considered the matter to be simoniacal and refused to initiate Eyre. ffytche had won his right to presentation before a Court of Common Pleas, but, as Cowper indicates, the House of Lords reversed this decision by a vote of 19 to 18.

Quamdiu se bene gesserit. 'During his good behaviour.' This is a clause frequently used in letters patent or grants of certain offices to secure certain rights provided that the grantees do not abuse those privileges.

71 *Mary to Anna*. Mrs Unwin to Lady Austen.

72 *the enquiry you purpose*. Unwin wishes to ask Joseph Johnson if Cowper's volume is selling and being well received by the public.

my Latin Ode . . . my English dirge. 'In submersionem navigii, cui Georgius, regale nomen, inditum' and the English version, 'On the Loss of the Royal George'.

73 *Gay's Ballad*. The ballad ' 'Twas when the seas were roaring' occurs in Scene viii of the 'Tragi-Comi-Pastoral FARCE' *The What D'Ye Call It*. This one-act play, which is probably by Gay alone and not a joint production of the Scriblerus Club, was first performed on 23 Feb. 1715 at Drury Lane.

Ballads that Bourne has translated. Among Vincent Bourne's translations were Gay's 'Black Ey'd Susan' and several poems by Prior. Bourne (1695–1747) was Cowper's master in the fifth form at Westminster. Cowper remembered him as an extremely pleasant but constantly dishevelled person. He was a poet of considerable accomplishment, and Cowper particularly admired Vinny's Latin poems and translated some of them into English.

Tibullus. Roman elegaic poet (*c*,48–19 BC).

74 *the versification of them serves to divert me*. The resultant poem was 'The Faithfull Friend'.

a piece of Mme. Guion. 'Scenes Favourable to Meditation' was enclosed.

Mr. Smith. See Biographical Register.

Shill. Shrill.

Mr. Palmer's House. Cowper's draper.

75 *George Griggs, Lucy and Abigail Tyrrel*. The Griggs and Tyrrels were related by marriage. George (d. 1809), a butcher, had married Alice Tyrrel on 20 Aug. 1754. Abigail (1736–87) was probably Alice's sister. There is no record of a Lucy Tyrrel, and Cowper may be referring to Mr Lucy, a townsperson whom he mentions in several letters.

a woman of the name of Jackson. Untraced.

Henshman. Edward Henscomb (d. 1788), a constable.

Daniel Raban's. Olney landowner and drunkard who died in 1784.

76 *One at Hitchin*. Five fires in this village in Hertfordshire were reported during Oct. Evidently, houses and barns were set alight with the purpose of robbing the inhabitants. Only one of the arsonists was caught—a servant girl who was hanged for setting her master's house on fire.

Sue Riviss. Untraced.

Goatham. Cowper's spelling of Gotham, a village proverbial for the stupidity and folly of its inhabitants.

77 *the woman I mention'd before.* In his letter of 3 Nov. 1783, Cowper had referred to 'a woman of the name of Jackson'.

Billy Raban, the Baker's son. Probably the William Raban (b. 1763) who served as churchwarden at Olney from 1793 until after 1808.

Junior Son of Molly Boswell. Francis (b. 1770).

Cart's tail. The back portion of a cart, to which offenders were tied for whipping as they were paraded through town.

from the Stone house to the High Arch and back again. This was the traditional whipping distance, which began at the prison, the Stone House (also known as the Round House), proceeded to the High Arch (the rise in the road near the Independent Meeting House), and then back again.

Henschcomb. See note p. 75.

78 *Swift observes.* In his Introduction to *A Tale of a Tub*: 'Whoever hath an Ambition to be heard in a Crowd, must press, and squeeze, and thrust, and climb with indefatigable Pains, till he has exalted himself to a certain Degree of Altitude above them. Now, in all Assemblies, tho' you wedge them ever so close, we may observe this peculiar Property; that over their Heads there is Room enough; but how to reach it, is the difficult Point . . .' (ed. A. C. Guthkelch and D. Nichol Smith, 2nd edn., Oxford, 1958, p. 55).

French Philosophers. Air balloonists. See note p. 91.

80 *the Revd. Doctor your predecessor.* Charles Plumtre (1712–79). At the time of his sudden death, he was archdeacon of Ely, rector of Orpington, Kent, and of St Mary Woolnoth. We have not been able to discover Plumtre's claim to the title of 'Doctor'.

81 *Eliza.* Elizabeth Cunningham, Newton's niece. After her mother's death in 1783 she was looked upon by the Newtons as their daughter and lived with them in London until her early death in 1785.

Sally Johnson. Mrs Newton's maid, whom Cowper had known at Olney.

82 *Mr. Bacon.* See Biographical Register.

83 *Mary Guthrie.* According to the parish register of Olney, a widow named Mary Gutteridge was buried on 8 Feb. 1784.

James Abraham's wife. Untraced.

George Knight. He was buried on 27 Jan. 1784.

Hoxton. The district of London where the Newtons lived.

before he dissolves the parliament. Cowper often asked friends to obtain franks from Members of Parliament, particularly when he wanted to convey galley or page proofs to London. However, franking could be practised only when Parliament was in session. Cowper was not aware that the King had dissolved Parliament four days earlier on 25 Mar., thus invalidating his frank. Therefore, Newton would have been charged for this letter.

84 *Mr. Grenville.* William Wyndham Grenville (1759–1834), later Baron

84 Grenville (1790), a cousin and supporter of Pitt. He was returned to Parliament.

Ashburner the Drapier. He died in May 1785.

85 *the dispute between the Crown and the Commons.* The Commons had asked the King to remove his ministers. The King refused, the Commons repeated its request, was refused again, and finally reproached the King in a 'representation' which carried by a majority of one (191 to 190).

Mr. Scott. See note p. 55.

86 *Mr. Grindon . . . is, I think a dying man.* Cowper's pessimism was justified: Maximilian Grindon was buried less than three months later on 13 July 1784.

your book. Apologia: or, Four Letters to a Minister of an Independent Church had been published in Mar. 1784.

Beattie's and Blair's Lectures. Dissertations Moral and Critical (1783) by James Beattie (1735–1803) and *Lectures on Rhetoric and Belles Lettres* (1783) by Hugh Blair (1718–1800).

87 *candidates for this County.* In addition to William Wyndham Grenville (see note p. 84), the candidates were Ralph Verney (1714–91) and John Aubrey (1739–1826); Grenville and Aubrey were elected.

a Merry Andrew's jacket. A merry andrew is someone who entertains people by means of antics or buffoonery, and Cowper is indicating that the rioter is dressed in a manner appropriate to his conduct.

Mr. Ashburner. See note p. 84.

89 *Miss Bunkham.* Untraced.

90 *Lady Coventry.* Mary Gunning, Countess of Coventry (1732–60). Cowper is referring to the rumour that she had died as a result of habitually painting her face with white lead.

Vive valeque. Be well and goodbye.

91 *an Uncle still alive.* Ashley.

your uncle. John Unwin (d. 1789).

Balloons. Hydrogen balloons were very much a topic of conversation in the early 1780s, and Cowper became enraptured with Lunardi, Blanchard, the Montgolfier brothers, and the other explorers of the air.

his elder Brother. Robert Throckmorton (1750–79).

his Mother. Anna Maria Throckmorton (d. 1791).

93 *poor Puss.* A common name for a hare as well as a cat.

94 *Puss, Tiney, and Bess.* According to a memorandum of 9 Mar. 1786 found among Cowper's papers after his death, Bess died young, Tiney lived to be 9, and Puss died at 11 years, 11 months.

95 *Vestris.* Auguste Vestris (1760–1842), the celebrated French acrobat and dancer.

97 *Marquis*. Marquis, Cowper's spaniel, died in Sept. 1787 and was succeeded by Beau, who lived only a few months, and then another Beau.

99 *Sum, ut semper, Tui studiosissimus.* I am, as always, most enthusiastically yours.

100 *near the End of the last book.* vi. 759–817.

101 *á merveille.* Marvellously.

Lunardi. Cowper is referring to the graceful and elegant portrait of Vincenzo Lunardi (1759–1806), the first traveller in the English atmosphere. The portrait was from a design by Richard Cosway and engraved by Francesco Bartolozzi; it serves as the frontispiece to *An Account of the First Aerial Voyage* (1784).

Miss Unwin. Mary Unwin (d. 1833). William's cousin, was the daughter of Henry Unwin, who had been a stationer in Pater Noster Row, London. At his death, William Unwin became one of her two trustees. Mary, who was heiress to a large fortune, lived with him and his family until she married John Hiley Aldington on 25 Oct. 1785.

be pleased to substitute Hill for Joe. The 'Epistle' as sent to Unwin read 'Joe' in line 45. The signature to this letter has been cut away.

John Gilpin. Cowper had enclosed this poem with a letter to Unwin, who sent it to the *Public Advertiser*, where it was published anonymously on 14 Nov. 1782. This version of the poem achieved remarkable success when John Henderson gave public readings of it at Freemasons' Hall during Lent 1785. A flood of chap-books, broadsides, and prints followed. Cowper acknowledged authorship of the poem when he allowed a revised version of the poem to appear in *The Task* volume in July 1785.

102 *Mrs. Bellamy.* The autobiography of the actress and prostitute George Anne Bellamy (1731?–88).

the learned Pig. In the Apr. 1785 issue of *A New Review*, the feats of this intellectual beast from Cheshire are facetiously treated: 'A gentle pig this same, a pig of parts, / And learn'd as F.R.S. or graduate in arts; / His ancestors, 'tis true, could only squeak, / But this has been at school—and in a month will speak.'

the Master of St. Paul's. Richard Roberts (1729–1823) was elected High Master of St Paul's in 1769.

Tirocinium. Cowper's poem on education, which was published in 1785 as part of the *Task* volume.

dance nor weep. See Matthew 11: 16–17.

two sheets in a. The remaining part of the letter is missing.

103 *an Apothecary, now dead.* Thomas Aspray (d. 1784).

the younger Harcourt. See note p. 8.

T. White. Untraced.

103 *Mr. Foy.* Untraced.

Mr. Teedon. See Biographical Register.

Sheridan would adore him. Thomas Sheridan (1719–88), actor, writer, and lecturer on elocution.

Theron and Aspasio. *Theron and Aspasio: or A Series of Dialogues and Letters upon the Most Important Subjects* (3 vols., 1755) by James Hervey (1714–58). Like many others, Cowper thought Hervey's style excessively florid.

104 *Miss Cunningham's illness.* See note p. 81.

Southampton well. Southampton became a popular spa resort in the 1740s; Cowper had visited there in the 1750s, often in the company of Sir Thomas and Lady Hesketh.

105 *Nettley Abbey.* The extensive remains of Netley Abbey, a 13th-century Cistercian abbey six miles from Southampton, are mouldered and crumbled in a Gothic fashion.

Freemantle. Freemantle House, in the east part of Southampton, was a wooded estate which became one of the town's chief attractions.

Redbridge. A short distance from Southampton along the shore, Redbridge was a popular place for an evening stroll.

Mr. Perry. In his letter to Newton of 27 Aug., Cowper had told him that Mr. Perry, the miller at Lavendon, was dying.

106 *Mr. Scott.* See note p. 55.

Mr. Jones. Lady Austen's brother-in-law, the Revd Thomas Jones, who had been expelled from St Edmund Hall, Oxford, for holding Methodist views, was curate at Clifton, near Olney, from 1772 to 1792.

Mr. Teedon. See Biographical Register.

Lord P. Charles Henry Mordaunt, 5th and last Earl of Peterborough (1758–1814), owned the living at Clifton; the quarrel, which concerned the enclosure of the parish, was amicably resolved in early Nov.

107 *Sally Johnson.* See note p. 81.

Hannah. See Hannah Wilson in Biographical Register.

Miss Cunningham. See note p. 81.

Miss Catlett. Betsy (d. 1807), Mrs Newton's niece.

a Letter frank'd by my Uncle. Lady Hesketh had written on 10 Oct.; her father, as Clerk of the Parliaments, had franking privileges.

108 *the Arabian Nights' Entertainment.* In the period when Cowper and Lady Hesketh had enjoyed the London theatre, there had been a vogue for exotic and spectacular productions, such as Garrick's elaborate pantomine *The Chinese Festival.*

personal kindnesses to myself, but the last testimony that he gave of his regard for you. Sir Thomas Hesketh (d. 1778) bequeathed £100 to Cowper, and an annual sum which varied between £800 and £900 to his wife.

109 *13 of those years.* Cowper is referring to his dream in the winter of 1773 in which he believed it was revealed to him that God had forsaken him.

three female descendents. In addition to Harriot and Theodora, Elizabeth Charlotte (d. 1805), who had married Sir Archer Croft (1731–92).

Manual occupations. Cowper's included carpentry, gardening, and drawing.

the Mirror. A bi-weekly newspaper comparable in subject matter to the *Spectator* which was issued every Tuesday and Saturday from Edinburgh from 21 Jan. 1779 to 27 May 1780.

Dr. Beattie. See note p. 86. Beattie was not a regular contributor to the *Mirror*; he wrote only two of its 110 issues.

110 *the Copy.* Cowper means copyright, and he is referring to the fact that he has to make a present of the copyright to Johnson as a condition for publishing.

several small matters. 'The Yearly Distress or Tything Time at—— . . .', Aug. 1783; Letter (on his hares), June 1784; 'Epitaph on an Hare', Dec. 1784; 'The Poplar Field', Jan. 1785; 'Sonnet' ('The Rose'), June 1785; 'Letter on the Defects of Pope's Homer', Aug. 1785; 'The Poplar Field' in Latin, Aug. 1785.

a small Spaniel . . . the great beast Mungo. Marquis was the spaniel and Mungo the bulldog.

112 *do not much exceed my own.* At this time, £20.

114 *Pope's Messiah.* ll. 67–70: 'The Swain in barren Desarts with surprize / See Lillies spring, and sudden Verdure rise; / And Starts, amidst the thirsty Wilds, to hear / New Falls of Water murm'ring in his Ear.'

your Note. A bank note.

the Writing-desk. The desk, actually a gift of Theodora, arrived on 7 Dec.

Sejour. Place of retreat.

Johnson's Poets. Cowper received the first of Johnson's *Prefaces* from Unwin in 1779. See note p. 37.

Extracts from Hayley's works in the Review. Hayley's *Essay on History*, *Triumphs of Temper*, and *Plays of Three Acts* had been reviewed in the *Monthly Review* in 1780, 1781, and 1784—each time with extensive quotation.

115 *the Quarto volume that you mention.* Hayley's works, except for *The Triumphs of Temper*, were often gathered together in composite volumes in which the poems of other authors were included. Lady Hesketh probably had one or more works of Hayley bound up in a volume with some work of Goldsmith's, and it was such a volume that she offered Cowper.

Shrub. A drink made from orange or lemon, sugar, and rum.

116 *Mrs. Montague.* Mrs Elizabeth Montagu (1720–1800), the queen of the blue-stockings.

116 *a friend of his* [*Samuel Johnson*]. Although it seems very doubtful that Johnson 'consigned' his office as critic of Cowper's poetry, it appears likely that Benjamin Latrobe (1725–86), the distinguished Moravian pastor, may have served as the intermediary who told Newton—and therefore Cowper—that Dr Johnson had read Cowper's poems. The review was by Edmund Cartwright (1743–1823), who was from 1778 to 1785 a principal reviewer for the *Monthly Review*.

a new Edition of Johnson's Dictionary. In the autumn of 1785 several cheap reprints of the *Dictionary* appeared; by the end of the year four editions were appearing serially. Cowper undoubtedly wished for the sixth edition printed by Strathan, which was to be published in eighty-four sixpenny numbers.

117 *reward their labours.* See ll. 607–9 of Cowper's translation of Book xxiii of the *Iliad*.

118 *the Common-scene in the Task.* ll. 526–33 of Book i.

the Doctor. Kerr. See note p. 58.

119 *Specimen.* Cowper was persuaded by his cousin, General Cowper, to prepare a specimen containing the speeches of Priam and Achilles at the end of the last book of the *Iliad*. This was printed with some copies of the *Proposals* for subscribers. See James King, *William Cowper: A Biography* (Durham: Duke University Press, 1986), 198–202, 205–7.

friend's strictures. Fuseli's commentary on the translation of Homer.

121 *in a Bag.* A small silken pouch to contain the back-hair of a wig.

a queeüe. A long plait of hair worn hanging down behind, from the head or from a wig. It would look like a pigtail.

the Snuff box. Cowper's three hares and a landscape are depicted on the lid of the snuff-box (now at the Cowper and Newton Museum, Olney).

123 *the rest is left to heav'n.* Cowper and Mrs Unwin moved to the Lodge, Weston, on 15 Nov. 1786. Cowper is loosely paraphrasing the last line of Pope's *Epistle to Dr. Arbuthnot*: 'Thus far was right, the rest belongs to Heav'n.'

Hirtius. The eighth book of Caesar's *De bello gallico* is attributed to Aulus Hirtius, one of Caesar's generals.

125 *the peaceful hermitage!* Il Penseroso, ll. 167–8.

had the honour to celebrate. The Task, i. 154–80.

126 *the Don.* Don Quixote.

Cadwallader . . . the Welshman threat'ned me. The Welshman is Walter Churchey (1747–1805), a Welsh attorney who sought Cowper's advice about writing verse of a Methodist cast. Cowper is sarcastically referring to him as Casail Cadwaladr (*fl.* 1590), the Welsh bard.

127 *partake the gale.* An Essay on Man, ii. 385–6.

the Howardian Committee . . . the poem called the Triumph of Benevolence. A proposal to erect a statue to honour the philanthropic activities of John

Howard (1726?–90). The poem which Cowper mentions was donated by Samuel Jackson Pratt (1749–1814).

our little Cousin at Kensington. George Augustus, afterwards 4th Earl Cowper (1776–99), to whom the translation of Homer was dedicated.

Mrs. Forrester. Untraced.

Mr. G. Maria Throckmorton, Cowper's friend, had two half-brothers, Thomas and John Giffard, and one of these is probably referred to here.

128 *Mr. H. Thornton.* Henry Thornton (1760–1815) was the third son of John Thornton and a close friend of William Unwin, who died while visiting him at Winchester.

Inscription. Cowper's inscription (now lost) was written in Latin. He was under the impression that Thornton had used what he wrote, but then he saw a letter in the Mar. 1793 issue of the *Gentleman's Magazine* which indicated that the inscription was in English and not of his devising.

129 *Sally Perry's case.* She may have been a daughter of Mr Perry of Lavendon Mills, a friend of Newton's.

130 *the Bark.* Quinine and other medicines extracted from cinchona bark were commonly used in the treatment of agues, fevers, and headaches.

Hoffman. One of the many compounds devised by the German physician Friedrich Hoffman (1660–1742).

Daffy. The celebrated elixir, made from senna, jalap, aniseed, caraway seeds, juniper berries, treacle, and water, which was invented by the Revd Thomas Daffy (d. 1680).

131 *my name-sake of Epsom.* William Cowper (1750–98), Maria Cowper's son, who in 1786 had bestowed £10 per year on Cowper.

Mrs. Carter. C is referring to *Rambler* 44 (18 Aug. 1750), which was written by Elizabeth Carter (1717–1806). Mrs Carter does not specifically state that dreams are 'the ordinary operations of the Fancy', but she does suggest that a frightening nightmare can be succeeded by a pleasant dream. She also describes how the beautiful creature who calls herself 'Religion' eschews those who dwell on melancholy thoughts. From the context of this letter, it would seem that Lady Hesketh, who was attempting to relieve her cousin from the depression following a series of nightmares, cited Mrs Carter's essay or discussed Cowper with this renowned expert, whom she sometimes entertained. In rebuttal, Cowper is telling Lady Hesketh that his experiences are vastly different from Mrs Carter's.

132 *Turchas.* Turquoise.

Rose. See Biographical Register.

133 *when you and I shall come together.* The London season usually continued unabated while Parliament was sitting, and Lady Hesketh does not wish to leave the city until the season is over.

134 *Chicheley.* Walter Bagot's brother Charles (1730–93), who assumed the surname of Chester, lived at Chicheley Hall, Bucks.

at Horton. Sir Robert Gunning (1731–1816), a retired diplomat, lived at Horton, midway between Olney and Northampton. He had two daughters; the elder, Charlotte Margaret, was a maid of honour to the Queen.

Mrs. Wrighte's is still consider'd as a melancholy case. Anne Wrighte, née Jekyll, the wife of George Wrighte, whose seat was at Gayhurst, five miles from Olney. She recovered from her mysterious illness.

green wax candle. Green is a reference to the freshness, not the colour; wax tapers were coiled on a vertical shaft and cut off when needed.

135 *Miss Moore was on the point of publication.* Hannah More (1745–1833) published her long poem *Slavery* and her prose treatise *Thoughts on the Importance of the Manners of the Great to General Society* in 1788.

I have already borne my testimony. Cowper is referring to ll. 137–243 from 'Charity', and to sentiments expressed in such lines as these (137–40): 'But, ah! what wish can prosper, or what pray'r, / For merchants, rich in cargoes of despair, / Who drive a loathsome traffic, gage, and span, / And buy, the muscles and the bones of man?' However, Cowper changed his mind (see note p. 143).

136 *Mrs. Trimmer's publication.* Sarah Trimmer (1741–1810), a popular writer whose work had been praised by Samuel Johnson. The book for Hannah Wilson must have been *Fabulous Histories: Designed for the Instruction of Children, Respecting their Treatment of Animals* (1786).

trial of a man. Warren Hastings (1732–1818) attended Westminster from 1743 to 1749. Hastings had been Governor-General of Bengal for 14 years when the House of Commons voted on 3 Apr. 1787 his impeachment on the grounds of cruelty and corruption in his administration of Indian affairs. Hastings's trial began on 13 Feb. 1788 and ended on 23 Apr. 1795 (the trial itself occupied 145 days) with his acquittal.

Sir Elijah. Sir Elijah Impey (1732–1809), also at Westminster (1740–51) with Cowper. Impey, who was Chief Justice of the Supreme Court of Bengal from 1774 to 1787, defended himself successfully at the Bar of the House of Commons in 1788 of six charges.

137 *Margaret King.* See Biographical Register.

terrible Curate. Possibly the Revd Laurence Canniford, who was preferred to the living of St Helen's Abingdon in 1811.

Andrew Fridze. The origin of this nickname not traced, and we have not been able to locate the advertisements.

Postlethwaite. Revd Richard Postlethwaite (*fl.* 1785–1816). He succeeded Thomas Scott as the curate of Olney in 1785. In 1787, he acquired a living in Essex.

at a Gaming table. Charles James Fox (1749–1806), the 3rd son of Henry

Fox, in a speech almost five hours long, moved the impeachment against Hastings.

Fort St. George. An outpost completed in 1640 which was the centre of British activity in Madras. Hastings served as second in council there from 1769 to 1772. In using the expression 'Governor of Fort St. George' Cowper is referring figuratively to British rule in India.

138 *Jessamy Hall.* A toilet.

139 *as Virgil says.* Aeneid, ix. 6–7.

Encoignure. Corner cupboard.

140 *Naples biscuit.* Perhaps a form of arrowroot.

141 *I could wish too with Dr. Johnson.* Johnson did not make such a statement regarding Thomson.

Non-naturals. A medical reference to those things (air, meat and drink, sleep and waking, motion and rest, excretion and retention, and the affections of the mind) which are essential to health but which, paradoxically, are liable, by abuse or accident, to become the sources of bad health.

142 *Deedy.* Actual, real. Cowper is the only source given by the *Oxford English Dictionary* for this definition of the word.

John Watson. Further unidentified.

Cousin Charles. Charles Cowper (1765–1820), who had been called to the Bar in 1788 and who would serve as Commissioner of Bankrupts from *c.*1789 to 1801.

Henry. Henry (1758–1840) was the 3rd son of General Cowper; he was appointed in 1785 Deputy Clerk of the Parliaments 2nd Clerk Assistant to the House of Lords.

143 *Tartar Emetic.* As he makes clear at the very opening of his letter to Lady Hesketh of 5 July, Cowper was taking a form of fixed salt of tartar which is made from crude tartar as opposed to emetic tartar which is derived from cream of tartar.

Ballads against the Slavemongers. Although Cowper had refused a similar request (see note p. 135) by Lady Hesketh in Feb. 1788, he wrote 'The Negro's Complaint', 'Sweet Meat Has Sour Sauce', and 'The Morning Dream' in Mar. 1788 at the request of Lady Balgonie for the Committee for the Abolition of the Slave Trade.

144 *Sephus.* Joseph Hill. See Biographical Register.

146 *Sto qui.* I remain here.

148 *in France and in the Austrian Netherlands.* Up to 1787, France had been attempting to control the Netherlands through Joseph II, the Holy Roman Emperor; England was pleased when power in the United Provinces (Holland) was restored to the Prince of Orange and in 1788 signed a treaty with the United Provinces calling for mutual defence.

149 *1789.* Cowper should have written 1790.

149 *Lodi*. Cheese. Lodi, a town in the Piedmont 20 miles from Milan, produces more Parmesan cheese than Parma.

Lord Howard's note. The note, presumably to Cowper, was from John Griffin Griffin (formerly Whitwell), Lord Howard de Walden (1719–97), who lived and died at Audley End, near Saffron Walden. Lord Howard has asked Johnny to celebrate his seat, and the resulting poem, a hackneyed pastoral eclogue reminiscent of Theocritus and Spenser, was written in couplets grouped in four-line stanzas. Lord Howard was a subscriber to Cowper's Homer.

150 *Kilwick wood*. A wood belonging to John Throckmorton.

Martyn. Thomas Martyn (1735–1825), the distinguished botanist, was Mrs King's cousin.

151 *Mrs. Howe*. The Hon. Mrs Caroline Howe (*c*.1721–1814) was a noted intellectual and a friend of Elizabeth Montagu, through whom Lady Hesketh had probably met her.

the only picture of my own mother. This portrait miniature (oil on copper) was painted by D. Heins.

152 *Should the wretch be detected*. Incident untraced.

Cambridge's conclusion. Unidentified.

Enfield's Speaker. The *Speaker*, founded and edited by the Revd William Enfield (1741–97), achieved great popularity from its first appearance in 1774 as an anthology of pieces for reading and recitation. Cowper published three poems in the *Speaker* in 1792.

153 *brother*. Roger Donne (1702–73), Rector of Catfield in Norfolk.

a Donne at all points. It is possible, but far from certain, that Thomas Dunne (d. 1592), the first Donne in Cowper's ancestry we can be sure of, was related to the poet John Donne's father.

154 *Hewitt*. Elizabeth Donne (1724–96) was the daughter of the Revd Roger Donne (1702–73) and his first wife Elizabeth Pacey (d. 1729). She married Thomas Hewitt of Mattishall in 1764.

Balls. Harriot Rival Donne (1736–1808) married Richard Balls, a Catfield farmer, in 1759. She was the niece of Cowper's mother.

Catfield. The centre of the Donnes in Norfolk.

Castres. The Revd Castres Donne (1744/5–89).

155 *without exception*. In Oct. 1786, Cowper's manuscript of his translation of the ninth book of the *Iliad*—on its way to Kingston where Cowper's cousin and literary adviser General Cowper lived—was lost when the entire cargo of a boat 'in which it was a passenger' was sunk.

future disappointments. Cowper is referring to Swift's letter to Pope and Bolingbroke of 5 Apr. 1729: 'I remember when I was a little boy, I felt a great fish at the end of my line which I drew up almost on the ground, but it dropt in, and the disappointment vexeth me to this very day, and I believe it was the type of all my future disappointments.' *Correspondence of*

Jonathan Swift, ed. Sir Harold Williams (5 vols, Oxford, 1963–5), iii. 329.

156 *Mrs. Unwin's use.* In her postscript, Mrs Unwin asked Lady Hesketh to tell her 'in what point I differ from you'; Mrs Unwin also said that she expected her poor health to improve.

157 *Keeping-room.* Sitting room.

New Norfolk Street. Cowper refers to Lady Hesketh's house in London.

Longinus has insinuated. Longinus made this claim in his treatise on the sublime.

158 *leisure.* Hill had obviously objected to Cowper's brief, impersonal note of 20 Mar. asking for money.

teste me ipso. As I can affirm from personal experience.

159 *your great loss.* Mary Newton had died the year before.

160 *The Clerk.* John Cox (d. *c.*1791) of the parish of All Saints in Northampton. Cowper wrote verses for the bills of mortality of 1787, 1788, 1789, 1790, 1792, 1793.

the late Sexton. Samuel Wright.

162 *Newspaper.* We have not found the newspaper account to which Cowper refers.

163 *Sonnet:* Hayley had composed a poem—enclosed with his letter—upon hearing that he and Cowper were '*hostile competitors*' in writing lives of Milton.

165 *Mr. Steevens . . . Adamo of Andreini.* George Steevens (1736–1800), a member of the Johnson circle, published various editions of Shakespeare (1766, 1773, 1778, 1793). He probably sent Cowper one of the Milan editions (1613, 1617) of *L'Adamo* by Giovanni Battista Andreini (1576–1654). Voltaire was the first person to suggest that *Paradise Lost* was influenced by this poem.

shield of Achilles. Cowper's reference is to the beginning of Ulysses' speech (ll. 159–68) in Book xiii of the *Metamorphoses*.

Comus . . . Job. Hayley must have called attention to the similarity between l. 597 of *Comus* ('The pillared firmament is rottenness') and Job 26: 11 ('the pillars of Heaven').

hermit. At times, Hayley referred to his reclusive existence in this manner. He also sometimes signed letters in this way.

166 *a poem of yours.* Cowper's reference is to the conclusion of Epistle iv to *An Essay on Epic Poetry* (beginning with l. 435), where Hayley recalls his childhood illness and his mother's unflinching devotion in nursing him back to health.

astrum. Odes, ii. xvii. 21–2: '. . . our stars agree in a marvellous way.'

a female oculist. Mrs Disney. At the age of 8, Cowper's eyes were weak, and he was said to be in danger of losing one of them. He was therefore

166 sent to the home of Mrs Disney, where he remained for two years. He subsequently recalled the oculist and her household without affection.

167 *your good handmaid of 40.* Cowper and Mrs Unwin did not object to the possible impropriety of Hayley travelling with a maid, Mary Cockerell.

little more. We have not been able to trace these lines to Pope; Cowper may be conflating passages from the *Dunciad* (see Book i, ll. 127–42, Book iv, ll. 319–20).

your own handwriting. Hayley sometimes used an amanuensis.

168 *fire and brimstone. Paradise Lost,* i. 50–74.

received that Being. See Acts 17: 28.

169 *Dr. Kerr.* See note p. 58.

Dr. Austen. Dr William Austin (1754–93), at this time physician to St Bartholomew's Hospital.

an Electrical Machine. A contrivance which produced static electricity by the friction caused by silk or leather being rubbed against a revolving glass cylinder; the sparks obtained were administered to the patient through the tongue or teeth or other parts of the body.

our neighbour Socket. A stationer and bookseller in London who habitually returned to his wife and son in Buckinghamshire when he experienced financial difficulties.

proposed amendments of thy friend. An untraced friend of Lady Hesketh had suggested improvements to the Wilberforce sonnet which forms part of Cowper's letter of 26 Apr. to her.

Hastings. 'To Warren Hastings'. See note p. 136.

170 *Steers's Opodeldoc.* This ointment, useful in the treatment of sprains, bruises and rheumatism, was sold by one H. Steers from his 'Medicinal Warehouse' on Old Bond Street.

171 *an aperient electuary.* A laxative.

Carwarden. See Thomas Carwardine in Biographical Register.

Murphy's book. Arthur Murphy's *An Essay on the Life and Genius of Samuel Johnson, LL.D.* (1792).

172 *her son.* Thomas Socket, jun. (1778–1859), who assisted Hayley in running the electrical machine, was invited by him to tutor his son at Eartham; through this connection, Socket met many influential people; eventually he went to Exeter College, Oxford, was ordained, and held three livings at the time of his death.

173 *notices.* The messages Teedon claimed to receive from God.

27 years ago. Mrs Unwin's 'atrophy' took place in 1767, not 1765.

174 *a physician and a parson.* Dr Austin and Thomas Carwardine.

the kind Donor. Mary Cockerell, Hayley's maid.

This cannot fail . . . to interest him. Hayley wrote to Lord Thurlow's daughter, Catherine, asking her if she would lend him one of the volumes of the set of Cowper's poetry which had been presented to her by Carwardine. When she complied with this request, he returned the volume to her with an eighteen-line poem inscribed on a blank leaf. In the poem, Hayley suggested that Miss Thurlow might assist in promoting the friendship of Cowper and Thurlow.

175 *I rejoice therefore. Henry V*, III. vi. 53.

your fine poem on History. An Essay on History in Three Epistles to Gibbon (1780).

the commission. The pension.

176 *so proper a compliment.* Cowper sent presentation copies of both his books of verse to Dr Austin by way of Hayley. On the flyleaf opposite the title-page of the earlier volume, Cowper inscribed his verses to Dr Austin; on the recto of the same leaf, Hayley wrote a poem of his own to the physician.

My Pourtrait. By Lemuel Abbott (1760–1803); it is now in the National Portrait Gallery. Abbott was the son of a Leicester clergyman and was largely a self-taught painter, particularly noted for his ability to capture the physical and emotional likenesses of those who sat to him. His portrait of Cowper shows the poet dressed in a green archery coat and buff waistcoat and breeches.

177 *remittance . . . annual one.* Cowper is enquiring about the payments made to him by his cousins Theodora and William Cowper.

Sam's wife. See Samuel Roberts in Biographical Register.

178 *jades of Asia.* Cowper is paraphrasing *2 Henry IV*, II. iv. 161–2, where Pistol is misquoting Marlowe's *Tamburlaine*, 2nd part, IV. iii. 1–2.

route. Cowper and his party left Weston on 1 Aug. and stayed at the Mitre Inn at Barnet that night; Rose joined them there that evening, and he journeyed to London with them; from there, the group went to Kingston and met General Cowper, and then on to Ripley where the group spent the night; the next morning they continued the journey, arriving at Eartham on the 3rd.

181 *Sir John Croydon.* This was Lady Hesketh's nickname for him, probably derived from misreading the name 'Corydon' in his poem 'Audley End'.

Pelbarto. Significance not known.

182 *the loss of his favorite sister lately dead.* Catharine, who had died on 7 Aug.

183 *Charlotte Smith's last novel. Desmond* (1792). Mrs Smith's pro-revolutionary sentiments made the novel controversial. Her next novel was *The Old Manor House* (1793).

in crayons. Now in the National Portrait Gallery.

184 *An admirable likeness.* Romney made several portraits of Hayley, and it is not known which he gave to Cowper.

184 *Hob-owchin*. Usually spelled hobhouchin; an owl. Cowper is referring playfully to the profile drawing of himself by John Higgins.

Sepr. 21. 1792. Cowper probably wrote this letter on Thursday, 20 Sept.; 21 Sept. 1792 fell on a Friday.

pardon it. The return trip began on Monday, 17 Sept.; Cowper and his party stayed at the Sun Inn at Kingston on the evening of the 18th and went to dinner from there at General Cowper's home at Ham; they left Kingston early on the morning of the 19th, went to Samuel Rose's home in London, where they took chocolate, were accompanied by Rose as far as St Albans, and arrived at Weston that evening.

185 *Socket's Letter is deliver'd and his parents are well.* See notes pp. 172 and 169.

187 *Evening Collect.* Teedon had recommended, among others, the Third Collect, for Aid Against All Perils (for Evening Prayer) from *The Book of Common Prayer*; it reads in part: 'defend us from all perils and dangers of this night'. The Third Collect, for Grace (for Morning Prayer) thanks God 'who hast safely brought us to the beginning of this day'.

188 *Jan. 2 1793.* Cowper misdated this letter, which was written in Feb.

189 *remarks.* Thomas Alphonso's corrections to Cowper's translation of the *Iliad*.

190 *Pindus*. A range of mountains in northern Greece associated with Apollo and the Muses.

Guy. William Guy (d. 1825), a Chichester physician, who was a good friend of Hayley. Cowper had met him at Eartham.

those lines. Hayley's letter to Cowper regarding Shakespeare is not extant, and we cannot provide information on the passages to which he referred.

Poetry-professorship at Oxford. Hurdis was elected in Nov.

Lippus. A man with sore eyes.

191 *the Great House.* This was an unoccupied mansion on the outskirts of Olney, where Newton had held services.

192 *war.* Against France.

Lawrance's sketch . . . by Bartolozzi. The present location of the drawing is a matter of dispute. Francesco Bartolozzi's engraving after Lawrence was not made until 1799 (only five copies are known to exist of the private issue).

a new edition of my poems with embellishments by Lawrance is in contemplation. Such an edition was not published.

preference of landed honours. Catharine presumably wished to retain some land she had inherited.

Clarke's notes. Cowper owned copies of the *Homericas* to the *Iliad* and the *Odyssey* by Samuel Clarke (1675–1729).

194 *Mundesley.* The coast at Mundesley, Norfolk, has many cragged cliffs and deep ravines.

North Walsham. Market town and parish, 15 miles north-north-east from Norwich and situated on an eminence on the road from Cromer to Norwich.

195 *Mattishall.* The village 5 miles south-east of East Dereham where Mrs Bodham lived.

Hazeborough. A large village—with a dramatically high cliff—20 miles from Yarmouth.

196 *the light-house.* At Happisburg, near Hazeborough. Two lighthouses were erected there in 1791.

the present occupant. John Fish.

the Trinity-House. The supervisory body in London of lighthouses.

201 *The country that you have had in prospect.* Clifton, near Bristol.

202 *what Mr. Johnson said of me . . . yesterday.* He was trying to arrange accommodation in Dereham for Lady Hesketh.

203 *the book.* Perhaps Newton's *Memoirs of the late Rev. William Grimshaw . . .* (1799).

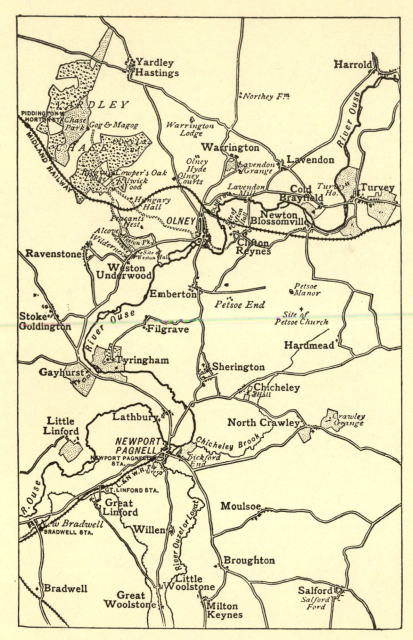

Map of environs of Olney

Redrawn from *The Correspondence of William Cowper*, ed. Thomas Wright (1904)

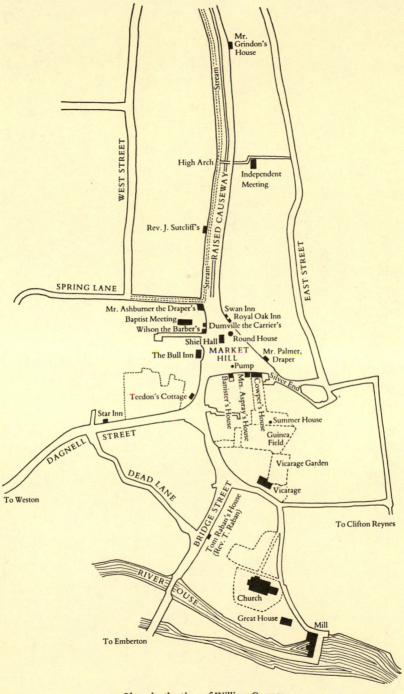

Olney in the time of William Cowper

From *The Correspondence of William Cowper*, ed. Thomas Wright (1904)

INDEX